First there was Wiseguy.
~~Then B~~

~~...other.~~

Death of an Enemy . . .

"Into the bathroom." The man put up no struggle as he was led into the bathroom, until they pulled his head down so that it was suspended over the toilet bowl. Griselda came in last. She was carrying a short machete.

The arms dealer knew they were going to cut his head off, and he screamed. "Please, please, shoot me; don't do this to me."

"Shoot you? No, I don't want anyone to hear the noise," Griselda said.

"There's a gun with a silencer under the seat of my car. Please shoot me, don't chop off my head."

"You have a gun with a silencer?"

"In my car, the black Camaro parked right in front. The gun's under the front seat."

Griselda sent Osvaldo to get the gun. When he returned she shot the arms dealer in the head. Then they dumped the body in the bathtub and hacked it into pieces. The pieces were put into green garbage bags and distributed into the canals and swamps around Miami.

THE GODMOTHER

RICHARD SMITTEN

POCKET BOOKS

New York   London   Toronto   Sydney   Tokyo   Singapore

An *Original* Publication of POCKET BOOKS

 POCKET BOOKS, a division of Simon & Schuster Inc.
1230 Avenue of the Americas, New York, NY 10020

ISBN: 0-671-70193-2

First Pocket Books printing November 1990

10 9 8 7 6 5 4 3 2 1

Cover design by Tom McKevney

Printed in the U.S.A.

This book is for Kelley Smitten,
My beloved daughter,
Who stood by me through the
Maelstrom of my life and
Never faltered in her love.

Of all the animals, man is the only one that is cruel. He is the only one that inflicts pain for the pleasure of doing it. It is a trait that is not known to the higher animals.

Mark Twain
[Samuel Clemens]

Cruelty . . . is one of the most natural feelings of man, one of the sweetest inclinations, one of the most intense he has received from nature.
Marquis de Sade

Table of Contents

Introduction   *1*

PART I: THE HATCHING

1. Birth of the Black Widow   *6*
2. Danger in the Desert   *25*
3. Griselda's Girdles   *33*
4. Girl Talk   *41*

PART II: SPINNING THE WEB

5. Operation Banshee   *48*
6. High Seas Hoax   *61*

PART III: DEADLIEST OF THE SPECIES

7. Hit List   *74*
8. High Tea and Diamonds   *80*

TABLE OF CONTENTS

9. White Powder Wars   *87*
10. *La Compasionata*   *96*
11. The Red Rose   123

PART IV: THE SPIDER AND THE FLY

12. The Handsome Informer   *128*
13. Betty's Bagboy   *147*
14. The Brazilian Link   *160*
15. The Reverse Sting   *171*

PART V: THE SPIDER GROWS WINGS

16. The Cop They Couldn't Kill   *188*
17. Greenback Stew   *200*
18. Boxes of Cash   *211*
19. Fresh-Cut Flowers   *214*

PART VI: THE CORNERED SPIDER

20. A Kiss on Each Dimple   *224*
21. Kickin' Ass   *238*
22. Raiders of the Lost Archives   *244*
23. Pulling the Tolls   *256*
24. Something Will Fall on Your Head   *274*
25. Deal with the Devil   *286*

INTRODUCTION

In 1987, DEA Special Agent Jack Toal spoke to me of a woman on whose dossier "The Godmother" was scrawled in bold black letters. He told me the Godmother was the most fascinating criminal the DEA had ever pursued. Her real name was Griselda Blanco, and she was the pioneer of the Colombian Cocaine Cartel, the deadliest group of criminals ever assembled. The DEA agents told me that she lived the legend of the black widow spider: She used her lovers and husbands, then killed them when they were no longer of use to her. Anyone who had ever come into contact with the Godmother felt compelled to talk of their experiences. I began to make queries about the Godmother, and soon I became so interested in her story that I decided to write a book about her.

In researching *The Godmother,* I conducted many interviews with people, such as María Gutierrez, who was Griselda Blanco's "best friend" and confidante. For example, it was María who said that Griselda told her she did not own a pair of shoes until she was thirteen and never owned a doll. María also told me of the attempted rape of Griselda, and of her subsequent beating by her mother. María was an intimate of Griselda's who not only got hard information on her drug activities, but also was privy to the secrets shared between women friends. The DEA found the information about Griselda Blanco they were receiving from María so incredible that they put her "on the box," that is, gave her a lie detector test. She passed that test; but even then they didn't believe her until one of their own was almost killed.

Bob Palombo, a DEA agent, chased Griselda Blanco over a ten-year period. He spent days with me explaining the innermost workings of his mind while he chased her, and of his feelings while battling within his own agency, and of the many times he had almost quit the chase. He relived for me his hopes, fears and trepidations during both Godmother trials.

Sergeant Al Singleton, a fourteen-year homicide detective, ex-marine, and veteran of the Miami Cocaine Wars, told me the never-before-disclosed details of the death of Chucho Castro's baby boy.

The words of the sons of Griselda Blanco are taken directly from more than a thousand pages of secretly taped conversations with undercover informants. The boys brag, whine, and complain about their mother dragging them into the business, but they are happy to spend the proceeds.

The vicious fight between Griselda Blanco and her husband Dario in Max Mermelstein's kitchen, which resulted in the death of Dario, was told to me by Max himself, who was an eyewitness to the event.

The Miami trial dialogue comes directly from court records and from the people who were there, such as Assistant U.S. Attorneys Steve Schlessinger and Arthur Mercado, and DEA agents Bob Palombo and Mary Cooper.

I have told the Godmother's story exactly as it was reported to me by those who knew her. When occasionally I had to recreate incidents involving Griselda, her family and her associates, the many sources available to me provided enough detail to allow me realistically to portray the events described. The reader should also be aware that many members of Griselda's "family" have never been convicted of the particular crimes described in this book. I have changed the names of certain people to protect the privacy, and in some cases the safety, of people described. It should also be noted that Griselda refused to be interviewed.

It took three years to research this story: I labored over thousands of pages of court reports, informant reports and tape recordings, interviews and transcriptions.

The old adage that sometimes "truth can be stranger than fiction" never applied more than to the story of the Godmother. You can be confident that what you are about to read is true. Although there may be times you doubt it.

With Special Thanks to:

Drug Enforcement Administration
Bob Palombo
Charlie Cecil
Bill Mockler
Jeff Behrman
Jack Hook
Rich Crawford
John Fernández
Steve Georges
Joe Keefe
Jack Toal
Mary Cooper

U.S. Attorneys
Steve Schlessinger
Lurana Snow
Larry Scharf
Dick Gregorie
Arthur Mercado

Griselda's Girlfriends
María Gutierrez
Carmen Cabán

Miami Metro-Dade Police
Sergeant Al Singleton
June Hawkins

and
Max Mermelstein

Without these people, there would be no story. And the Godmother would still be in business.

and

My great gratitude to Sherry Robb, my agent and friend, who fought like hell for this book.

RICHARD SMITTEN

PART I

THE HATCHING

CHAPTER 1

Birth of the Black Widow

She sat huddled in a dark corner of the one-room shack, coiling herself as tight as a spring, pulling her legs up under her chin until they squashed her small breasts flat against her chest. She heard the mewing and moaning of her mother and the grunting of the man on top as he thrust up and down into her.

She knew from experience that it wouldn't take long until the man was spent, unless he was drunk. She had noticed that sometimes when the men were drunk, they went for a long time, or sometimes they just collapsed on top of her mother like deflated balloons and fell asleep snoring. The other two children, Carlos and Olga, were sound asleep, each in a different corner.

Griselda never slept until her mother slept.

She looked down at her feet and hated them. They were flat and wide, peasant feet. She was thirteen now, and she had never owned a single pair of shoes. She leaned down and felt the bottoms of her feet. They were thickly padded and tough, like shoe leather. She could walk across the hottest streets in Medellín and the steaming surface would only tickle her soles.

She looked up. All of a sudden it was quiet. Something was wrong. The man was off her mother and crawling around on the floor on all fours, checking out the corners of the room.

"Griselda? Where are you, my pretty little one?" the man whispered playfully.

His teeth were white against his swarthy skin, framed by his thick black moustache. The teeth flashed in the darkness, occasionally flickering in the light of the single candle.

"*El Lupero,*" she whispered and started to shiver. The four-legged form reminded her of a wolf. The fear came from somewhere deeply buried in her primeval memory.

"*Oye, Lupero,*" her mother yelled from her crumpled sheets on the dirt floor. "*¡Veni!*"

The man gave up his quest, returning to Griselda's mother like an obedient dog.

Gradually, Griselda stopped quivering and her heartbeat returned to normal. She knew it was only a matter of time until *El Lupero* returned. But maybe he would leave, especially now that her mother was pregnant. The men always left just before the babies came.

But this one was different, more dangerous, she thought. Then she realized—she was the one who was different.

She was thirteen now, and a woman.

Bob Palombo sat at the kitchen table and listened to his father and grandfather discuss him like he wasn't there. They were both powerful men in his eyes. The women, his mother and grandmother, sat at the table and listened quietly, speaking whenever they felt it necessary.

Just two nights before, Bob had come home with bruises and lumps and his father had said, "We took you up to Westchester County, and look at you. We could have stayed in the Bronx. What did we come up here for? You come home all lumped up like a street kid!"

"You should have seen the other guy," Bob answered, attempting a smile.

"Well, I see you, and that's enough. Let's get you cleaned up before your mother sees you, and Bobby . . ."

"Yes, Dad?"

"Tell her you fell."

Bob Palombo sat feeling his bruises and listening. He was about to enter high school, an important event within the family. Bob was a high-spirited boy who loved running the streets, getting into scraps now and then, but never any real trouble.

"So! It's decided, then," his father said, and surveyed the faces that looked at him, avoiding his son's. He counted the nods.

"Good. Bobby, you will go to Eastern Military Academy in Huntington, Long Island, in the fall." All the faces looked at the boy for a reaction.

The only thing Bob felt bad about was that he would miss his best friend, Bob Presioso. The military life held a fascination for him. He knew he would get a uniform; maybe they would let him shoot a gun. He could live in a dorm or even a real barracks. He looked over at his mother and saw tears welling up in her eyes. She hated to see him go. For a second he thought about refusing, then his father spoke again. "Well, Bobby, what do you think?"

Bob just shrugged and stood up. He walked over to stand next to his mother and put his hand on her shoulder. "Sure, I'll give it a try," he said softly.

His mother put her arm around his waist, hiding her tears by laying her head on his chest.

Griselda Blanco was born in Santa Marta, Colombia, on the estate of Señor Blanco. The estate was called Magdalena; it was located near the Caribbean coast close to the Guajira Península, home of the fierce Guajiro Indians. Señor Blanco was half Guajiro himself.

The Guajiro Indians were smugglers; they were so fierce that even the Colombian army refused to enforce the law in "the Guajira." The Venezuelans agreed. They owned the land on the other side of the peninsula, and they also refused to enter the no-man's-land inhabited by the Guajiro. The Guajira Península became a natural border between Colombia and Venezuela. It was a lawless land that governed itself.

Griselda's mother was a servant on the estate of Señor Blanco. She became pregnant by him. When the last days came, she hid in a small cottage and delivered Griselda into the world. A few days later she wrapped Griselda in a shawl and walked with her newborn daughter to the Grand House. She asked to see the master, and waited. He finally walked out onto the porch to see who was calling.

Griselda's mother extended the baby to Señor Blanco as an offering, a smile on her face, reflecting pride in her beautiful baby daughter. Señor Blanco parted the shawl and looked at the child. He said nothing and went into the Grand House. Minutes later he came out with a handful of *pesos*. He stuffed the paper money into her hand and pointed down the long unpaved plantation road that led into Cartagena and said, *"!Ahora, vaya!"* Señor Blanco spun on his heel and walked into the Grand House, slamming the door shut behind him.

When Griselda was two, her mother decided she was old enough to help her make a living. She dragged the child around the city, pointing at her and screaming, "My poor child, she is dying, starving for food; please give us some money for food." If Griselda protested or struggled, her mother beat her unmercifully, and yanked her back into the streets crying; a crying child collected more than a smiling one.

As more children were born, they also were pressed into service, begging in the streets. Griselda was constantly assailed by her mother. Not one day went by when she wasn't beaten. Once Griselda picked up a doll that belonged to another child; the doll was pulled out of her hand and returned to its owner. She was beaten severely for her boldness. She never received a single toy as a child, nor a new dress.

The family wandered through towns and cities, living in the rough *barrios,* and always there were new men with her mother. When the babies came, the men disappeared. The family always lived in one room— no privacy, no relief, on the edge of survival.

As the years passed and Griselda grew, she tried to please her mother, partly to stop her daily beatings and partly because she wanted her mother's love. She improved her begging techniques and was always able to spot those people who might toss them a few *centavos* for food. But it never stopped the constant beatings.

Once in a while her mother found work, and Griselda was left on her own to wander around the city. She walked through the *colonias* and marveled at the beautiful houses and the shiny cars. And many of the houses had their own *seguridad*—armed guards who patrolled the property, and iron bars that protected the inhabitants from the outside world. As she walked past, the guards glowered at her as if she could do some harm.

And always she had to leave her *Casas Fantásticas* and return to her own *barrio* of filth and squalor. But at least she had seen them, the "Fantasy Houses" and the "Fantasy People." An idea was slowly forming in her brain. Maybe she too could live such a life, but how? It seemed *imposible.*

Bob Palombo was born in the Bronx and resided there until he was eight. He lived on Purdy Street in a house with his parents, sister Loretta, and grand-parents. Bob went to Catholic grammar school and ran freely in the streets. His grandfather, Joseph Duva, had been in the restaurant business since 1905. He had two prosperous bars, each located by an airport. His grandfather, "The Mayor of Morris Avenue," loved politics and was always helping some-one, particularly immigrants who needed their papers.

Bob's father worked in the post office. He was stern but fair, and kept a strong hand on his active son. When Bob was eight, sensing the pending demise of the Bronx, the family moved to Yonkers, and later to Westchester. It meant a long commute to the city for his father and to Queens for his grandfather, but the family was worth it. The family came first.

Bob, for all his life, would remember the Sundays when his mother and grandmother cooked in the kitchen, laughing and chatting about the men over the strong smell of garlic, tomato sauce, oregano, and basil. The men read the newspapers in the living room, and argued over the baseball scores.

Bob was thirteen when he entered military school in Huntington. He attended for one year and enjoyed the regimen of military life, the orderliness, and the tradition. He didn't know why he liked it, but he knew it had something to do with keeping him under control, channeling his energy and shaping his manhood.

But at the end of that year, Bob Palombo explained to his parents that he wasn't going back to the military academy. At first his father was disappointed, but he knew that his wife had missed her son badly while he was away.

"Well, if you do come home, you're not going to public school. You're going to go to a good prep school, where you're going to learn something and not go crazy and get into trouble."

"And where is that, Dad?"

"Iona, that's where. You're going to Iona."

And he did. At least he got to see girls once in a while.

Griselda Blanco was thirteen when she first met Carlos Trujillo. He was what was known in the *barrio* as a *mafiosa,* a man of the underworld. Carlos specialized in false papers and importing illegal immigrants into the United States. He operated out of the small Colombian *barrio* beginning to form in Queens, in New York City. He flew regularly between Queens and Medellín, Colombia.

Carlos was attracted to the pretty Griselda Blanco. He understood why she wore old dresses and had never had any shoes; he was a product of the same environment. They talked often and became friends. Griselda knew what he did for a living, and wondered if some day he might make "papers" for her.

One afternoon she came home early, something she never did when her mother was working. She pulled aside the worn fabric curtain that acted as a door and almost fell on *El Lupero,* her mother's boyfriend. He was sitting at the table in the center of the small room, drinking.

She gasped when she saw him and sprang for the loose curtain that was swinging in the hot tropic air. But she wasn't fast enough. He grabbed her arm and pulled her toward him.

"Why are you in such a hurry?" he whispered, his teeth bared.

"I must go. Let me go."

"Here, first you have a little drink." He held the bottle up to her lips. She swiped it aside with the back of her hand and it spilled onto the dirt floor.

He hit her a crashing blow that drove her into a corner. She huddled, crabbing deeper into the corner as he came and stood over her. He was smiling. He leaned down, groping at her young body, trying to feel her breasts. He dropped to all fours; his hand darted underneath her loose tunic and onto her thigh.

12

Then something snapped inside her. She ripped her hand across his eyes, scratching his face. Dark blood started to ooze out of his cheeks. He stopped to feel his face and look at his hand, now covered with blood. It gave her the chance she needed to rise. But she didn't run. She stood there and waited for him to spring to his feet. Then she kicked with all her might, the way she had seen the whores do it on the street. Her toughened bare pointed foot landed right in his groin, driving his testicles up into his body. *El Lupero's* eyes opened wide, almost crossing, as he lurched forward. He fell at her feet.

For a split second she thought about kicking him again but decided against it. She ran.

She ran to where her mother was working, on the edge of the *colonia,* cleaning one of the big houses. She streaked past the security guard and found her mother in the kitchen, cleaning the floor.

Breathlessly, she explained to her mother, "He tried to touch me, to violate me. I escaped."

Her mother rose from the kitchen floor she was cleaning and stared at her daughter, speechless.

"Mama, he tried; I swear, he would have stuck me with his thing. I know it! You must believe me."

The first blow almost knocked her out. Her eyes were so full of tears she didn't see it coming. It drove her all the way across the kitchen to the edge of the sink. Then her mother was on her, flailing her unmercifully. "You lying little *puta,* he would never do such a thing! It is you, you *puta!* You are trying to take my man away!"

Griselda was hovering on the edge of unconsciousness, dizzy from the blows. The security guard and the other servants pulled her mother off her. Slowly she arose and made her way out of the kitchen.

This time she ran deep into the *barrio* looking for Carlos, praying that he would be there. She found him in a cafe. He quickly took her up to his apartment, where he washed her cuts and bruises and put her into bed. When he thought she was asleep, Carlos returned to the cafe.

But she only feigned sleep. The endless, recurring nightmare raced through her brain. It was not only the nightmare of *El Lupero* and her mother beating her; it was her life, a never-ending nightmare. She took deep breaths to calm down and tried to block the demons from her brain.

Slowly, Griselda calmed down and her heart started to pump in a regular rhythm. Now she was determined never to depend on anyone again, except herself. The thought soothed her, made her feel safe. Yes, it was within her, she had power within her, and if she could harness it, she would be safe because she would be powerful. Weakness was being dependent upon other people.

And she had a great strength that she had never known she had: She wasn't afraid to die. Why would she be afraid to die? Maybe it would bring her peace.

Carlos Trujillo told his friends in the cafe that they were to say nothing about what they had just seen. He knew they wouldn't; his word was law. He knew he would have to wait for her face to heal before he could take her picture for the passport. She was very beautiful. He knew it would be a good picture, and she would be a good lover for him in New York. And his instincts told him she was a smart girl. He had friends who would teach her how to be a pickpocket; she would quickly pay for her keep.

He smiled and sipped his *aguardiente* and asked if anyone would like another game of dominoes.

Bob Palombo had wanted to be a G-man for as long as he could remember. In eighth grade he and his friend Bob Presioso were totally fascinated by Eliot Ness and "The Untouchables." They watched every show, almost memorizing the dialogue. To the boys, "The Untouchables" *was* the FBI. There was no differentiation between federal law enforcement agencies; all G-men worked for the FBI, and that was it. Mystique, mystery, and action were synonymous with the FBI.

Then there was the magical day for both of them. Bob's aunt worked for Fordham University, in the Registrar's Office. She worked with the FBI agents that came to Fordham to recruit, and she knew of the boys' interest in "The Untouchables." She arranged for a tour of FBI headquarters in New York on 69th Street. The tour was a dream come true for the boys. They felt privileged. They absorbed everything they were told as they walked through the inner sanctum of the Federal Bureau of Investigation. They felt the power of the American flag, and their eyes widened as they saw the badges and guns the men and women carried. After their tour, both boys decided they wanted to become G-men.

Bob Palombo enrolled in Pace University and took accounting, because at that time the FBI required either a law degree or an accounting degree. But there was one major problem: Bob hated accounting. His friend Bob Presioso was having the same problem. But another friend, who had done research on government agencies told them, "Don't be depressed, guys. It's not only the Department of Justice that does law enforcement! Treasury has five agencies: U.S. Customs; the IRS; Secret Service; Alcohol, Tobacco and Firearms; and Inspections. All you need is a college education, not necessarily law or accounting."

The young men's dreams were resurrected. In their last semester they went to the post office together and took the test for the Treasury Department. As they handed in their tests they were told, "It's a big list. You'll have a long wait, fellas, but don't be disappointed. If you pass, you'll go on the list." Both boys just shrugged and left, not optimistic about their prospects.

Bob went home and told his parents what he had done.

"My God," his father said. "After prep school and four years of college, he was going to be a teacher. Now he wants to be a cop. Forget it! For a smart boy, you can be so stupid sometimes."

Bob's mother slipped her hand into her husband's and looked up at him.

"All right, all right," his father said. "I know everyone has to go his own way. If nothing else, if you decide to do it, it's good retirement and steady pay. It's a safe civil service job."

Things moved quickly. Richard Nixon had declared war on drugs, and had passed the Safe Streets Act in 1968. It was now 1970; a lot of money was being allocated for hiring. Two months after their tests, Bob Palombo and Bob Presioso were called down for interviews with U.S. Customs. They were interviewed and hired the same day, March 10, 1970.

On March 23, 1970, they were both sworn in as Customs Agents. After the swearing-in ceremony, they walked out into the New York streets, and as one, gave an earsplitting war whoop.

They had made it.

It was the late sixties, and Griselda Blanco had been enrolled in the Colombian crime college now for nine years. She was living primarily in Queens, and she had learned to become an expert pickpocket and forger of documents: visas, green cards, and passports. Together with Carlos Trujillo, Griselda forged the papers in Colombia and sold them in the United States.

She was still living with Carlos. By now, it was difficult to tell who worked for whom.

Carlos Trujillo was a mulatto. He was the father of Griselda's sons: Dixon, born on April 2, 1960; Uber, born on November 15, 1961; and Osvaldo, born May 5, 1962. All the boys were born in Medellín.

Griselda had grown into a pretty woman, and to

make herself even more attractive, she had undergone plastic surgery to remove the deep cleft in her chin. She also had had her dimples filled in. But none of this could improve her slight stutter. She tried to stay away from those words that twisted her tongue, but behind her back some people called her *La Gaga,* The Stutterer.

Carlos introduced Griselda to Alberto Bravo, an associate, who was the son of a highly respected Colombian businessman. Alberto was an educated man from the upper class, and had the excellent business brain of his father. He was interested in something more than false papers. He was interested in the business of the future—in cocaine. He explained it to Carlos and Griselda. Carlos shrugged it off, but Griselda listened to his every word.

Their love affair began shortly afterward.

Griselda also met María Gutierrez in 1968 in Queens. María had a travel agency in Medellín and was from one of the famous first families of Colombia. Her cousin had been president of the country. María had been an Olympic swimmer and a concert pianist. She embodied a great fantasy for Griselda—what Griselda herself might have become under different circumstances.

Griselda decided immediately that María would become her girlfriend and confidante. She needed one person, just one, in whom she could confide—a person she could trust because that person had nothing to gain from her. Griselda promised to visit María in Medellín and use her travel agency sometime in the future. María smiled, and agreed, "Whenever you want, just come by and see me." Griselda filed that away in her brain for the future.

In 1970, Carlos Trujillo found out about Griselda's affair with Alberto Bravo. He beat her severely and ordered her to stop.

She didn't have to stop. Shortly after her beating,

Carlos was taken to the hospital in Queens. He was diagnosed as having cirrhosis of the liver and hepatitis. Shortly after he was admitted, he died.

Griselda did not mourn his death. She flew to Colombia to be with Alberto Bravo. She now had the forgery business to herself, along with a new interest —cocaine.

In 1970 the U.S. Customs Service had narcotics divided into two groups. One was "soft narcotics," which was primarily marijuana and hashish. The second group handled "hard narcotics," which consisted of cocaine and heroin. Both Bob Palombo and Bob Presioso had been vocal in their interviews. They hated drugs and had lost some good friends to drug abuse. Both of them got assigned to the "hard narcotics" group.

They were in the first group, twelve in all, that went directly from college to become Customs agents. There were only 375 Customs Special Agents throughout the world at the time. Normally, the Customs agents were promoted out of the patrol divisions that worked the piers, the airports, the borders, and the patrol cars. These men and women had labored years to become agents. Many were veterans of other police forces with tremendous experience in Customs law enforcement. The boys were just twenty-three years old, and they faced some strong resentment from their elders on the force.

Al Seeley became their mentor. He took an immediate liking to the boys and decided to teach them "the business." But first he tested them—for an entire year.

Al Seeley reminded Bob Palombo of Edward X. Delaney, the hero of many Lawrence Sanders novels. Al Seeley was precise and very organized. He left nothing to chance, and he wanted anyone who worked with him to do the same. Before joining the Customs service, Seeley had been an NYPD homicide detective, first-grade. He loved to teach, providing the pupils responded.

And Al Seeley was the master of conspiracy. He sat the boys down and explained.

"You guys wanna learn?"

"Yes, sir," the boys responded.

"For the next year you fellas are gonna do whatever anyone asks you to do. And you're not going to ask why, just do it. If after a year, you still don't know why you're doin' something, then you can come and ask me." Seely winked at them and continued. "You two are going to be running rap sheets, getting photographs from the BCI [Bureau of Criminal Investigation], working to get information out of other agencies, running credit checks, and pulling phone records. You are going to make contacts, and if you handle yourselves right, they will be good contacts for years to come."

The boys leaned forward, listening to Seeley's every word. "You don't start from the top; you start from the bottom and work your way up. Remember, this isn't like going out for coffee. You're going to be pros; this is your living. You gotta do it right."

At first the boys thought maybe he was giving them the gears just to run them ragged. But the deeper they dug, the faster they knew that Al Seeley was the real article. And as 1970 passed, they found themselves getting more and more interesting assignments until Seeley started to let them in on some of his secrets. They found out that Seeley's secrets were 10 percent inspiration and 90 percent perspiration.

And there was a little humor on the job once in a while.

A Customs patrol officer watched a suspicious-looking Colombian clear Customs. He intercepted the man near the exit door and casually patted him on the back to show him the way out. The "pat down" was an old Customs trick to see if he had anything hidden under his jacket. The man's back felt kind of lumpy, so the officer said, "Come with me for a second inspection."

The Customs officer ordered the man to remove his jacket. "What's your name?" he asked.

"Manuel Restrepo," the man answered, handing the officer the jacket.

The Customs officer removed the shoulder pads, and sure enough, they were full of cocaine. The officer called Bob Palombo and his partner. A few minutes later they arrived at the scene and took the man into custody. They took Manuel Restrepo downtown to fingerprint, photograph, and book him. Before he was sent off to the West Street Federal Detention Center, they decided to do a thorough search.

"Take off your shoes," Palombo ordered. The man slipped out of his high-heeled platform shoes and handed them to Palombo. Palombo took out his knife and split the soles; they were full of cocaine; so were the heels.

"Do you have any more drugs on you?"

"No más, no más; no more, no more," Restrepo answered.

"Take off your belt and hand it to me," Palombo said. He examined the belt. It had a zipper in the back. Palombo unzipped the belt, and it was full of marijuana cigarettes.

"What else are you carrying?" Palombo continued.

"Nothing, *señor,* nothing."

"Gimme your tie," Palombo ordered. He examined the tie, and it was full of marijuana. "Strip, right now!"

Almost every article of clothing the man had on was full of drugs. The man stood stark naked in the examination room and burst out laughing as the agents piled up the dope. He held his arms out from his bare body, palms up, and said, *"No más, no más."*

"Bullshit," Palombo said. "Bend over and spread 'em." And sure enough, there was one more container of dope. Palombo turned and looked at his partner, shrugged his shoulders, and they all burst out laughing. Manuel Restrepo could have turned on the entire West Street jail, if the U.S. Marshals there hadn't found the dope. And if they *had* found the dope, Palombo and his partner would never have heard the end of it.

One day Seeley said, "Fellas, we got a real bad problem with heroin coming up from South America, particularly from Argentina. The bad guys are using false-bottomed suitcases, sealed food cans, every goddamn thing they can think of. There's no rhyme or reason to what's happening."

"We know," the boys said.

"Well, maybe there is some pattern," Seeley grinned. "Every foreigner coming into the United States on a visa would have to have an I-94 Immigration Document, right?"

The boys nodded. They knew they were being set up, but they didn't care. Seeley continued, "So why don't you guys pull all the I-94s coming from Santiago, Chile, and Buenos Aires, Argentina, and have them segregated. There can't be too many of them, maybe two flights a day. When you have them catalogued, we will sit down and see what we can see."

Seeley pointed out to the boys that they should be particularly interested in B-2 visas, who were short-term visitors, especially if they stayed in hotels. "Hey, here's what I mean. Look at this, this guy lists himself as a laborer. How the hell can a laborer afford to come to New York for three days. Hell, I can't afford a trip to Buenos Aires for three days. Put this joker on the 'soundex,' the lookout file for Immigration."

That was before computers; painstakingly, they compiled a list and watched as a pattern formed. The list came alive in their hands. These men and women were couriers, returning often to the United States. They forwarded the list to Immigration. And just as

Al Seeley had predicted, the arrests came like clock-work. Seeley just smiled and said, "And they don't know how we're nailing them. We'll do great for about six months, until they figure it out. But by then they will have lost so much money from us confiscating the heroin that they will be out of business anyway."

The boys were ecstatic, electrified by the thrill of the chase. "Hey, relax," Seeley said, seeing their excitement at the arrests. "This is just the beginning. Now we gotta flip 'em. Wanna come and see how it's done?"

The boys went and observed. It was just like they thought it would be, only easier. The good-cop–bad-cop routine was played out in front of their eyes. Seeley was great. He could take either role: calm and accommodating, as if he cared; or tough and belligerent until he left them shaking, on the verge of tears. Inevitably they flipped, and then Seeley went to work. He made a deal with them. It depended on how high he thought they were on the crime ladder. His ultimate objective was to get to the top: "You kill rats by cutting off their heads!" Seeley often used the informants, he extracted all the information he wanted—names, places, times, and amounts—verified the information, and then after rounding up the people he was after, deported the informant.

Then it was Bob Palombo's turn. It started out as a small case. Two beautiful American girls got nailed at Customs in New York; one a black girl, the other an Italian. The black girl was a stunning model. The girls were coming up from Colombia with a complete set of encyclopedias, animal encyclopedias.

The Customs inspector said, "This is a beautiful set of encyclopedias, girls. *Hablan español?*"

The two girls looked at the inspector with no response. "Do you girls speak Spanish?"

"No," they chorused.

"These books are written in Spanish. Why don't

you come with me, ladies." The inspector took them aside and he probed the books, cover to cover. The bindings were full of cocaine.

Palombo got the call. The two girls were taken down to the jail on Greenwich Street, the house of detention for women. They were processed there and told they would be sent to Rikers Island the next day. The Greenwich Street jail was rough enough but the thought of Riker's Island petrified the girls. Bob Palombo let them spend one full night in jail and talked to them the following morning.

They flipped immediately. They led Palombo and his partner to a Colombian living in Queens. The girls corroborated each other and had supporting documentation. Palombo arrested the Colombian.

Palombo was so excited about the case he went to Seeley and explained the case to him. "And this is what I want to do, Al . . ."

"Hey Bob, you're a big boy now. Just tell me when you have a problem. It's time for you to fly on your own. I'll be here for you if you need me. But if you're looking for a pat on the back every time you find something out, I'm too busy. So, you know, unless you really need my help, Godspeed, and go knock yourself out."

"Right, Al," Palombo said, leaving.

"And Bob."

"Yeah?"

"If you weren't ready, I'd tell you."

"Thanks, Al."

The Colombian they arrested started them on a chase that lasted six months. They arrested the recruiter, the middleman, and the boss. This one case was a great experience for Palombo because it covered the gamut: It showed them how to talk to defendants, follow up on the leads, and work with corroborating individuals.

It also taught him that Colombians had no fear of

being arrested. Palombo arrested Colombians who were sleeping like babies in the backseat of the car by the time they got to the jail. And they did not flip on each other, for one very good reason: If they talked, their families in Colombia would be hunted down and killed or kidnapped. Palombo learned that when a Colombian was arrested, it was the end of the trail, unless he carried some helpful documentation that might lead somewhere else. But they were careful people. In most cases, their telephone numbers were coded and their records were coded, and they never talked in anything but code on the telephone.

From these techniques, Seeley shaped and formed some great conspiracy cases, and Bob Palombo was one of his best students.

CHAPTER 2

Danger in the Desert

Griselda Blanco had a brilliant business mind. It was 1971 and she knew there was an enormous demand building for cocaine in the United States; it was supplying that demand that was the problem. A distribution network had to be established once the cocaine hit United States shores.

She dealt with the problems one at a time. Together with Alberto Bravo, Griselda had bought several ranches in Colombia, which they quickly converted to the production of cocaine. The paste came in from Bolivia and Peru, and it was processed into cocaine hydrochloride at these ranches.

The inventory was backing up.

Three of them sat around trying to figure out how to get more cocaine into the United States. José Antonio Cabrera was there; his nickname was "Pepe." Pepe was a friend of Griselda's and had good distribution contacts in the United States, particularly in Queens. Alberto Bravo, her lover, was there. And Griselda Blanco was there.

"Let's bring it in in a dog cage," Pepe offered.

25

There was silence. Griselda spoke, "Let's bring it in in bras and girdles." The three of them looked at each other and silently nodded. "We can conceal it by sewing it into the undergarments. We will put it in small plastic bags and actually sew it in."

They knew that Griselda knew how to handle the false papers. And getting "mules," human couriers, was easy. For a few hundred dollars' payment each, they would have a line of eager mules standing by. And there would be little chance of rip-offs because the mules all had family in Colombia; if they took what didn't belong to them, their families faced death. If the mules were caught, they would most likely just be deported.

"How much can they carry?" Pepe Cabrera asked.

"At least a kilo each," Griselda offered. "And let's do the shoes. Platform heels and soles are perfect; we could put at least half a kilo in each shoe."

"Dogs," Alberto asked. "What about dogs?"

"They don't use dogs at the airport; this we know from people who work the airports."

The assent was unanimous. Soon afterward, Griselda visited a Colombian brassiere factory, a girdle factory, and a shoe factory. Every manufacturer she spoke to was happy to fill her request for custom-made goods.

Bob Palombo had been working exclusively on Hispanic cases, particularly Colombians, and the Customs service offered a seventeen-week immersion course in Spanish in El Paso, Texas. He talked to his friend Bob Presioso, who had just returned from the course. Neither of them had ever been away from New York before.

"Well, what do you think of the course?" Palombo asked.

"El Paso sucks. Man, you can't get any Italian food that's made by Italians; you can't get any Chinese

THE GODMOTHER

food that's made by Chinese. Everything is made by
Mexicans down there; it's ridiculous!"

Bob Palombo's laughing was interrupted by his
superior. "Hey, Palombo, cool it; you're goin' next,
you leave next week. You wanna catch Colombians,
you gotta understand Spanish."

In July of 1971, Bob Palombo went to El Paso, and
got through sixteen weeks of the course without
incident. In the seventeenth week, the El Paso Customs office called him. They covered the border, and
they were having a problem. They had a case going,
and they needed a New Yorker to do some undercover
work.

"Okay, I'll do it; what do you want?" Palombo
answered. He had never done any undercover work;
up until then he had handled historical conspiracy
cases and control and deliveries.

"It shouldn't be difficult; act like a doper and talk
with a New York accent. That shouldn't be too hard
for you," the commanding officer said.

"A lot of dese, dose and dems, huh?" Palombo
offered.

"Yeah, that's it," the officer drawled.

"Act like a wise guy? Sure, I can do it."

"We got a crew of nasty bastards who're ripping
people off. We don't know much about them, and we
need someone to bring 'em out in the open. You have
to let it be known that you're in the market for
marijuana and some cocaine."

"How do I do that?" Palombo asked.

"We've already done it. And you'll have a partner;
you'll meet him when we get there."

"Does he have undercover experience?"

"No, he's a virgin, like you. Now we have to hurry
to test out the bug. The bad guys are coming to the
motel in a few hours. We've got the room bugged.
We'll be right next door."

"Let's go! I'm in your hands; this is your turf,"
Palombo said, swallowing deeply.

27

The meeting was held, and it was agreed that on the following night the dopers would return and take the two agents to a stash car where money would be exchanged for drugs. The agents would drive away with the stash car and leave the car keys at the motel after the car had been emptied of the drugs.

"So?" Palombo asked the commanding officer after the dopers had left. "What do you think?"

"Sounds fine. Just go with them, and don't worry, you've got backup surveillance."

At ten o'clock the next night one of the dopers appeared, a scrawny, disheveled thug. "I'm going to take you toward the airport," he said.

Bob slipped into the backseat while the other agent climbed into the front. The surveillance car headlights reflected back at him in the rearview mirror. His fingers rested on the cool metal of the .25 automatic stuck in his groin; it was cocked, no hammer. He then checked the Smith and Wesson .38 in his waistband.

The car sped along for ten minutes and headed into the desert. They were now on a single strip of highway that stretched out into the night. The trailing headlights still gleamed in the rearview mirror.

"Where are we going?" Bob asked.

"Not far, we're going down out of the way. We can't do this deal out in the open. We're going out past the airport."

Another ten minutes passed, and Bob looked up once again for the surveillance car. It wasn't there; no headlights in the mirror. Slowly, Bob turned to look out the back window, squinting his eyes, hoping that the following agents had only turned off their lights to avoid detection.

Suddenly, the car pulled off the highway and stopped. The headlights shone on the dark form of a second car, hidden in the night. "That's the load car. You two get out; our guys will meet you and do the deal."

Bob and the other agent slowly got out of the car

and walked toward the parked car. Suddenly a second pair of high-beam headlights lit up the darkness, illuminating the two agents, leaving them exposed halfway between cars.

The dry silence of the desert was cracked by the clear rack-rack of a pump shotgun being cocked. It was a sound like no other. "You guys got guns?" a voice from the dark asked.

"Course we got guns; we're here to do business. Wouldn't you have a gun if you were coming out here to meet some people in the middle of the fucking desert?" Palombo answered.

"Lose 'em."

Palombo looked around quickly. There was a deep ravine off to the side of where they were standing. He could take a dive, but no, all they had to do was pump some rounds down there and he would be dead. Besides, he felt the cold metal of the hidden .25 automatic in his groin. The agents dropped their guns.

"Put your hands up," the voice from behind the lights said, as two men, wearing stocking masks, emerged, silhouetted in the high beams.

For a brief second, Bob thought that these were his own people, playing a training game, tuning them up for undercover work. But the thought passed quickly, and he knew deep down that the cavalry wasn't coming. He was on his own and he'd better do something, fast.

"Get down on the ground! Where's the money? Where's the money?" the man with the shotgun asked.

The agents dropped to the ground. Palombo took a deep breath and said a fast prayer; then he started screaming, reaching down into his Italian New York heritage, and as he screamed, his anger rose. "What the fuck's the matter with you? You think I'm going to bring the fucking money out here, you assholes?"

"Where's the money?"

"In the safe in the motel. You don't believe we would bring it with us, do you? Look what you fuckers are doing to us!" Palombo screamed at the top of his lungs.

"You son of a bitch, I ought to kill you. Maybe you got it on you, you asshole." The man who had been talking kneeled beside Bob and roughly started to search him, looking for a money belt.

Palombo's mind raced as he thought of the hidden gun in his groin going off and blowing off the family jewels. He couldn't take the chance. "Take it easy, there's a fucking gun down there."

"What? You've got another gun, you son of a bitch." The gun was removed. "I ought to kill you! What are you doing with another gun?"

"I've got it for protection, what do you think?"

Suddenly, Palombo's arm shot up and swiped at the pistol. The gun flashed in the night. The desert absorbed the sound. It sounded like a child's cap gun going off. Palombo didn't feel the round graze his arm. Everyone was shocked at the sound of the gun; they just looked at each other, stunned.

Two headlights appeared in the distance on the black strip of road.

"Who the fuck is that?" the man with the shotgun mumbled. "Okay, you guys get down in the ravine. Don't say a word."

The agents crawled and crabbed their way to the edge of the ravine and took a dive. They rolled and tumbled down the slope until they hit the barbed wire crumpled on the bottom.

"Shit, there's barbed wire here!" Palombo had torn his legs from his knees to his shins, but felt nothing. His adrenaline was pumping. They huddled and heard the screaming of tires as the two cars above them hit the highway and disappeared into the night. The oncoming lights kept right on going; just a motorist on his way somewhere.

Slowly and carefully they climbed out of the ravine and walked onto the highway. They stood in the center of the highway illuminated by the moon and shook hands.

"Shit, we're still alive. This is unbelievable!" Bob's partner said.

"Oh yeah, this is great, just fucking great. My pants are torn to shit, not to mention my legs. My shirt's got a big hole in it, and I got this huge gaping wound in my fucking arm. And there's nobody here to pick us up; no one even to hitch a ride with. This is lovely, just fucking lovely!"

They had to walk six miles to a power station. Bob Palombo listened as the other agent explained what they had done; he told Palombo that his ranting and raving had probably saved their lives.

Palombo turned to his fellow agent. "No shit, I did that?" He didn't remember a word.

Palombo got on the phone at the power station and was patched through to the surveillance team. "Where the fuck are you? What happened?" Palombo asked.

"We're out by the guy's house, the guy that picked you up. We lost you."

"No shit!"

"We wanted to sit back real far so we wouldn't burn the surveillance, and because we were back so far, we lost you. You made a turn off the main road and we couldn't find you."

Palombo let the silence hang on the line before he spoke. "Just get out here and pick us up. I want to be there when those assholes return."

By the end of the night they had rounded up the entire gang. The shotgun-toting criminal made the mistake of resisting arrest, but that gave little gratification to Palombo. The pain from the wound to his arm would flare up for the rest of his life, particularly when things got tense.

Palombo finished Spanish immersion school and returned to New York, where his superior officer greeted him with a tirade. "What the hell is the matter with you? A couple of virgins going up against a gang of rip-off artists? You crazy? You could have wound up with one of the shortest careers in Customs history."

"Wait a minute, what are you chewing me out for? I was ordered to do it."

"Who told you to?"

"The special agent in charge of El Paso; he's the boss. He said he called and cleared it with New York."

"Well, he didn't! Next time, you call yourself and get clearance. Christ, I can't believe it."

In the coming weeks, Palombo's mind would often return to that night in the desert. He had finally experienced the "shoot 'em up" he had seen so often on television, and the real thing was nothing like the film version. He remembered the tiny popping sound the deadly pistol had made in the desert air, like a cap pistol. It was something he would always remember. He talked to experienced undercover agents, and they told him he should have pulled his gun when the surveillance car disappeared, stuck the gun in the driver's ear and said, "Turn around, we never agreed to this. Let's go back to the motel." He would have kept control and kept the cover.

He squeezed his healing arm and said to himself, "Never, never again, will I let control of a dangerous situation slip out of my hands . . . never."

CHAPTER 3

Griselda's Girdles

Carmen Cabán was Pepe Cabrera's mistress. Petite and pretty, with dark brown eyes, she talked in a voice so soft that you had to pay attention to hear what she was saying. She looked like the last person in the world to be mixed up with gangsters.

The first time Carmen saw Griselda Blanco was in Central Park in 1971 when she was taking a walk with her girlfriend, Amparo Restrepo. Griselda was already famous in Colombia. Carmen's girlfriend grabbed her arm and said, "Don't look now, but that is the Godmother over there."

A little on the heavy side now, Griselda had dyed her hair blond and wore a lot of jewelry. Griselda was with her lover, Alberto Bravo, walking through the park just enjoying the day.

Carmen's head automatically turned in the direction of Griselda. "No, Carmen, don't look at her. She is the evil one I told you about," Amparo said.

Carmen looked at her friend with a bewildered look on her face and raised her eyebrows.

"She is the one who killed the two girls in the hotel room here in New York," Amparo whispered.

"Why?" Carmen asked. "Why would she do such a thing?"

"She owed them a lot of money, so she killed them."

"So she wouldn't have to pay the debt?" Carmen asked, trying to steal a glance at Griselda.

"Yes, now do as I tell you. Don't look at her," Amparo insisted.

Carmen took a quick look at Griselda anyway. Then the two girls scurried out of the park.

In 1972, Griselda Blanco spent every moment of every day thinking up ways to smuggle cocaine into the United States. She, Alberto Bravo, and Pepe Cabrera had decided they would be wholesalers. Their involvement would end when the white powder entered the United States. They knew distributors who would eagerly buy the 90 percent pure coke, dilute it with speed or vitamin B, and resell it for much more than they had paid. It didn't matter that their customers made great profits. Griselda believed the real money was in moving weight. She couldn't read or write very well at the time, but her mind was fast with numbers. She knew that every one hundred kilos at $10,000 a kilo net profit meant a million dollars to her organization. It was simple: Deliver the coke and collect the cash—no street problems.

The money started to pour in. It was like a tidal wave of cash, twenties turned into hundreds, hundreds turned into thousands, and thousands turned into millions.

She couldn't quite believe her good fortune until one day she looked into her closet and saw three hundred pairs of shoes. Many had never been worn; some designs were the same, but in eight different colors; and some were designer shoes from Italy that she remembered had cost more than a hundred dollars a pair.

THE GODMOTHER

Carmen Cabán next saw Griselda in August 1972 in Medellín, Colombia. Carmen had traveled from New York to Colombia with Pepe, her lover at the time, who was carrying cash down to Griselda. She was also visiting her young son, who was being raised by her mother. At that time, Carmen was working in a New York nightclub called "The Club Mambo" on Broadway.

Carmen went to Griselda's house and delivered the cash. Griselda immediately asked her, "Why don't you take some cocaine back to the United States on your body?"

"I'll think about it, but I'm very nervous," Carmen whispered.

Carmen spent a few nights out, dancing and dining with Griselda, Alberto Bravo, and Pepe Cabrera. Griselda was a well-known person in Medellín. She spent money freely and was welcomed wherever she went, heralded as *La Madrina*—the Godmother. One night when they were out, Griselda bragged to Carmen that she had a good way of dealing with anyone who crossed her. "I kill them," she said. "Anyone that crosses me dies; that keeps it simple."

"Surely not everyone," Carmen said softly.

"If my mother does something to me, I'll kill my mother, too. You understand?"

Carmen sat with her mouth open, too shocked to answer.

One time Carmen was invited to go with Griselda to the Barrio Antioquia to visit the girdle and bra factory where they sewed the cocaine into the undergarments. A bra and girdle held one kilo. The showroom was covered with bras and girdles of all sizes and shapes. It was the fitting room for the female mules who would carry the coke.

Diana, a pretty Colombian woman, was in the showroom. Griselda told Diana to try on a bra and girdle, then slip her dress on so that Carmen could see how well the undergarments were fitted and how

35

difficult it would be for U.S. Customs to detect the coke.

"Maybe you will fly with Diana, and both of you can carry product for us, no? We will fit you out here, then you will meet with me again in my house with the other girls when we are ready, and you will all be dressed together and sent on your way."

"Maybe," Carmen said, fascinated. "Maybe; I will give you my final decision tomorrow."

But that night she saw Pepe Cabrera in Medellín, out on the town with another woman. She had a fierce argument with him that ended in Carmen's refusal to carry the coke.

Carmen did not see Griselda again until December of 1972, when Pepe asked her to travel from New York to Colombia to take some bank money orders to Griselda to pay for the cocaine he was receiving.

Griselda was now the main Colombian connection for New York. She brought finished cocaine in from Peru and Bolivia, and also processed cocaine on her own ranches.

Griselda greeted Carmen warmly. The Godmother had just returned from Brazil, where she had had some minor plastic surgery done on her face, and also a "tummy tuck." But basically she looked the same.

Griselda asked Carmen if she wanted to go with her to visit the forger who made the passports and visas.

"Sure, why not?" Carmen said.

They drove to the apartment of Bernardo Roldán. It was a large apartment, and the entire living room was given over to his work. New Colombian passports and visas were stacked up on the main desk. It was obvious that he had a good source of supply for new passports.

He had a complete photo booth for Polaroid passport pictures, along with other camera equipment. Entry and exit stamps were piled up neatly on a nearby table. Griselda also supplied "papers," for a fee, to people other than those inside her own organization.

Carmen watched in awe as Roldán worked his magic. First, he used a razor blade to pry loose an old photo from a passport. He gently removed the photo and laid it back to back with a new photo of a different person. He trimmed the new photo until it was exactly the size of the photo he had removed, then placed it on the rough area where the original photo had been. Satisfied that it was a perfect match, he carefully glued it into place. Roldán waited a couple of minutes for the glue to dry, then he compressed the photo tight to the page with the official embossed seal of the Colombian government.

It was not uncommon for three or four people to use the same passport. Once the person was inside the United States, Griselda would collect the passport and have it sent back to Colombia for a new photo to be attached. Roldán was also an expert on the visas that had to accompany the passports for entry into the United States.

Carmen was astounded; the Godmother had her own passport office, only it was quicker and more efficient than the Colombian government office.

That night they went out to a nightclub to party. Carmen was shocked when Griselda proudly announced that Alberto Bravo now owned the national soccer team.

In 1973, Carmen finally decided to carry drugs, but only inside the United States, never from Colombia. She traveled many times to Puerto Rico and Miami from New York to pick up coke. Griselda would call Pepe from Colombia and tell him of the shipment details. Platform shoes were a favorite way to send the dope.

Often a ship from Colombia would pull into the port of Miami with a crate of one hundred to two hundred pairs of shoes loaded with cocaine. Griselda would know in advance the shoe sizes of the people who were to pick up the merchandise. Carmen and her male companion would wait for a signal to board the ship, passing time either in a bar or the parking lot.

Inside their car, they would have up to one hundred pairs of shoes each. Once they received the "all clear" signal, they would board the ship as visitors. On board, they would slip into a stateroom and swap shoes, leaving behind their shoes and slipping on the coke-filled shoes they were given. To avoid suspicion, Carmen and her companion would repeat this routine up to ten times a day for a period of as long as five days, until they had removed all the loaded shoes from the ship.

The shoes would then be taken to a rented apartment or motel room and sliced open; the cocaine would be carefully removed, weighed, and poured into plastic Ziploc bags. Then Carmen would give the dope to Pepe Cabrera to distribute to his anxiously waiting customers.

On one occasion Pepe accompanied Carmen to Miami Beach, and they stayed at the Fontainebleau Hotel waiting for a man called San Cocho, who was coming in from Puerto Rico with a shipment of Griselda's cocaine. Puerto Rico was a good pickup spot, because once in Puerto Rico, it was not necessary to clear U.S. Customs again.

San Cocho arrived, and he was short eight kilos; he gave Pepe only two. Carmen flew the coke to New York. When Alberto Bravo saw that eight kilos were missing, he and Griselda decided to kill San Cocho.

San Cocho arrived back in Medellín, Colombia, a few weeks later and was executed. This was a vivid lesson to Carmen that things had to be done right in the drug business. There were no second chances.

On the average, mules now made a thousand dollars a trip. And they often carried cash on their bodies down to Colombia. In March of 1973, Carmen watched Pepe strap $120,000 onto the bodies of two girls; $80,000 in money orders and $40,000 in cash. It was fitted into special bras and girdles. The money was to pay Griselda for the coke she had sent.

For this trip, Pepe accompanied the girls himself. On the plane, Pepe told the girls to go to the washroom and remove the money from their bodies and give it to him. He put the money in a plastic box. Pepe had a friend in Colombian Customs who he believed was going to clear him with no inspection. After they landed in Medellín, Pepe handed him the box and watched the man disappear. The Customs man never returned, and the money was gone forever. Later, as the business grew, this amount of money would be a lot less important, but at that point it was critical to Griselda's organization.

Griselda was waiting at the airport with Alberto. When Pepe told her, she flew into a rage, "I told you to use the girls to carry the money. I sent you special underwear for them to hide the money. Why did you not use them? Why did you do this on the plane?" Pepe stood in silence listening to Griselda.

Griselda was shaking, her eyes black with rage. "Pepe, if you do not give me this money, I am going to kidnap your son and kill him."

Pepe knew that this was no idle threat. He had seen Griselda's unleashed violence with his own eyes. "I will give you my Mercedes car and my house, my beautiful house."

"Enough! I do not want your car or your house! I want the cash that you owe me. That money was your responsibility."

The matter was settled. Pepe paid, but Griselda never supplied Pepe Cabrera again, and she told Alberto not to ship to him. But Alberto disregarded Griselda's wishes and continued to ship to Pepe, in secret, risking his own life.

This relationship worked out well for a while, until late 1973 when Pepe killed one of Alberto Bravo's nephews over a dope deal gone bad. At that point they ceased doing business.

Things were getting hotter in New York. In the early part of 1974, Griselda, Alberto and Pepe could feel the breath of the NYPD and the Feds on their necks. Pepe left New York for Miami, and Alberto went to join Griselda in Colombia.

It was at this time that Griselda met the Sepúlveda brothers, who were to play a large part in her life. Paco and Diego were the shooters and dealers who worked for her out of New York; and Dario, a famous bandit, bank robber, and drug smuggler who operated from Colombia, would later become Griselda's lover and husband.

Colombia was also becoming dangerous for Griselda; she was making strong enemies with her repeated use of violence. There was a string of murders and destruction that could be traced to her doorstep. It was inevitable that sooner or later she would have to leave Colombia.

CHAPTER 4

Girl Talk

María Gutierrez was not surprised when Griselda Blanco walked into her travel agency in Medellín in 1973 with a handful of passports, visas, and a list of itineraries. All the destinations were the same—New York.

María had first met Griselda in 1968, in Queens, and they had met socially a few times after that. María Gutierrez was from one of the first families of Colombia; her cousin had been president of the country. María was a celebrated concert pianist in South America, as well as a championship swimmer who'd competed on the Olympic team. She moved in the best social circles in Medellín. Somehow she knew that drugs would be the scourge of her country, and she was determined to do all she could to stop the *narco-traficantes.*

María knew that Griselda was a *narco-traficante* and that her partners were Alberto Bravo and Pepe Cabrera. Griselda did not live with Alberto Bravo; he traveled in higher social strata. His family was prominent in Colombian society, and Griselda Blanco was not invited to join the group. She kept a private residence in Medellín where Alberto visited and sometimes stayed the night, but she never visited Alberto.

María also knew that Griselda had five ranches now, where she processed the cocaine base into cocaine hydrochloride. The process was run by "cooks" who used ether, aviation fuel, and a lot of human labor. Griselda had hundreds of employees on these ranches. They all brought their babies to her for her blessing, and many asked her to stand godmother to the children.

María inspected the papers and found them to be in order.

"I will have much business for you, María," Griselda said. "Do you want to handle it?"

María looked at her and smiled, her brain working quickly. "Yes, of course, that's why we are in business." She examined the papers more closely and knew they were all forged, but it was excellent work. The forgeries would be undetectable to the authorities, and even if they did discover the papers were false, Griselda would simply pay them off.

"So, that's good. You will be my exclusive agent; it's good for both of us. Maybe we will become friends," Griselda said.

"I'm sure we will," María said.

"When will you have the visas processed?" Griselda asked.

"I'll have the plane tickets and the visas ready tomorrow afternoon."

"I'll see you then; perhaps we will go for coffee after," Griselda offered. "We'll have a little girl talk."

"Yes, I would like that." María watched as Griselda walked down the street to her waiting bodyguards and car. María's heart was pumping so hard she almost swooned as she raced back to her desk and scooped up the documents. She hurried out the back door and ran straight to the U.S. Embassy.

George Meyer, the American consul, listened quietly as María spilled out what had just happened to her. When she had finished, he explained that a new agency had just been formed, the Drug Enforcement Administration, and that its people were the ones to contact. María sat there as he called Bill Matthews, the special agent in charge of the brand-new Colombian office. Matthews came immediately with Special Agent Charlie Cecil in tow. Charlie, an easygoing, good-looking agent, spoke perfect Spanish and had a natural way with people.

María repeated her story. Matthews and Cecil knew who Griselda Blanco was. Charlie had labeled her dossier "The Godmother," since all the locals called her that. María explained about the false passports and visas, and how Griselda would be bringing documents to her on a regular basis.

The DEA agents asked her why she wanted to help; what was her motivation?

María Gutierrez hated *narco-traficantes*. She knew the potential human destruction, and that it would ruin the Colombian people. It was the small people who would be used as mules and processors, and only a few would reap the profits. It would ruin her country.

The agents looked at each other, wary that perhaps they were being set up.

"What would you like me to do?" María asked the agents.

"Let us photocopy these documents, and we will take it from there," Bill Matthews said.

The documents included itineraries. The agents knew that it would be easy enough to see if the itineraries were followed. The mules could be picked up in the United States and tailed.

"Go ahead and process the visas," Charlie Cecil said. "Do you think you could get any closer to her, become her friend, provide us with more information?"

"No problem; I think she wants to become my friend," María responded.

"So, you will help us?" Charlie Cecil asked.

"Yes, I will help you. Maybe we can make a difference."

"Maybe, just maybe, we can," the agents said, after they had Xeroxed the documents and walked her to the door. They stood at the window, watching her and wondering, as she hurried back to her office.

The original DEA office in Colombia was made up of six agents, including Bill Matthews, Charlie Cecil, and Annabelle Grimm. In ten years' time, events would get so violent and murderous that the DEA would have to shut down the Colombian operation and return to North America.

María immediately promoted her friendship with Griselda. It started slowly at first, with coffee, shopping, getting their hair done together, talking about children, and doing business.

Finally, Griselda began to open up to María. She took her on drives to her many ranches, where Griselda spoke to her people who oversaw the processing of the cocaine base into cocaine. María felt that Griselda, in her way, was trying to impress her. María just smiled and nodded, letting her carry on.

Then one day Griselda picked María up, and together they went to visit some factories. Griselda explained to María that she personally oversaw the operation to ensure that things were done correctly.

They arrived at the brassiere and girdle factory, and Griselda opened the trunk of her car and showed María boxes of small glassine bags, each bag the size of a silver dollar. She carried the boxes into the factory and gave them to the plant manager, who got right to work. The cocaine was never out of Griselda's sight. She explained to María that the cocaine packets were sewn in at the factory so the garment seams would be perfect. The cocaine was strategically placed so that the brassiere looked like a slightly padded bra, and the tight elastic girdles were designed to pull in the female abdomen in order to make room for the half-inch layer of cocaine.

At the shoe factory, María watched as hollowed-out heels and soles were filled with bags of cocaine, then carefully and perfectly glued together so no one could find an unnatural joining.

They visited the bird cage factory where false bottoms were welded on after the cocaine had been enclosed. The cages could only be opened with a welder's torch.

Then Griselda took María to her home, where María watched Griselda's young sons, Dixon, Uber, and Osvaldo, now aged 13, 12 and 11, as they worked like experts on two Samsonite suitcases that lay on the floor. They tore out the interior shell of one suitcase and set it aside. They loaded coke into the untouched second suitcase, and then fitted the loose interior shell into the second suitcase over the coke. They used a rivet gun to reseal the shell. The new suitcase looked perfect; no one could tell there were two interiors with a layer of coke in between. The only difference between the modified suitcase and the original was that the new suitcase weighed an additional five kilos. This could only be done with the Samsonite hard-shell suitcase. Griselda had thought of the idea, and she was very proud of herself and of the proficiency of her sons.

The DEA officials were impressed with her originality, too. They knew that Griselda was using female mules, but they didn't know that the mules were wearing factory-made undergarments full of cocaine until María told them.

Charlie Cecil was building up an extensive rogues' gallery of Griselda's organization. As María received the passports, itineraries, and visas, she would bring them to Charlie, who would photocopy them and pass the intelligence on to DEA headquarters in Washington. María was providing precious information. It furnished exact details of who, where, and when the couriers and the coke entered the United States.

In 1973, the DEA was only beginning to be able to handle the intelligence it was receiving. Computers were in their infancy, and the NADDIS (National Narcotics and Dangerous Drug Information System) was not yet born.

Sometimes this information was passed on to the proper areas within the DEA; sometimes it wasn't.

PART II

SPINNING
THE
WEB

CHAPTER 5

Operation Banshee

In July 1973, as far as Bob Palombo was concerned, he was in the right place at the right time. The government decided to merge the Bureau of Narcotics and Dangerous Drugs with certain divisions of the U.S. Customs Service, now to be called the Drug Enforcement Administration. Government officials came through the Customs Service and examined the case load of every agent to determine what the predominance of the cases were. If most of the cases were narcotics, the agents went over to the new agency, like it or not. For Bob Palombo, it was the greatest thing in the world. Then, too, he was now engaged to a terrific woman named Grace, who worked as a medical secretary. His career and personal life were going extremely well.

That summer, Bob Palombo was transferred into Division 20, a wild, rock 'em, sock 'em division that was made up of groups 21, 22, and 23. Group 23 worked the streets undercover, and was known for long hours—weekends, nights, holidays—"just bring in the bad guys." The agents in Division 20 liked the job.

However, many agents wanted to avoid being moved into Division 20, so much so that they would avoid running into superior officers whenever possible. It became a joke with the superiors. "Hey, who's that? He looks like a good recruit for Division 20, don't you think?"

"He looks perfect to me."

The agent they were discussing would quickly disappear into the nearest washroom in a panic as the jokers walked on.

The first case that Bob Palombo worked on after the merger was the Omar Hernández case. Bob was doing buy-bust operations in Queens. The undercovers would buy a few small amounts of narcotics, then request the largest amount they thought the doper could handle. The doper would show up with the coke and the agents would grab him.

One afternoon the DEA was notified by Customs that a kilogram of coke had been grabbed and the doper wanted to make a deal. A kilo of coke was a major bust in 1973. Bob Palombo's new supervisor came to him and said, "How do we handle this? You've had a lot of experience with this kind of bust."

"It's just a typical control delivery. The guy wants to do the right thing; let's get him in here." They brought in the doper and debriefed him. He told everything he knew. They set him up in a hotel room in the Taft Hotel, and told him to call his contact, Omar Hernández. He made the call, but the contact wasn't biting. "Come to Queens Boulevard. I want to have a look at you, to meet you," Omar said.

Palombo decided not to let the informant go; he might flee. The doper called back. "Hey, where were you?" Omar asked.

The informant answered as he had been instructed. "I got lost. I'm a stranger here. I got the stuff in a hotel, and this is where I'm staying. You want the goods, you come here. I'm not going to walk around New York. I'm a foreigner; I'll get arrested. You want the goods, you come to me."

"Fuck you!" the voice on the other end said. But eventually he called back, and a meeting was set up. When he came in to make the buy, he was arrested. He was carrying a whole set of phony identification. Omar Hernández was really Jaime Bermudas Botero, a dealer for Griselda Blanco.

He was brought before a magistrate in the Southern District of New York, which had had little experience with Colombians. Palombo pleaded before the Magistrate not to give bail, but his pleas fell on deaf ears. The bail was set at $15,000 cash. The money was posted and Omar Hernández slipped back into the maze of New York City, skipping out on his bail. And he went right back to work for the Godmother.

Palombo was picking up a steady stream of intelligence on the street, all pertaining to a large group of Colombians who were acting like the mob; they were getting organized, and there was a powerful woman involved. He just didn't know who the hell they were.

Bob's days were busy. The Colombians were creeping through New York, spreading the cocaine cancer. The demand was building every day, and so was the supply. The newly formed DEA had its hands full dealing with the intelligence the agents were receiving from Colombia and New York.

And there were potential conflicts with other agencies, primarily the NYPD, New York's finest. The New York Police Department was just beginning to wake up to the fact that it had a plague on its hands: Colombian rats bearing white powder on their backs had come to New York.

Whatever *could* go wrong usually *did* go wrong. This was proven once again when Bob Palombo's Group 23 and the NYPD were both working the same doper, only they didn't know it.

Group 23's undercover was a roly-poly American

who was buying from a Colombian female, Elena Ramirez. Bob and the rest of his Group wondered how anyone could sell to him, he looked so much like a cop. The NYPD was also working her, using Luis Ramos, a narcotics officer who looked the part of a doper. They were both buying eighths of a kilo daily, trying to get Elena up to a kilo so they could nail her.

On one occasion, both undercovers were in her apartment at the same time, each buying an eighth. They stared at each other and thought, "Wait a minute, this guy looks like the heat; could it be we're both undercover? Shit!"

When they got out of the apartment, they returned to their superiors and began to compare notes; phone calls were made at the highest level. "Are you guys working on Elena Ramirez?"

"No."

"Bullshit; come on, my undercover saw your undercover in her apartment today."

"Yeah, okay, so we're working her. Luis was sure there was a DEA agent in that apartment with him."

"Well, we want to work her."

"Get real, we're already working her, and we're going to bust her ass."

"You can't do that; we're the DEA."

"Congratulations, that and fifty cents will get you a cup of coffee. We're the NYPD, and Queens is fucking part of fucking New York, in case you hadn't noticed."

After this exchange, the two groups agreed to share information to see what intelligence they had on these Colombians. The NYPD had wiretaps, and the DEA had incredible intelligence coming up from Colombia that was being fed to them by Charlie Cecil.

What unfolded before their eyes was amazing. They had a major cocaine ring on their hands. These people were organized and moving a lot of weight. They had infested Queens like a rabbit warren. They changed addresses and names on a constant basis. They drove old cars, always with false IDs. They were paranoid, yet they didn't fear the police. The worst that could happen if they were arrested was that they would jump bail and go back to Colombia. Bob Palombo knew what they were: a new form of criminal. You could throw the police manual out the window. A new one would have to be written to catch these people. Three names were now appearing on a constant basis: Griselda Blanco, Alberto Bravo and Pepe Cabrera. These people were the source of the cocaine.

The long hours, weekdays and weekends, put a strain on Bob's pending marriage plans. Grace was left to plan the wedding basically on her own. When the two families were to meet for the first time at Grace's house, Bob was unexpectedly called away to do a drug bust on the Grand Concourse in the Bronx. He called Grace later and said, "How did everything go?"

"They met, and everyone got along fine. We talked a lot about you; they understood why you weren't here," Grace said. "I understand, too."

It was a trying time for both of them, but Grace never faltered in her support for her future husband.

Frank White, the slightly sarcastic supervisor of Group 23, put it succinctly: "Bob, you couldn't have picked a better group to come into than the 23rd. If Grace can put up with this bullshit while you're engaged, then she'll put up with it for the rest of your lives, because there is no crazier division, and no crazier group *inside* the division, than yours."

"Thanks for the exquisite logic, chief."

"You're welcome, Bob, anytime."

To handle the growing Colombian problem, they decided to form a task force that included two narcotics divisions of the New York Police Department: Manhattan North, and the 17th Division. The task force also included the New York State Police and the Drug Enforcement Administration. The primary targets were singled out: Alberto Bravo, Pepe Cabrera, and "The Godmother," Griselda Blanco. The operation was named "Banshee."

Bob Palombo and his partner, Bob Nieves, were sent from Group 23 to the task force on loan. Palombo was hearing Griselda Blanco's name over and over on the streets. She was mysterious, like a whisper in the dark.

And there was murder floating in the air; dead bodies kept surfacing. The word was out that to belong to the Godmother's gang of killers, *Los Pistoleros,* you had to remove a piece of the dead victim's body, then take it to her main shooter, Paco Sepúlveda. The gang would then look for the newspaper account of the killing to see if it mentioned a missing ear, finger, or hand.

These stories were not really believed until there was a gruesome murder in an apartment in Queens. The murder was believed to have been committed by Jorge Rivera, who was known as "Riverito."

The killers entered the apartment of a Colombian dope dealer and shot him. They wanted to remove the body from the scene, but they were afraid that the blood would leave a trail down the hall and steps of the apartment building. They decided the best way to handle it was to hang the victim by his feet over the bathtub like a side of beef, slit his throat, and let the blood go down the drain.

They relaxed in the apartment, playing cards while the body drained. After an hour or so, they scooped up the living room carpet and wrapped the bloodless body inside. When this was completed, one of the killers slung the carpet over his shoulder and walked out of the apartment house to his car, threw the body into the trunk, and drove away.

Palombo knew the Godmother was the main link, the linchpin that held everything together. And now with Operation Banshee, they had a chance to nail her.

As Palombo and Nieves walked out the door, the

other members of Group 23 yelled after them. "Hey, guys, you gotta be goin' up in the world! You can't get any lower than Division 20. You must be sad to be leavin'."

"Yeah, yeah," Palombo said.

"Don't forget, kick a little ass for your old pals, will ya?"

"Kick your own ass! Get your feet off the desk and get out in the street; that's what you get paid for," Palombo said as he closed the door behind him. He was excited. He could feel the adrenaline filling his body. Operation Banshee was big stuff—there was no question about it.

It was the first operation of its kind, an official amalgamation of several police agencies to work on one specific case, even though the case involved, as they were later to learn, hundreds of Colombian players.

The commanding officers of Operation Banshee did not like what they saw. As the more-than-fifty-man task force blitzed the Colombians with wiretaps, surveillances, and undercover buy-bust operations, they soon realized that they were up against a giant conspiracy that had its roots in Queens but permeated almost all of New York City.

It was October of 1974, and the investigation had been under way for eight months. The wiretap that had been issued to NYPD Narcotics District 17, in Queens, had been terminated early in Operation Banshee, and the surveillance had gone stale. Colombians are the most difficult of all criminals to trace, because they change identities as casually as Americans change shirts. On any given day, a Colombian might show up with a new address, new car, new driver's license, and new registration. Bob Palombo had been working Colombians almost exclusively since 1970, and he knew their habits. He had burst into apartments where the eggs in the pan were still hot yet the place was abandoned, lock, stock, and fried egg. Colombians left clothes in the closet and water in the bathtub. If a surveillance went cold, then it most likely meant that he would have to start all over again. Colombians would never return to a house that was "hot."

And that was exactly what happened with the cold wiretap. Most of the addresses and phone numbers were stale, and the agents knew it.

But the situation was a lot more complicated at the senior level, where politics crept into play. The longer the agents waited, the more chance they had of additional surveillances going cold. And if it came out that they had had a major conspiracy in their grasp and it had slipped through their fingers, the media would crucify the senior officers for incompetency and indecision.

There had been no bigger case of drug conspiracy ever discovered. No matter what happened in terms of arrests, the senior officers understood that the case would garner enormous press coverage, and with good press coverage came instant promotions.

But the men in the field, the Indians, knew more than the chiefs. They knew that the best way to kill a rat was to cut off the head, and this rat had three heads: Griselda Blanco, Alberto Bravo, and Pepe Cabrera. They were lying low in Colombia and Miami. Somehow, they had to be lured up to New York, and nailed. There were ways to do this; the agents just needed a little more time.

The agents saw it differently from the street. It was really a giant, complicated maze of multiple conspiracies, with one common denominator—Griselda Blanco and her organization. She was the queen, and the Colombians in the New York *barrio* were like soldier ants working to the will of their monarch. It was 1974 and because of demand, Colombia was no longer producing the bulk of the coke. It was primarily a transshipping and processing point, with much of the cocaine coming from Peru and Bolivia as a finished product and cocaine base. Griselda had her ranches, but they were still just starting to produce. She was a giant wholesaler, supplying other smaller wholesalers, but it was clear that she was the source.

The field agents needed more time to figure out a way to lure the three to Queens; they were so close to nailing them.

But there was no more time.

The men had been on loan now for almost nine months from the DEA and the NYPD. They were the best men in their squads, the "case makers," and their supervisors wanted them back.

"Operation Banshee is over—arrest the assholes, and send me my guys back." That was the word coming from headquarters. "Operation Banshee was supposed to be a task force, not a new department; send my boys back!"

And so it was on Columbus Day in 1974 that the final order came down: "Showtime! Let's roll."

The "war room" was the training room for the NYPD at 555 West 57th Street. Extra men were called in who had not participated in the actual investigation; all together there were more than one hundred men.

The room was as wide as a gymnasium, and could easily accommodate the officers. Few people were privy to exactly what was going to happen, until it happened. It was "need to know" only, to avoid security leaks; even the officers of the 110th Precinct, where a lot of the arrests were going to take place, only knew there was going to be a takedown; no details were given.

The meeting was run by a Deputy Inspector from the NYPD, and by James Hunt, the Associate Regional Director of the DEA. They handed out the criminal complaints and arrest warrants from the U.S. Attorney's office.

"Okay, men, listen up. Your teams are listed on the board by table; go to the table and pick up the arrest files," James Hunt said. The arrest files were complete dossiers on the individuals who were to be apprehended. The files, when possible, included surveillance photos, mug shots, fingerprints, addresses, maps, favorite bars or hangouts, car license and description, and addresses of girlfriends.

"What's the color of the day?" an officer yelled.

"Orange," the Deputy Inspector retorted. In order to identify a cop, especially an undercover cop, the NYPD used a color code. If an undercover officer was caught in the sweep, he was supposed to say, "I'm on the job, and the color of the day is orange." This was usually enough to identify himself, and the appropriate action would be taken.

The arresting officers were all dressed in casual civilian clothes. The DEA wore identifying armbands, and the NYPD wore jackets with POLICE printed across the back.

It was essential to be identifiable when making arrests, especially in apartment buildings and private homes throughout many precincts. Sometimes a neighbor would call in a complaint, saying, "There's a bunch of guys running around my building carrying shotguns and handguns," and a radio car would be dispatched to the scene. Missed communication could be deadly.

Palombo was a team leader, one of three who stayed in the command center and orchestrated the raid. He rose and spoke to the group, "I'm Bob Palombo, the coordinator of case 0416. We've got about thirty defendants to pick up. Contact me at the base on extension 213. I want to know when the arrest is made, the exact time, and you guys mark it down as well. And I need to know if you are on your way back here to 57th Street with the prisoner. And when you get to the lockup, let us know that you are in safely. That's it from me; good luck."

Boards were hung with the names of the defendants in bold letters and as they were arrested, the names were crossed off. There were only three names that really excited Palombo: Griselda Blanco, Alberto Bravo, and Pepe Cabrera. Maybe, just maybe, they would be up visiting from Colombia, and they would get caught in the sweeping net of arrests.

The arrest teams were handpicked. They were experienced officers who knew the ropes. They knew not to just knock on someone's door and say, "Hey, are you Julio? This is your picture, you must be Julio. You're under arrest." Palombo and the other officers had been trained that the last thing to do is knock on someone's door, because once alerted, a Colombian will vanish. First, they would put the person's place under surveillance, then try to spot the car on the street somewhere in the vicinity. If the building had a garage, they would go down in the garage and use a phony reason for being there if they encountered a neighbor or a security guard: "Hey, I'm with auto theft; we are looking for a yellow Cadillac," when a brown Chevy was the true objective. Once the car was spotted, the officers would know the suspect was probably nearby.

Often, a female officer would call the house and ask for the Colombian; if he came to the phone, they'd nab him. If the information on the dope sheet included his favorite bar, an agent with an Hispanic accent would go to find him and keep an eye on him until he left. Once he went outside, he could be nailed. If he made it to his car, the officer would follow him until he stopped and got out. The officers were told to avoid conflict and confrontation; to be patient and nail the suspect on turf where the good guys had control.

Throughout the operation head counts were added up by the senior officers: "What are we up to? What's the arrest count?"

"Sixteen arrests and teams A, C, and F are transporting. Each is on its way back to 57th Street with a defendant."

"Everybody's got arrest kits, right?" the officer asked.

"Yes, sir."

Arrest kits were made up of Ziploc bags to hold evidence, and four separate fingerprint cards. The first fingerprint card was for the DEA; the second was for the FBI, to be run through the National Crime Computer; the third set went to Interpol, to coordinate with the Colombian police; and the fourth was for Immigration.

The arrest kit also contained photo instructions. Four photos were to be taken of the defendant for the files. A 202, which is a pedigree sheet, was included. All the particulars of the defendant were listed: age, description, and criminal history. In addition, an exact, detailed arrest report had to be made out by one member of the team. The arrest report was a complete summary of what happened during the course of the arrest.

And finally, each arrest team was responsible for reading the Miranda warning in Spanish, collecting any evidence, and placing the evidence in the Ziploc bags. Evidence included all pieces of paper with phone numbers, diaries, address books, airplane tickets; anything that might lead the agents further in the investigation.

The final count was eighty-eight arrests. The next day, banner headlines broke in all the major New York newspapers: "Major Drug Bust," "Giant Ring of Cocaine Smugglers Nabbed," "Major Cocaine Conspiracy Busted."

The higher-ups—in the U.S. Attorney's office, the NYPD, and the DEA—fell all over each other to accept the kudos for the success of Operation Banshee. Meanwhile, the agents had a mountain of paperwork to deal with.

Some of the wiretap evidence was later thrown out on technicalities; several state charges were successfully tried. In 1975, the U.S. government tried twelve people in the original Operation Banshee trial, and they were all convicted. But as far as Bob Palombo and a lot of other agents were concerned, the big fish got away. Griselda, Alberto, and Pepe swam right past the arrest teams. Nevertheless, there were major results from the Operation Banshee bust: It was proven that a large complex conspiracy designed to sell cocaine did exist and was flourishing in New York. Griselda, Pepe, and Alberto, along with forty others, were now fugitives on a United States federal arrest warrant. And things were so hot for the Godmother in New York that she moved her operation south to Miami.

Bob Palombo's shoulder hurt him. He squeezed his bicep where he had been shot, and the pain shot right through his shoulder. His arm always hurt when things didn't go right. And as far as he was concerned, they had not cut off the source of the problem, Griselda Blanco, the Godmother. The rat's head was still intact. "But that won't always be the case," he thought. "Our paths will cross again, Señora Blanco! Sooner or later, I'm going to pull your empire down."

What Palombo didn't know was that it was going to take another ten years of his life.

CHAPTER 6

High Seas Hoax

It was 1975, and Griselda was splitting her time between Miami and Medellín. María Gutierrez was informing Charlie Cecil of the Godmother's every move, and Charlie was telling the DEA.

María had told him of Griselda's bookkeeper, Luz Marina. Luz was married to Conrado Valencia Zalgado, a vicious shooter and dope dealer called *El Loco*. He lived in Miami and Queens. Sometimes he worked for the Godmother, and sometimes he worked freelance. *El Loco* was later involved in the famous Turnpike Shoot-Out that occurred in Miami in 1979.

Charlie Cecil picked up Luz Marina's trail, and they followed her to her own house in a small suburb of Medellín. Charlie was able to talk the DAS (Departamento Administrativo de Seguridad) into raiding the house. They did, the next night. Charlie and Annabelle Grimm went in right behind the DAS. The DEA agents knew immediately what they had, but the DAS didn't; to them it was just a mass of meaningless paper and some cash.

Charlie and Annabelle looked at each other for a

second and grinned. Charlie spoke up. "Can we have these papers for a while?"

"Yeah, take them, we don't want them," the commanding officer responded.

Charlie and Annabelle scooped up the papers and rushed to their office, where they worked through the night to Xerox the records. Early the next morning, the DAS was there demanding the papers back. "We've got to have those papers back now," the commanding officer said.

Griselda was incensed that the DEA would manipulate the DAS into raiding her bookkeeper and have the audacity to go through her books. It angered her so much that on three separate occasions, she would try to kill Charlie Cecil.

The first time, in front of María, she talked of hitting Charlie and Annabelle. María immediately went to call Charlie and said, "Griselda is crazy with anger; you and Annabelle should leave Medellín for a while, right away, Charlie."

The next morning Charlie and Annabelle headed out for Bogotá. They were driving a souped-up Dodge Charger, the only one like it in Colombia. It was a car well-known to the *narco-traficantes*. Just outside of Medellín, Paco Sepúlveda, one of Griselda's shooters, passed by driving in the opposite direction. Charlie and Annabelle were sure they had been spotted. Annabelle climbed into the backseat with the shotgun and got ready for Paco and his group to return, but they didn't; they just became a spot of dust on the horizon and finally disappeared.

The documents that they had taken to copy confirmed, once again, that the magnitude of Griselda's operation was in the millions of dollars. Annabelle Grimm returned to Miami with many leads to follow up.

The relationship between Alberto Bravo and Griselda was beginning to deteriorate. Griselda never got over the insult of his having two separate residences and of her never being invited to Alberto's parties. And now there was Bruno Bravo, Alberto's brother, to contend with.

Bruno wanted to become an equal partner with Griselda and Alberto, and Bruno hated Griselda. She knew what would come next. If Bruno got into the group, he would form a triumvirate; there would be two against one, and she would be out in the cold. But Griselda had plans of her own.

She secretly arranged to have Bruno Bravo kidnapped and held for ransom; the ransom demanded was nine million pesos, 250,000 U.S. dollars.

Griselda encouraged Alberto to pay the ransom and get his beloved brother back. Alberto followed the advice, produced the ransom, and Bruno was returned. Griselda cried tears of joy at his return and banked the $250,000.

A month later Griselda ordered Bruno's death, and he was killed. It became just another unsolved Colombian murder.

A few months after that, the DEA tried to make a deal with the Godmother. Charlie Cecil was given the assignment. Charlie called Griselda's lawyer, Jorge Valencia, at his office. "Hello, this is Charlie Cecil. You know who I am?"

"Yes, you are the *molestia* of an American agent who is always bothering my client. She has spoken often of you."

"We want to offer her a deal."

"I don't think she wants to make a deal."

"Well, you should listen anyway," Charlie said.

"Go ahead, I'm listening."

"Not over the phone. Meet me this afternoon at Kevin's Disco up on the hill. I'll be at an outside table," Charlie said and hung up.

A few hours later Charlie watched as Jorge Valencia's Mercedes rounded the snaking curves that led up the mountain to Kevin's Disco. Kevin's sat high on a mountaintop that overlooked the city of Medellín. The twisting road that led to the top worked its way through the verdant green countryside. The picture from above was pastoral and tranquil, a far cry from the violence and intrigue that was boiling below in the real Medellín. Two motorcycles escorted the Mercedes up the hill. Jorge pulled into the parking lot and each motorcyclist took a strategic position that would overlook the men.

Jorge walked over and sat down. "So, señor, shall we hear your offer?"

"Before I give you my offer, I want you to know that underneath this newspaper in front of me is a .45. It's cocked and loaded, and it's pointing straight at you. If those two monkeys you brought with you make any moves, if they even so much as sneeze, you're going to go first. *Comprende?*"

"*Sí.*"

"We are prepared to offer your client immunity on the charges against her if she will testify against all the other main defendants, especially Alberto and Pepe."

"I think your offer will be refused. Even if she were inclined to talk, her family would be placed in grave danger." Jorge rose, signaled to his motorcycle escort, and left in his car. A few days later he called Charlie Cecil and said that his client refused to entertain any notion of a deal.

A few months later Griselda tried a second time to kill Charlie Cecil. Charlie had passed her in his car. He stuck his head out of the window and called, "*Hola, Gorda,* how are you?" and waved.

In Spanish, *gorda* means heavy, and Griselda was infuriated if anyone said she was fat. She went into a rage. Not only was Charlie constantly causing her problems in her business, but now he was insulting her.

That night Charlie got a frantic phone call at home

from María. "Charlie, please, I need to speak with you. It's very important. Meet me in the Inter-Continental Hotel in Medellín."

"It's late; can't it wait until the morning?"

"The morning will be too late."

Charlie showed up twenty minutes later at the Inter-Continental with Annabelle Grimm.

"Tomorrow you are going with the DAS agents to the south?" María asked.

"Yes."

"One of the DAS agents has told Griselda your route. She will send people to kill you."

Charlie and Annabelle just looked at each other. María's information had never been wrong. There was no need to doubt it now. Tomorrow they were to head a long way south on a lonely road where there were no homes, no buildings, no people: a perfect area for a murder.

"Maybe I shouldn't have called her *'La Gorda,'*" Charlie joked. Nobody laughed. They canceled the trip south.

Griselda's sex life was changing. One day she showed María pictures of a party she had held in her apartment the night before. She kept the apartment for "The Bacchanal," and the bacchanals were turning into orgies. The apartment was covered in mirrors. Griselda liked to look at pretty girls dressed in bikinis or nothing at all. Both boys and girls would come to the parties, and then Griselda would ask the girls to take their clothes off or to model skimpy swim-wear. The boys would also watch, but most times Griselda would send the boys home, and the girls would stay for more fun. Cocaine was always freely available, and if it was necessary to pay the girls, they would get cash. Sometimes Griselda would give her lovers special presents: cars, and diamond or emerald rings.

* * *

At this time Griselda was using a new trick for getting the drugs into Miami, one that involved paying off baggage handlers and stewardesses. A ticket would be purchased on Avianca, the state airline, and a suitcase loaded with cocaine would be checked in at the gate, but the ticket holder would never get on the plane. In Colombia, the Samsonite suitcase would be code-marked XXX in red chalk on the side. The lock combination and ticket number would then be passed on to the baggage handlers in Miami by the stewardesses in case they missed the XXX. The baggage handlers would pull the luggage, bypass Customs, and deliver it to an address in Miami. Each piece of luggage sent this way contained seven kilos. At Christmastime in 1975, Griselda had each plastic kilo bag marked *Feliz Navidad,* as a joke. It was her present to the United States; she sent up the coke from Colombia and the United States sent down greenback dollars.

Sometimes the greenbacks were sent down to Colombia in Pampers disposable diapers. It was common for Colombian women to bring back packages of Pampers, particularly women with small children in tow. They would get quick clearance through Colombian Customs, and often the Godmother would be waiting in her car at curbside. The 24-size box of Pampers could hold a cool, dry $300,000. One day María was in Griselda's car when she made a pickup at the airport. "Griselda, look," she said, "I have a new camera; maybe I should take pictures of everything we do?"

"Why? Why do you want to take pictures?" Griselda asked.

"For the future. When we are old women, we can look at the pictures, and we will feel good."

Griselda thought for a while. "Well, maybe it's okay, but I get to look through them and throw away the ugly ones."

"Sure, sure, that will be fine. Who wants the ugly

ones, anyway?" María asked, and they both laughed. The DEA received copies of all the photos María took, even the ugly ones.

That Christmas, 1975, Griselda received a special present from Alberto Bravo. The box was carefully wrapped with a big bow. Griselda tore the paper off and opened the box. Everyone watched as she withdrew the present. She held it up for everyone to admire. It was a gold-plated Ingram Mac-10 machine pistol, the fastest firing weapon made, a favorite with the Colombian shooters.

The gold-plated body of the weapon was encrusted with emeralds and a few small diamonds. The Godmother reached back into the box and withdrew the empty clip. She slipped the clip into the magazine and slapped the base with the palm of her hand, military-style, to ensure that it was well-seated; then she handed the weapon around for the Christmas revelers to admire. Everyone oohed and aahed as they handled and caressed the shiny gun. María passed it quickly to the person next to her; guns made her nervous.

And there was more. Alberto Bravo handed Griselda a second box about twelve inches long, a thin jewelry box of red felt. It wasn't wrapped. Griselda flipped it open. Inside was an exquisite necklace of large, perfect emeralds, interspaced with perfect three-carat "D flawless" diamonds. The necklace was easily worth more than a million dollars. She gasped in astonishment and delight. The necklace and the Mac-10 made a wonderful Christmas for Griselda, and kept Alberto Bravo alive for a little while longer.

Business had never been better. Griselda and Alberto were moving a steady two hundred kilos a month, and the price was holding up at $40,000 a kilo. This equated to $8 million a month in income to the organization. Yet it wasn't enough, because the demand was growing, and if they didn't supply, then someone else would.

They needed more ways to get the dope into the United States. The ever-creative Godmother came up with another new idea. It was 1976, and the United States was celebrating two hundred years of freedom. A major part of the celebration was the "Parade of Tall Ships," large-masted sailing vessels from all over the world. Most of the ships were national training vessels used by their navies.

The Colombian government was invited to send the *Gloria,* their big, beautiful, wooden-masted training ship. The three-masted *Gloria* was built in 1968, and was kept in the port at Cartagena. Two hundred fifty feet long, with a beam of thirty-five feet, she was the pride of the Colombian navy. Her permanent crew numbered sixty, as well as fifty additional cadets.

"We'll pack the *Gloria* with cocaine; we can easily get a thousand kilos on board," Griselda explained to Alberto.

"What about the navy?" Alberto asked.

"Pay them off."

"And the crew?"

"Diplomatic status; they'll all have diplomatic status," Griselda countered.

"Well, they'll never search the ship," Alberto mused. "But there is no way we can finance one thousand kilos. Suppose something happens and we lose the load?"

"Partners, let's take on partners. It will be to everyone's benefit," Griselda offered. "The ship will parade first in Miami, then Washington, New York, and Boston, all good ports of call for us and our partners." Griselda smiled.

"What was that party they had in Boston in their revolution?" Alberto asked.

"A tea party," María said.

"Forget the tea; we'll give them a cocaine party in 1976!" Alberto said, and they all laughed.

Griselda assembled the partners and the thousand kilos, and had the cocaine shipped to Cartagena.

María volunteered to travel to Cartagena with Griselda and her gang, in order to gather information for the DEA. Griselda wanted to oversee the operation of loading the thousand kilos of coke onto the ship. María stayed by her side the whole time.

The inside panels of the *Gloria* were stripped and replaced after hundreds of kilos had been stuffed behind them. Hatches were lifted to get access to the bilges, and the bilges were stacked with kilos wrapped in waterproof bags. The wall boards and flooring in the heads were removed, and the heads were packed with kilo bags. The galley was dismantled, and cocaine was placed in every available opening. María and Griselda were on their knees on top of bunks with screwdrivers in their hands as they helped the loading crew screw the paneling and fixtures back into place. There was almost no spot on the ship that did not have coke hidden in a secret compartment.

When it was over, Griselda stood back and admired her handiwork. There was $40 million worth of coke safely on board the *Gloria* when she was done, and the buyers were all standing by in the United States, waiting, cash in hand.

María could hardly wait to return to Medellín to tell Charlie Cecil the news. Charlie passed the information on to a disbelieving higher echelon in the DEA. Little was done with the information. Two hundred kilos were busted in Miami, and $1.7 million was confiscated in cash in Boston, but it was a political hot potato that no one wanted to field. No one in high office wanted the bad publicity, or to offend the Colombian government.

The Godmother had called it exactly right. Diplomatic immunity would raise its ugly head, and no one wanted to cast a pall on the bicentennial celebration by exposing the Colombian "gift" of one thousand kilos of coke.

* * *

The Godmother was becoming even more sophisticated in her operation. She used a code. No one in her operation ever used numbers in their books for phone numbers, addresses, or to keep track of debts or deliveries. The DEA was having a hell of a time trying to break the code, until María broke it for them.

Charlie Cecil asked her, "María, we need to find out what the code is. Can you help us?"

A week later, María came back to Charlie. "The key to the code is the Spanish word *murciélago.*"

"*Murciélago* means "bat," doesn't it?"

"Yes. Since it is a ten-letter word, M is 1, U is 2, R is 3, and so on, until you reach O, which is 0."

Charlie took the word IELURUG, which had been found in a coded address book. He spelled out the phone number 5672329. Griselda never found out that the DEA had broken her code, and she continued to use it.

Griselda's love of cocaine was growing, not only because it was making her a fortune; it also gave her personal pleasure. Smoking *bazuko* cigarettes was the way she ingested the drug. These were regular cigarettes from which the tobacco had been removed and mixed with base cocaine (processed cocaine just at the last stage before it became cocaine hydrochloride), then reloaded into the papers. Highly addictive, the base cocaine Griselda used led her to hallucinations and paranoia. It was the predecessor to crack.

María never partook of drugs, but was there to watch as Griselda's people waited for the Godmother to fall under the influence of the cocaine; then they approached her to sign documents and issue orders. Often, she signed what was put in front of her and went along with what was suggested; much was stolen from her when she was "under the influence."

Her three sons, all fathered by Carlos Trujillo, followed their mother's example. When Osvaldo was only nine years old, he was smoking coke or inhaling it. María observed that each son reacted differently to the drug.

Dixon, the eldest, would slip into depression. Often he would cry, "My mother is responsible for this; she must stop. Please, Mother, help us."

Uber would become angry and full of energy. He would take his motorbike and roar through the streets of Medellín, going through red lights and speeding down sidestreets at full speed. He would say to Dixon, "No! Stop always talking about Mother; you are always blaming Mother."

And Osvaldo just drifted off to sleep, escaping into a dream fantasy known only to him.

As the boys grew older, on Friday nights, Griselda would give them each two thousand pesos (about fifty dollars) for the night, and a vial of cocaine. She even had special hollowed-out pens that she gave them as presents, to carry their coke.

Griselda's crime organization in Miami was growing. Some of her mules were turning into distributors and dealers. Carmela Salcedo was one of those. An attractive girl, she acted as a courier for Griselda on several trips, and began to live with Domingo Hernández, a prominent Colombian coke dealer in Miami. One day Domingo hit and killed a woman with his car.

The accident was reported in the newspaper, and Domingo got scared; he fled to Colombia, afraid to return because of the hit and run. Carmela took over the business and built it up even better than Domingo had done. They were good customers of the Godmother. The Miami police learned from María that Domingo had killed the woman, but they were never able to do anything about it. It stands today as an open vehicular homicide in Miami.

Some of Griselda's people were not too bright. Dorance Salazar was one of those people. He acted as a thug for Griselda, taking care of small unpleasant businesses. She fed him, paid him a small salary, and kept him on a short leash. He was constantly complaining that he had no real responsibility, and that no one trusted him to do a "real job." So Griselda decided to send him from Medellín down to Cali with $50,000 in cash. The Colombian police got wind of the delivery through their informants. They followed Dorance Salazar to the airport and watched him check his luggage. They retrieved the bag and emptied it of the $50,000 which they pocketed for themselves. Then they placed the luggage in the plane's hold.

Dorance arrived in Cali, picked up the suitcase, and went to make the delivery, only to find the suitcase empty when he opened it. He was sent back to Medellín to stand trial before Griselda and her people. The consensus was that he was too stupid to initiate anything like what had happened, and he never would have completed the delivery if he had been in on the rip-off. He would have just vanished with the money. But he had to be punished. So Griselda sent him to one of her farms to guard the dogs, and that was all he was allowed to do, guard the dogs. He would stand at the fence and call to Griselda or her people as they went by and say he was hungry, and they would send a little food every couple of days.

PART III

DEADLIEST
OF THE
SPECIES

CHAPTER 7

Hit List

The Godmother's vengeance was unrelenting. One of her chief money launderers was *El Duque*—The Duke —Duquero de Jesús Velásquez, who had an office in Miami. María was in Miami on a business trip, and she dropped by to visit *El Duque*. He showed her a list he had received from the Godmother, a hit list of seven DEA agents who were to be assassinated. The names included Annabelle Grimm and José Marín in Miami; Richie Crawford in New York; Tom Sepeda, Dave Knight, Charlie Cecil and Paul Provencia, who were in Colombia. *El Duque* said that they had already tried the night before in Queens; their first victim had been selected. It was Richie Crawford.

María left the office of *El Duque* dazed and shaken. She immediately called Charlie Cecil in Colombia. "They are going to hit you, Charlie. They are going to try again to kill you; last night they went after Richie Crawford in New York."

"Let me check it out, María. You stay in Miami."

Charlie immediately called Crawford. "Richie, did anything strange happen to you last night?" he asked.

"Yeah, I was in Queens last night in several bars on Roosevelt Avenue looking for some fugitive Colombians, you know, just checking the neighborhood. While I was sitting at the bar, I spotted this guy staring at me, but I didn't pay any attention to him.

"I went into the bathroom, and the guy that was staring at me follows me in. That's when the shit started, Charlie. It got nasty."

"Hey, man, you the police?" the Colombian asked Crawford.

"No, I'm just here having a drink, like you. So why don't we leave it at that," Crawford answered, turning around.

"You look like the police, man, they got a certain stink to them, you know," the Colombian smiled. "Like pigs."

"Hey, just cool it. I don't want any trouble," Crawford said, and decided it was time to leave. As he went to the bathroom door, the Colombian blocked his path.

"Hey, get out of the way; you're blocking my way."

"Fuck you, man," the Colombian said.

"Listen, if you don't get outta my way, you're going to have a serious problem."

"Fuck you."

With that, Rich Crawford took out his badge and flashed it. "All right, I'm the heat, so move it over. Get outta my way."

"Hey, fuck your badge too, man."

Crawford's fist drove into the man's chin and he fell to the floor with a heavy thud. Rich shoved him aside and tried to open the door. The man resisted, and Crawford pinned him to the floor as he tried to get the door open. The noise was heard from within the bar, and the manager and some patrons forced the door open from the other side.

Crawford tossed the Colombian into a stall and pulled the manager aside. He flashed his badge. "Look, I don't know if this guy's drunk or fucked up, or what the hell he is, but just keep him out of my way. Unless you want to have a real problem in here when I call the cops."

"Naw, naw, naw, don't you worry. I take care of it *pronto*. It's over, no more trouble."

"Fine," Crawford said. He paid for his beer and went to leave the bar. As he did, the Colombian followed Rich out onto Roosevelt Avenue with three of his friends.

Once Crawford hit Roosevelt, the Colombian ran after him and grabbed his arm, spinning him around. Crawford said, "Hey look, what the hell is it with you? I told you who I am; now just leave it alone before you wind up in big trouble." One of the friends moved in beside the Colombian. Crawford addressed him. "Look, take this guy outta here; what the hell is the matter with him?"

With that, the Colombian reached into his pocket and withdrew something. He swung at Crawford, the object in his hand shining in the dim streetlight. Rich raised his hand to block the blow and felt something sharp bite into his hand.

Crawford whipped out his gun as the man flung his arm behind his back. Rich was sure he had a knife. "Drop it," Crawford yelled. "You others stand back; you don't want any part of this."

The Colombian kept moving forward. Crawford was a weekend rugby player and in good shape, but he wasn't in the mood to take on four of them. The Colombian kept coming; with all his might Crawford drove his shoe into the man's balls. The man collapsed in a heap on the pavement. As the Colombian fell, his hands reached for his bruised testicles and the object he was holding fell to the ground. It was a ring of keys on a leather strap. Crawford heaved a sigh of relief that he had not shot an unarmed man, or unarmed perpetrator, as the New York cops would say.

"That's it, asshole, you're goin' to jail." As

Crawford tried to slip the handcuffs on the man, he came alive, struggling to his feet; he took another swing at Crawford. Rich stuck his gun in his waistband and grabbed the Colombian by the back of his coat, took three steps and ran him headfirst into the iron grating in front of a liquor store. This time he didn't resist as Crawford dragged him over to his parked car. The three friends remained, moving ominously in the shadows.

Rich saw a passing cab and shouted, "Hey, police!" He flashed his badge as he unlocked the car. "I got some problems. Call the cops and tell 'em I need help." The cabdriver, instead of using his own radio, got out of his cab and ran around to reach in and grab Crawford's radiophone, which was connected to his base.

"Anybody there?" the cabbie asked as he activated the radio. "Good. I don't know who this guy is or what the hell is going on, but one of your guys needs some help."

With that, the Colombian made another attempt to escape. He wriggled out of Crawford's grasp, but didn't get far; Crawford grabbed him again. This time Rich got on the microphone, identified himself, and talked to his base. "Call 911 and get some precinct help here. I need some backup right away. I got a prisoner here and three of his friends circling me like sharks. Nobody's hurt at this point, but I need some assistance."

"Roger."

As he hung up the radiophone, the three friends moved in closer. Crawford spun around and leveled his gun on them. "This guy is under arrest; you try and interfere and you're also under arrest. Just stay the fuck out of this or you're all going to jail." The Colombian gave it one last try, kicking at Crawford. When Crawford turned for a second, one of the others cracked him in the back of the head, stunning him momentarily. The prisoner took off down the street with Crawford after him, both men running at full speed.

As he reached full stride, Crawford kicked the man's back foot out from under him. The Colombian hit the pavement face first and somersaulted three times down the block. As he was rolling, a New York plainclothes car pulled up to the curb. The cops jumped out, picked the Colombian off the sidewalk, and stuffed him into the backseat of the squad car. When his three friends saw the cop car, they took off, running in separate directions.

"What do we book him on?" the cops asked.

"Assault on a federal officer, for starters. Where are you guys from?"

"Hundred and tenth precinct. This guy don't look too good," one of the cops said.

"Don't let that fool you. He's like the fucking Terminator, every time you think he's finished he comes at you again," Crawford laughed.

"Well, this time I think he's goin' to take a little break before he charges again. Don't worry, we'll take him right to the lockup."

Rich finished telling his tale to Charlie Cecil and waited for a response. There was a long silence before Charlie spoke. "Rich, that guy was trying to delay you. I'll bet there were some shooters on the way to the bar. Someone in that bar knew you and fingered you, and called the shooters in. I don't like this much . . . this fuckin' hit list stuff stinks."

"It's not a lot of fun," Crawford agreed.

Cecil confirmed with María; he was right. Shooters had been called, and there was a car on the way to do the job on Crawford. He had escaped by only minutes.

After Crawford's verification, Charlie immediately called the Miami office. The DEA people there weren't sure they believed the story of a hit list. So they called María into the Miami office and put her on "the box," a lie detector. She passed. Now they believed that she had seen the list. They didn't like it, either.

The next day, *El Duque* was visited privately by two DEA agents in his swank offices in Miami. They went through the foyer and entered the office unannounced, to be greeted by the oily smile and arrogance of *El Duque*.

"Do you have an appointment?" *El Duque* asked.

"Yeah, with you, because you have a problem, a real serious problem," the DEA officer said in perfect Spanish, closing the door and sitting down.

"And what might that be?" *El Duque* asked, starting to fidget in his chair.

"I'm going to kill you, that's your fuckin' problem."

El Duque went ashen gray.

"We know that there are contracts out on certain DEA agents," the agent continued. "These are important people to us, like family. A lot more important than you, you fuckin' sleazebag. If any of those agents even stub their toes or get a bad cold, we are going to come back here and settle with you. *Comprende?*"

El Duque was too frightened to speak. He just sat there nodding.

"All the rules are out now and all bets are off, if anything happens to anyone on that list, here or in Colombia. Remember, any agent gets hurt, and we will be back to blow your fucking brains out. You're dead as dogshit, no matter where you are, scumbag."

The agents left, sure that *El Duque* now understood.

The DEA office in Colombia had become the hottest office in the world.

CHAPTER 8

High Tea and Diamonds

The life of a money launderer was a dangerous one when a client was ultraparanoid, especially if the money launderer was stealing from her. *El Duque* was a polished, slick charmer who had met his match in Griselda Blanco. Griselda knew he was cheating her. He was skimming the money by overcharging her on the laundering commissions. On the volume of cash that was flowing through *El Duque*'s hands, these small percentages ranged up into millions of dollars over a long period. *El Duque* had $5 million of hers that was "in transit," being laundered. She was prepared to take action when she got that money.

El Duque called from Miami to say that he would be down to Colombia for a visit. "Tomorrow I will see you, my friend, my first friend."

"I can't wait to see you. I'm counting the minutes," Griselda answered.

"I have presents for the children and presents for you."

"And the five million."

"It should be there by the time I get there tomorrow. I left my normal commission out as you asked. I will pick it up in cash while I'm down there."

"Good, my friend; my heart pounds with anticipation."

"As does mine; *te amo,*" El Duque answered, and hung up.

The next day *El Duque* arrived with expensive presents for everyone, including jewelry and perfume for the Godmother. He handed them out, and everyone made a fuss showing their presents to one another.

The next day, instead of receiving his commission on the $5 million as he expected, *El Duque* was shot to death in the Barrio Belén in Medellín.

Griselda could be generous when she wanted to. On a whim, she decided to buy her key people 4-wheel-drive Nissan jeeps in white. She told them it was a raffle to determine who got the new cars, but she just picked the winners herself. She gave out seven white ones—and one red one to Emilio Rojas, a bodyguard. She told María she thought it was a cute joke to give out the one red Nissan, since *rojas* means red.

By the beginning of 1978, Griselda's trust in María had grown to the point where she invited María over for tea one day and brought out the best silver. Tea was served on a beautiful tray with a silver teapot, creamer and sugar bowl, and on a sideboard in the dining room were twelve more silver trays, one of which held a silver coffeepot.

The tea was poured into fine bone china cups; little silver tongs were positioned on the sugar bowl to lift the cubes. María moved the teapot from the center of the silver tray and traced the beautifully regal, embossed seal with her fingernail and looked questioningly up at Griselda, who smiled and asked, "Do you like it?"

"Very beautiful and very old. What does this fancy coat of arms stand for?" María asked.

"It is the coat of arms of the Queen of England."

"Queen Elizabeth?"

"Yes." Griselda put down her cup of tea and walked over to the sideboard. "When she was visiting in Canada, this service was stolen by Colombian thieves. They came to sell it to me, but they wanted too much so I sent them away."

"How much did they want?"

"Three hundred thousand pesos is what they wanted. They finally returned and took the two hundred thousand pesos I had offered."

María got up to look at the silver trays. "That's a very reasonable price, two hundred thousand pesos; only five thousand American dollars, less than a tiny amount of cocaine."

"Yes, and I have sold three of these trays to my friend Gabriela for a good price. She also wants to drink tea from the Queen's silver."

María walked around, touching the silver and wondering how far back it went, perhaps to Queen Victoria, maybe even further. Now it rested in the home of a drug queen who had risen from the *barrio*.

Weeks later, Griselda came over to visit María with several bodyguards. She and the bodyguards carried three overnight cases about the size of makeup cases. "María, I must leave Colombia; it's too dangerous for me now. I want you to do me a favor. I want you to look after my jewelry."

Griselda dismissed the bodyguards and put the three cases on the coffee table in front of them. She opened the lid of the first one. It was packed to the top with jewelry, like a pirate's treasure. The rings, bracelets, necklaces, brooches, loose stones, and earrings were heaped in. Griselda reached in with two hands and scooped out as much as her hands could hold, then she did it again and piled her booty high in front of María. María sat dumbfounded, unable to believe what her eyes beheld. María fingered the jewelry, looking for earrings that matched, trying on emerald, sapphire and diamond rings, spotting a clear red ruby and holding it up to the light.

Griselda opened the second case. It was like the first, packed solid with precious gems and designer watches encrusted with jewels and gold.

She held one hand on the top of the third case. "In here are my two favorite pieces." With a slight flourish, she opened the case. Lying on top of everything else, in the center, was a diamond about the size of a small egg. It was surrounded by twenty-one perfect one-carat diamonds. Griselda handed it to María and watched her reaction.

"It was Eva Perón's. Each of those diamonds is for one of the provinces of Argentina."

"My God, I have never seen such a thing as this." María held it in the palm of her small hand. It seemed to glow with a life of its own. María half expected it to feel hot to the skin, but it felt cool. It sent tingles up her wrist and forearm.

"And this also I love," Griselda said, handing María a large brooch about the size of two cigarette packs. The brooch was cut in an irregular way. María examined the design.

"It is cut perfectly in the shape of Argentina. The big diamond is for Buenos Aires, and the smaller diamonds indicate other smaller cities."

María's eyes scanned the brooch. She counted more than fifty-five diamonds. María calculated that there was over $20 million worth of jewelry in the three cases.

"This is too much for me to watch over. I cannot take responsibility for this."

"You must; it is what I want."

María thought for a second, then said, "As you wish, but I must keep them in a safe deposit box in the bank."

"I know you will take care of them, María. There is

no one else I trust like I trust you. Now you see what I mean by my actions. I give you my most precious possessions, after my sons, to look after. I am going away soon, and I can rest assured that everything is well, because my friend María will look after it for me."

Griselda got up and kissed María on the cheek and together the two of them closed the cases.

Alberto Bravo was killed. It was unclear whether Alberto was murdered by Griselda's orders or whether she killed him herself, as she would later boast.

Dario Sepúlveda, the most powerful of the Sepúlveda brothers, had become Griselda's new lover. Paco and Diego Sepúlveda were Griselda's shooters and dealers. In August 1978 Griselda delivered Michael Corleone, her fourth child, Dario's son.

María, Griselda, and Dario were out one night at an upscale restaurant owned by Griselda. Three tough *pistoleros* from a rival gang came into the restaurant and sat in a red leather booth across from them.

Griselda and her group had not even ordered their food when the taunting began.

"Do you see any assholes in here?" one of the gunmen asked his companions.

"Only the three assholes sitting across from us. Two female assholes and one *puta* whose manhood we question."

"Yes," the third gunman said, "he looks like a fag, an asshole who can only shoot his enemies in the back."

María was scared; she started to shake so badly that she could not hold her menu steady. "Dario," María whispered over the top of her quivering menu, "we must leave. These men will not leave us alone, please let's leave. We want no trouble."

"Dario, she is right," Griselda added. "We can deal with these men later when we have our own men with us, or we will send them visitors."

THE GODMOTHER

"Look at the *puta* sissy, as he confers with the women. Perhaps he needs them to tell him what to do," one of the *pistoleros* said in a loud voice.

"Perhaps you are right; tonight is not the time to deal with this. Let us leave," Dario said quietly, ignoring the men in the opposite booth. He slid out of his seat and waited for María and Griselda to move out and start toward the door.

The women were a few feet ahead of him when Dario turned to face the men. As he spun, he whipped his Beretta automatic out of his waistband and fired. The first bullet hit the mouthy gunman square in the face, obliterating his nose and teeth. Dario's second bullet passed through his throat. The gunmen on each side went for their pistols. Dario took out the man on his left first with two fast shots to the chest. The third gunman was firing now. Two shots whizzed past Dario. One of the bullets flew right by María's ear and into the wall behind her. She was on all fours. Griselda was next to her as they scrambled on their hands and knees under tables, pushing chairs aside, while bullets flew overhead. Other shooters were involved now. Almost every man in the restaurant carried a gun, and many of them started firing wildly, randomly, hitting the ceiling and walls.

María looked over her shoulder and watched the third *pistolero* take two shots in his chest.

"María, out the back door; let's go out the back through the kitchen," Griselda yelled to María, and she disappeared out the back. Dario was only steps behind her, the kitchen door slamming shut behind them. María crawled behind the bar and scrunched in the corner out of sight. The police arrived and did a cursory investigation. The dead bodies of the three *pistoleros* were removed, and the restaurant went back about its business. It was only another shooting in Medellín. María knew that tomorrow Griselda would contact the police and pay them off to close the case.

María decided that would be the last time she was

seen in public with Dario and Griselda. Things *were* getting too hot.

It was 1978. Dario Sepúlveda and Griselda headed for Miami. But it was also hot in Miami; the cocaine wars were just starting to smolder. When Griselda arrived, they would reach the boiling point.

CHAPTER 9

White Powder Wars

Griselda wore violence like a bloody boa.

It was 1979, and the homicide departments of the Miami and Metro–Dade police were never busier. There was a murder a day in Miami or its suburbs. The cocaine wars in Miami were building to a crescendo, and the Godmother was orchestrating the lethal symphony. The Spanish names of the "cocaine cowboys" that appeared in the *Miami Herald* were a mysterious hodgepodge that baffled the investigating officers and the public.

Colombians changed names, addresses, official IDs, and alliances so often that it became like following the plot of a Russian novel to keep track of their identities. The Colombians banked on this as a way to keep the cops off balance; half the cops couldn't even pronounce the names, never mind remember them.

But the Colombians finally went too far. The famous "Turnpike Shoot-Out" and the "Dadeland Massacre" were the two cases that pushed America's tolerance over the edge.

Germán Panesso was a very powerful supplier of

cocaine and a feared man in Miami. Griselda owed him a great deal of money, over a million dollars.

On April 17, 1979, Germán Panesso's maid, Ester Ríos, was discovered in a field in Dade County. Her body was in an advanced state of decomposition when it was found. Ester had been handcuffed, her mouth taped with duct tape, and a rope had been tied around her neck and connected to her ankles. As Ester had moved, kicked, or rolled, the rope had bitten into her neck, until with her own movements, she had choked herself to death.

Ester had made the mistake of seeing Jaime Suescún, one of Panesso's employees, rip off twenty-five kilos of coke, so Suescún had killed her.

Panesso found out about what had happened.

On April 23, 1979, Suescún was lured to a meeting by his boss, Germán Panesso, on the pretext of doing a dope deal. Suescún was slightly suspicious, so he brought two shooters with him as bodyguards, Diego Restrepo and another Colombian called Panello.

"Wait in the car," Suescún ordered, leaving his bodyguards in the white Grand Prix and walking into the house.

Inside the house, waiting for Suescún, were Panesso, Álvaro Palacio, and the famous hitman with the mad eyes and the muscular build, Conrado Valencia Zalgado, better known as *El Loco*. Suescún was grabbed and handcuffed; duct tape was slapped across his mouth. A rope was quickly noosed around his neck with a short connecting tail that was tied to his ankles. He was picked up and thrown into the trunk of an Audi 5000, the shiny black trunk was slammed shut, and the garage door electronically opened.

Suescún's two shooters, Restrepo and Panello, who were waiting outside in the Grand Prix, saw the garage door open and the Audi move quickly out of the driveway. They realized immediately that something was wrong, and they followed the Audi out onto the Florida Turnpike.

It took only minutes for *El Loco* and Panesso to realize that they were being followed. *El Loco* leaned out the window of the Audi and let off a burst from his silenced Mac-10 machine gun at his pursuers. The pursuers shot back. The shooting went on for ten miles, with both cars pushing their speedometer needles to the limit. What neither car realized was that a third car was behind them with an off-duty cop inside. He observed the entire shoot-out, but without a radio he was powerless to intervene.

The high-speed chase finally ended when the shooters exited the Turnpike at U.S. 1 and Caribbean Boulevard, where both cars stopped at the light, between them an innocent motorist.

El Loco jumped out of the Audi and started to fire from behind a concrete post. The Grand Prix answered with a volley. The motorist in the center, angered by the shooting, reached under his seat and yanked out his own pistol. He fired four bullets to his right at the Audi and three bullets to his left at the Grand Prix, and then sped off through the red light into the Florida midday sunshine, leaving the Colombians clear shots at each other.

The shooters suddenly heard police sirens in the distance and fled. Germán Panesso headed on foot for the giant Cutler Ridge Shopping Mall, as did *El Loco*. The black Audi, with Álvaro Palacio driving, turned down Cutler Ridge Boulevard. First to the scene was a single police car; the cops chose to pursue the black Audi and let the Grand Prix go.

They were led on a wild chase through the residential neighborhood of Cutler Ridge. They finally came upon the Audi, but the driver was missing. They called in other cars and combed the area. The officers spotted discarded clothes on various lawns: a shirt, a belt, a pair of trousers, socks, even a pair of shoes. When they rounded a corner, they came upon Álvaro Palacio, the driver of the Audi, running down the sidewalk in his underpants at a nice leisurely pace.

They pulled the police car up over the curb in front of him and hopped out with drawn guns. They could see by the way he was dressed that he was unarmed. Palacio was arrested on the spot and handcuffed.

"What the hell were you doing out here?" one of the arresting officers asked as he put him in the rear of the police cruiser.

"Jogging, just jogging," was Palacio's answer.

The arresting officers looked at each other, rolled their eyes, and drove Palacio off to jail.

Back at the Audi, other police had opened the trunk and found forty kilos of sugar and Jaime Suescún, dead by asphyxiation, choked to death by the rope eating its way into his throat as he moved, finally cutting off air to his windpipe.

Germán Panesso was not found, but *El Loco* was apprehended inside the Cutler Ridge Mall. The police learned that *El Loco* was married to Luz Marina, Griselda's bookkeeper. They did not know what to do with the information. It was later discovered that *El Loco* was simply working on his own, freelance.

He was booked and his bail was set at $500,000, later reduced to $100,000. The bail was posted in cash, and *El Loco* walked out of jail. He disappeared until he was caught in California in 1983. He was tried and sentenced to 135 years in total. Palacio was not convicted.

One of Griselda Blanco's great strengths was to seize an opportunity when it was presented to her. She had a real opportunity now to deal with her debt to Germán Panesso. He was weak now, and on the run from the police.

But the police heat was building, and public awareness was never higher. Finally, America was awakening to the fact that it had been infected by a new strain of criminal, worse than any virus. The Colombians had brought a pestilence that would permeate American society and bring it to its knees. In future years, billions and billions would be needed to fight the scourge of the white powder. But in 1979, the American public was just getting its first glimpse of what was ahead.

Observing the violence in Miami at that time was like looking into the only window of a building burning from the inside. There was a whole new hell waiting for America.

And the Godmother, pioneer of the cocaine cartel, would provide her share. Griselda enlisted the help of Paco Sepúlveda, Dario's brother and her chief shooter and distributor in New York, to organize and plan the hit on Germán Panesso. She had no intention now of paying Panesso the money she owed. It was easier and cheaper to kill him.

It took the police—using informants, court testimony, and eyewitnesses—almost ten years to figure out who was in the van and what really happened in the "Dadeland Massacre."

July 11, 1979, was a standard beautiful, sunny South Florida afternoon in Miami's Dadeland Shopping Mall, the largest mall in Dade County. It was a mall that was designed for the elite of Miami, those who shop simply to pass the time.

Germán Panesso and his twenty-two-year-old bodyguard, Juan Carlos Hernández, drove up to Crown Liquors in a new white Mercedes sedan. Tossed on the floor by the backseat lay a loaded .9mm Browning high-powered automatic. Panesso and his bodyguard were relaxed and dressed casually. Panesso sauntered up to the clerk and asked him for a bottle of Chivas Regal scotch.

"Over there," the clerk, Thomas Capozzi, said, pointing to a shelf at the far end of the store. Panesso tossed his head as a signal for his bodyguard to go fetch the bottle.

Seconds later, the clerk looked up to see a windowless white Ford van, with "Happy Time Party Supply" printed crudely on the side, pull up to the front door.

The back door of the van popped open. There were many men inside, but only two jumped out. They took the curb on the run and slammed open the liquor store door, guns blasting.

The first shooter spotted Panesso and opened fire with a silenced Baretta .38. The second shooter was right behind him, spraying the store with a Mac-10 machine gun.

Morgan Perkins, an eighteen-year-old stockboy, was eating his lunch in the back room. He heard the noise and came out to see a man blasting away with a machine gun.

Panesso was running for the front door when he was caught in the head by five .45-caliber slugs from the Mac-10. He fell backward with what was left of his face staring up at the white fluorescent-lit ceiling.

The bodyguard, Hernández, died where he stood, at the scotch shelf. His bullet-perforated body fell forward; the bottle of Chivas Regal fell with him and rolled away from his elbow, unbroken.

The shooters were high with their bloodlust and the pungent smell of cordite. They turned their attention to the bottles in the store and the two remaining people, Thomas Capozzi and Morgan Perkins.

Liquor bottles exploded on the shelves in a hail of bullets; cases of liquor were shredded; wine bottles exploded and bled red on the floor while bullet holes were engraved into the walls and ceiling.

Capozzi ran for all he was worth, but as he reached the front door, a stray bullet caught him in the right shoulder and ripped through his chest. He staggered out the door and weaved away, falling in a heap on the sidewalk.

The shooter emptied the clip and slapped another clip into his Mac-10 and looked around as Morgan Perkins crawled for his life, crabbing on all fours behind the counter, then made a final run in the open for the door. He made it outside, unhit, and scrambled under a parked car.

The shooter with the Mac-10 emptied the second clip, dropped the weapon inside the liquor store, and ran outside, the other shooter on his heels. They jumped into the cab of the white van.

Inside the van, a man with a .30-caliber carbine spotted Morgan Perkins hiding under the car and opened fire.

Morgan Perkins crawled and squirmed farther under the car, yelling, "Why are they shooting at me? I didn't do anything." His words changed to screams as two bullets from the carbine tore into him, one in each foot.

The shoppers were hysterical.

"Somebody's hit in the parking lot!"

"My God, oh my God, there's shooting everywhere!"

The women in the beauty parlor next door to Crown Liquors thought at first the slugs hitting the wall were teenagers playing a prank. When they saw the carnage unfolding around them, the manager yelled to the receptionist, "Call the police!"

Still the shooters were not done. To cover their escape, they opened up on the mall parking lot. Parked cars were raked with bullets; plate-glass windows of shops were shot out, the glass shattering like millions of tiny beads of rain; gas tanks were riddled and gas spilled out, flowing onto the hot tarmac, the fumes rising in the blazing Florida sun. A stray bullet whizzed by a screaming pedestrian's ear.

The white "Party Time" van finally disappeared. The scene of death and destruction had been played out in less than three minutes from start to finish. The shooters left behind two dead and two wounded. It was amazing that more had not been killed or hit.

Sergeant Al Singleton of Metro–Dade Homicide was one of the first people on the scene. Considered an expert on Colombians and murder, even he had never seen anything like this before. Neither had his bosses. So they did something that they never do; they allowed the press on the crime scene to examine a piece of evidence. They had found the white Ford van behind the Jordan Marsh store in the south end of the mall, abandoned, less than half a mile from Crown Liquors.

Singleton explained to the press, "This is a real war wagon; the walls are made of reinforced quarter-inch stainless steel plates, and these bulletproof vests hanging from the ceiling come down with the door when it's closed, to act as armor. You can see that gun ports and peepholes were drilled in the sides and back of the van, for shooting out. The van also has two gas tanks and black one-way glass. And the thugs are armed to the teeth." Singleton pointed at an array of weapons on the floor in the back of the van that included two M-1 carbines, shotguns, Mac-10s, silenced handguns, and thousands of rounds of ammunition.

"And every weapon has been fired," Singleton added.

He let the inference hang in the air. These guys were real "cocaine cowboys" as in the days of the old wild West; they all had to shoot off their guns, even if they didn't hit anything.

For a long time, Singleton would wonder what would have happened if the war wagon had run into the police that day—especially one single, lightly armed, marked patrol unit, answering a 911 call for help.

The thought made him shudder.

That night before going home, Singleton went out and bought a fourteen-shot .9mm Browning high-powered automatic. He retired his .38-caliber Model 19 blue-steel Smith and Wesson that was standard issue for the Dade County police. Singleton, an ex-Marine, decided that if he was going to go toe to toe against these players, he was going to carry a gun that had some stopping power. If they wanted to wage war, he was ready. He was getting very tired of hearing the name Griselda Blanco almost every time he found a dead body.

Miami was written up as the murder capital of America, the most violent city in the United States. Miami made the front pages of both *Time* and *Newsweek* as a dopers' paradise, featuring death in the streets daily.

But the Dadeland Massacre was the beginning of the end of the cocaine wars, although they would rage on for another few years.

The Medellín Cartel in Colombia was just being formed, and its members were not happy with Griselda. Miami was a giant maw open and ready to take in endless quantities of cocaine, and Griselda Blanco was inadvertently shutting it down by her reckless "gangster" actions. The Cartel passed the word to her that she had gone too far.

So Griselda came up with an idea. She bought a casket and had a nameplate attached to the coffin, engraved with her name. The coffin was sent from Miami to Colombia as physical proof of her death. She paid a reporter for the Colombian newspaper *El Tiempo* to write a story of her death, and the Customs and Immigration departments were bribed to provide official verification. The scheme worked perfectly until the coffin was opened and found to be full of car parts.

But Griselda was no fool. She was in serious trouble and she knew it; she and her husband, Dario Sepúlveda, dropped out of sight for the next few years and ran her empire from underground. She didn't surface again until 1982 in Miami and California.

CHAPTER 10

La Compasionata

"Griselda Blanco orders death the way other people order pizza."

That's what Max Mermelstein had heard on the streets of Miami from the Colombians he hung out with.

Max Mermelstein had been born in Brooklyn of middle-class Jewish parents. After finishing college, he moved to Puerto Rico and met a beautiful Colombian girl whom he later married.

In 1977, Max and his new wife moved to Freeport, Bahamas, where Max was the chief engineer at the Princess Hotel. His sideline business was bringing illegal Colombian aliens into the United States through Florida. From this humble beginning, Max rose in the next ten years to become the most important American advisor to the Medellín Cartel. Many of the "illegals" he brought into the United States later became major smugglers.

Max was brilliant and well-educated, especially compared to the Colombians he dealt with. He was a robust figure, at five feet nine inches, weighing more than 250 pounds. He had an outgoing personality with enormous energy. In many ways he was the Cartel's mastermind, able to show the Colombians new and better business techniques. He opened major new windows into the United States through which massive amounts of cocaine poured. Over a five-year period, he paid his pilots $100 million in cash.

Max worked directly for "Rafa," Rafael Cardona Salazar, who was a member of the Medellín Cartel. Rafa had a powerful cocaine empire with bases in Florida and California.

Griselda Blanco was an old friend of Rafa's. He knew her from when he had been a young car thief, before he got into the white powder trade.

She had warned him of a planned assassination in 1979. Rafa's car stopped at a light in Medellín; he was driving, with his bodyguard sitting next to him. A man approached the car on foot, but Rafa was extra-alert because of Griselda's warning and picked the man up as he entered his peripheral vision. The shooter still managed to reach into the car and shoot him in the shoulder, but Rafa sped away. Rafa felt he owed the Godmother a favor, and unlike Griselda, he paid his debts.

Rafa knew that Griselda was having financial difficulties. She had been operating her empire from the deepest cover, often using her three oldest sons to do her bidding. The constant cocaine battles had drained her war chest to the point where, by 1982, she was in serious financial straits.

"She has been at war for so long against so many people that she has not had time to really work her business," Rafa explained to Max just before the Godmother walked into Max's life for the first time. She entered his house with her entourage: Jorge "Riverito" Rivera; two more shooters; Dario, her husband; and Osvaldo, her son.

Max gasped when he saw Osvaldo. He knew him. He remembered well how they had met.

A year before, in 1981, Max had been ordered by Rafa to take Osvaldo to California and teach him what was involved in a "pickup"—where dope was delivered and cash picked up.

"Why do I want to take this punk kid with me to California?" Max had asked Rafa.

"Because I'm asking you to do it as a favor to me."

"How old is this kid?"

"About fifteen."

"Fifteen! This is nuts. I'm supposed to take a fifteen-year-old kid to L.A. and teach him the business?"

"Maybe he's sixteen."

"Rafa, that doesn't make it any better."

"Just do it; okay, Max?"

"Who the hell is he, anyway?"

"His name is Osvaldo. That's all you need to know, Max. And he's not so much of a kid as you think. He has already killed two people."

"This kid? A punk kid has killed two people? I can't believe it."

"Believe it. He killed the first time when he was fourteen."

Max did as he was asked. On the flight to Los Angeles, Osvaldo actually bragged to him in detail about the people he had killed. Max ignored Osvaldo. It gave him chills to listen to this boy; there was no doubt in his mind that the boy had killed.

When they arrived in Los Angeles, they went right to work, delivering thirty kilos to a supermarket parking lot in the San Fernando Valley area. Normally the coke was put behind the side panels of the car. In this case the coke was in the trunk because the side panels could not hold it all. The two drove to the delivery spot in separate cars, a lead car and a trail car; there was a Colombian waiting to pick up the car with the dope. Osvaldo stood beside Max, observing the transaction.

"Did you put the shit in the compartments?" the Colombian asked Max.

"No. It wouldn't fit. It's in the trunk."

"Then I'm not going to accept the car."

"What the fuck do you mean, you are not going to accept the car?" Max asked.

"I'm not going to accept the car; the stuff has to go in here," the Colombian said, pounding on the side panels.

Max walked away to think. Osvaldo walked with him. "Max, I'll drive it for the kid, I'll take him."

"No, you don't go to the stash house. Where he's taking it is none of our fucking business. From this point on the shit is his responsibility. We don't want to know, believe me."

Max walked back and threw the keys on the floor of the car carrying the cocaine. "It's yours. If you want it, take it. If you don't, don't. I'm calling Colombia right now. I made the fucking delivery, and it's going to be paid for. Period. Pay for it any way you want to. You pay for it in cash or you pay for it in blood. Either way, it's going to be paid for."

Osvaldo started to argue with Max. He'd got out only a few words when Max's thick bejeweled hand glinted in the California sun. The back of Max's hand caught Osvaldo square in the face, knocking him across the tarmac. He landed on his back, stunned, blinking in the hot afternoon glare.

"Pick him up. We're leaving," Max snapped at Edgar Díaz, one of Rafa's men who was also along for that trip.

And now here was the lioness with her cub, standing on his threshold.

Max decided to discuss the incident with Griselda. He took a deep breath, swallowed hard and said, "I'm sure you are aware of what happened in California."

"I am aware of it. I guess he deserved it. Business is business; you weren't doing it for anything else but to teach him what he had to learn. You did the right thing. So we will forget it."

But Max never really believed it was completely forgotten. To Max Mermelstein, Griselda Blanco was the *consummate* actress and charmer. He knew that she could laugh or cry at will.

She had dyed her hair blond in those days, and always wore a kerchief tied around her head. Tilted back on her forehead were big sunglasses, which she pulled down to cover her eyes.

Max was surprised at how heavy she was, and how little she seemed to care about her appearance, especially because she loved to go to the beauty parlor. Often, through the months that followed that meeting, she would go places with Max's pretty Colombian wife, Cristina. Griselda did not drive, and when she wanted to go somewhere, she would call Cristina and ask if she would drive her. Griselda was at the beauty parlor every second or third day, having something done to herself—fingernails, toenails, hair, waxing. Even though Cristina drove her, Griselda was never without her bodyguards and shooters in a following car or idly waiting for her outside.

Max learned that Griselda was a woman of dramatic mood swings. She could be extremely generous and charming, then without warning turn cold and deadly. She was very conscious of other people's moods and desires, and she was not afraid to spend money. On Max's birthday, she bought him an expensive leather jacket.

Rafa could match her generosity when he was in the mood. One Christmas, Rafa showed up in his brand-new black Mercedes 450, the biggest model made, with all the toys and options. Griselda looked at the car and said, "This is beautiful; where did you get it?"

"Forget where I got it. It's yours." He handed Griselda the keys. "Merry Christmas!" he said, and went into his house without another word.

* * *

Max first met Dario Sepúlveda in a Fort Lauderdale hospital room, where he was surrounded twenty-four hours a day by his *pistoleros*—his bodyguards and hitmen. Surgeons had just removed a cyst the size of a golf ball from his throat. The doctors told Dario it was a direct result of the nonstop freebasing he and Griselda had been doing for the last several years.

"Four million dollars of coke, that's what we did, Max," Dario said in a raspy voice, like sandpaper on glass. "And that's at *our* cost, so it's like eight million dollars we inhaled over three years. Never, never again will I do it." And he never did do it again.

Dario Sepúlveda was about five feet, ten inches tall, handsome, with salt-and-pepper hair; his dark complexion was always enhanced by a strong suntan. He was an elegant dresser, impeccable in his appearance. He always wore a good pair of silk or linen pants, an open-collared dress shirt, and Italian shoes.

Dario drove a white Cadillac El Dorado Biarritz. He loved the car; it was his trademark. When you saw the white El Dorado coming, you knew it was Dario.

On July 24, 1982, Dario and Miguel Pérez killed Domingo Hernández, a Colombian who owed them money. They nailed him in the bleachers of a Miami soccer field. This murder was later referred to by the Metro–Dade homicide squad as the "Pelé Single" because a month later another murder ordered by the Godmother took place at the same spot; that one was called the "Pelé Double."

Dario had to get rid of the white El Dorado because he was driving it when he and Pérez shot Hernández to death. He told Max that it really hurt him to have to give up that car.

Dario also loved the ladies, especially young dancers and showgirls who performed in the topless and bottomless clubs around Miami and Fort Lauderdale. Max believed that there were at least eight unsolved murders of young disco dancers that could be traced right to Griselda's smoking gun.

Dario was afraid of nothing. Dario was one of the original bandit bank robbers; nothing bothered him. He was not from Medellín; he was from the town of Parera. Colombians have an expression: Nothing comes from Parera except whores and hitmen. Most of the heavy-duty hitmen in the drug business came from Parera. Dario had no fear of Griselda; if he had to, he could be just as vicious as she.

Dario was never without his gun. The only time he ever took it off was when he entered Max's house. Max had a rule: "no guns in the house." It was a rule that everyone obeyed. When he came to Max's house, he would slip the gun, a Walther PPK, out of his waistband and rest it on top of a wall unit in the living room. It was the ultimate sign of trust; Dario's life depended on that gun, and by setting it aside, he was showing Max the highest respect. But for insurance, he always had two armed shooters standing outside on the porch.

Griselda was often in the company of Doris. Doris was a cousin of Papo Mejía, a sworn enemy of both Griselda and Rafa, Max's boss. Doris had been kidnapped several years before Max met her. Griselda had turned her into a slave, and now she was constantly in the company of Griselda; wherever Griselda went, Doris went.

Chava, Griselda's maid of many years, confided in Max one afternoon. Chava was a trusted woman. Often she was asked to look after a stash house. She was very poor and sent all her pay down to her family in Colombia so they could live. Chava explained to Max that when Griselda went to sleep, she had to have someone to hold on to, and she kept girls like Doris around for that purpose. If Dario was away, she slept with one of these girls.

Chava had also slept with her many times, she explained to Max. "The ghosts and spirits of all the people that she has killed come to visit her at night and haunt her. They creep into her dreams and try to murder her. That's why she must always sleep with someone." Her sleeping companions had to hold Griselda tight all through the night, like a baby, something that her mother had never done.

Rafa started in business with Griselda by giving her a credit of up to ten kilos a week. Max was instructed to remove the goods from the stash house, collect promptly, and keep accurate records of every transaction. In the beginning, she kept the payments up to date.

Max was shocked when he first met Little Michael, Griselda's youngest son. "Max, I would like you to meet Michael Corleone Sepúlveda, my youngest son."

"You mean like Michael Corleone from The Godfather, the movie?"

"Yes, that's the name. Dario and I saw the movie, and we thought it was absolutely great. He's going to grow up just like Michael Corleone did."

Max just shook his head and walked away. He wondered what Al Pacino would say if he knew what a powerful impact his performance had had on Griselda Blanco and her husband.

Griselda, her sons, and Dario watched *The Godfather* movie on videotape, over and over, as they did *Scarface,* and all "The Untouchables" videotapes made from the old television series. They had memorized the dialogue from many scenes of *The Godfather* and *Scarface.*

Dario and Griselda fought often, and when they did, they pulled no punches. They would bicker back and forth—who had killed whom and who shouldn't have killed whom, and who was meaner and more treacherous. Once Dario screamed at Griselda that she had killed all of her ex-husbands and every lover she had ever had.

It took Griselda aback. She stared at Dario and said, "Well, Alberto Bravo wasn't my fault."

"Bullshit!" Dario roared.

Griselda said, "Alberto was sitting in the car, and I was standing next to the car. We were talking through the open window, fighting. I don't even remember what it was we were fighting about. He said some very nasty things to me. I said to him, 'Those words will never come out of your mouth again,' and then I stuck the barrel of my gun in his mouth and just pulled the trigger. It wasn't really my fault; it was just a reflex."

"Yeah, a reflex that blew the back of his fucking head off," Dario snorted back.

"You should shut up, you have killed many also," Griselda snapped.

"Maybe so, but I never shot a pregnant woman in the stomach like you did. I wouldn't do something like that. Nobody could be lower than somebody who would shoot a pregnant woman in the stomach."

Max watched as Griselda's anger turned to black rage. Griselda rose and said nothing; she stormed out of the room. For a while Max was in great fear that she would return and shoot Dario right on the spot. But she did not return.

One of Griselda's favorite pastimes was to sit around while having a couple of drinks and talk about all the people she had killed and how she had killed them. She often bragged to Max of how she and Dario had planned the "Dadeland Massacre" and how well everyone had performed that day in the parking lot, especially her son Dixon, who she said was in the van. She was proud of how easily they had escaped and hidden in a nearby apartment.

Once, she told Max of a time when she was trying to buy arms, and the arms dealer let it slip that he was also selling guns to Papo Mejía. She told Max this story to explain why some called her *La Compasionata.*

The arms dealer had no idea that Mejía was her most hated enemy. "I just sold arms to someone you might know, Papo Mejía," the arms dealer bragged.

Colombia. She said she was once a local "beauty queen." She showed Max and Cristina pictures of herself as a beautiful young woman of about seventeen, winning the contest. She spoke of how she had grown up in Barrio Mario Andopia in Medellín, a poor, rough neighborhood that produced the initial drug dealers who made up the Cartel.

Max observed that like Rafa, his boss, and Mafia chieftains he had read about, Griselda never got involved directly in any dealings with dope. She made the arrangements, gave the orders, and then waited for her lieutenants and flunkies to carry them out.

She taught Max a few tricks. The double-walled suitcase was one of her standard gimmicks. Max had a load of cash to send to Colombia.

"Try it with the suitcases," Griselda said. "Dixon will show you."

Max liked the idea so much he incorporated it into the Cartel's regular bag of tricks; it was deceptively simple and effective. A 27-inch Samsonite case with double walls on both sides would take $750,000 in hundred-dollar bills.

Max explained to Griselda that bills weigh one gram each; it takes twenty-eight bills to make an ounce. After that, when Griselda was in a hurry, money was weighed, not counted.

Rafa's coke came directly from the Ochoas. The Ochoa brothers, Jorge, Juan David, and Fabio, along with Pablo Escobar and Pablo Correa, formed the original Medellín Cartel. They were the largest, most powerful suppliers of cocaine in the world. Rafa, with Max as his main man, controlled their South Florida business and much of the coke that entered California.

Rafa was supplying cocaine to Griselda at his cost, no profit, until she got back on her feet. He believed that he owed her this because she had saved his life.

Griselda made Max nervous, and he told Rafa so. "She's always at war, and she seems to love it, even though it costs her millions of fucking dollars. And that Dadeland shooting was just about the stupidest thing I ever heard of. Jesus Christ, she must be out of her mind. She's like a damn gangster out of the thirties who just gets pissed off and shoots the shit out of anything and anybody that gets in her way. The Dadeland Massacre, the Kendall Six murders . . . she's nuts, and she brings the heat, incredible heat. Christ, we even have George Bush, the Vice President, in the act now with his Drug Task Force. She's trouble, Rafa, real trouble, and like I keep telling you, one day she'll come after your ass."

"Relax, *compadre,*" Rafa said to Max. "She did the Kendall Six as a favor for me. Just relax; she will be on her own soon and become a good customer like everybody else."

Max was shocked to hear that Rafa had been behind the grisly "Kendall Six" murders. Rafa told him that Griselda had located a hated enemy of his, Nicolado. Years before, Rafa had shot and killed Nicolado's brother Chino. Griselda asked Rafa if he wanted her to take care of Nicolado for him.

"Yes, do what you have to do!" he told Griselda.

What she did was so ghastly and brutal that even Rafa was stunned when he read the account in the newspaper. Griselda's shooters, led by Riverito, had gone in and killed all six people in the house. All the adults were strangled, two females and four males. The baby living in the house was missing.

The baby remained missing for three days, until an anonymous phone call to the police announced, "Go to the Dadeland mall and look on the bench for a baby."

The police acted on the call and found the baby sound asleep on a bench inside the mall.

Max wasn't placated by Rafa's reassurances. "Rafa, these wars cost fortunes; she is constantly changing locations, constantly changing vehicles. She's on the move nonstop, so she can't move the merchandise; she can't pay attention to business, she's too busy looking over her shoulder for who's going to blow her ass away. Shit, it's just stupid business.

"And guns, she's always buying arms and ordnance. I hear she's looking for hand grenades, for Christ's sake. Where the hell is she going to use a hand grenade in Florida or California? That's all we need is for her to start tossing fucking hand grenades. We won't know what heat *is* if she starts shit like that. We're all going to be out of business in a heartbeat."

"Max, *compadre,* please. It's my coke, my cash, so it's my decision. Everything will be okay."

"The hell it will," Max said quietly.

But Max did as he was instructed, and for the rest of '82 and the beginning of '83, little by little, Griselda got back on her feet again and also developed her own routes from Colombia for the cocaine. The demand for the white powder was overwhelming. As fast as she could get the dope delivered, it was sold. Rafa had also opened up a separate line of cocaine credit for her three sons in California.

Dario was very concerned with Little Michael's schooling. "I want my son to be educated," he told Max. "He will go into the business, but he will go in as an educated person, not as an ignoramus, like Griselda and her other sons. None of those sons went to school, Max. They can barely write their names to fill out an application."

"They have no problem counting money," Max said, trying to break the tension.

"Weighing drugs, counting money, and killing people; in those things they are well-educated. But for *my* son I want more," Dario said, drifting off in thought.

Max had strong opinions about the three boys. Dixon was dark, brooding and sinister. He was quiet but deadly. His nickname was *El Negro,* the black one. He was the tallest, at five feet seven inches, and had dark skin with kinky hair. He was an expert motorcyclist, but according to Max, his specialty was acting as the backseat shooter in motorcycle "drive-bys," a technique that was invented by his mother. Two riders would approach their victim on a motorcycle. The backseat rider would be carrying an automatic weapon, either a Mac-10 or a fully automatic Uzi. When they got close enough, they would spray the victim and anyone nearby with bullets, and then scream off on the motorcycle down back alleys and twisting side streets, and quickly hide the bike and the gun. It was a deadly execution method that was eventually adopted by other Colombians as a killing method, but it was the Godmother who had invented it, and Dixon was her best pupil. Dixon and Griselda both bragged to Max of his exploits. Dixon had killed people in Colombia, and at least two people in New York.

Uber was the second oldest. Short at five feet four inches and slight of build, he was the only one that Max felt had any hope of becoming a decent human being. He was sensitive and observant, and was determined to do things his own way. Whenever he heard that his mother was on a drug binge, he would go crazy trying to find her and stop her.

As her habit increased, she began to dip into their coke stash, so much that the sons asked Max to deliver the dope directly to them. "Max," Uber told him, "sometimes you deliver a full kilo of a thousand grams to my mother and she only turns over eight hundred grams and keeps two hundred for her own habit. Please deliver the shit directly to us. I don't want my mother using drugs." Uber did no drugs himself.

Osvaldo was the worst of the boys: a cold-blooded killer who had killed often and seemed to enjoy it. And he could go off at any time into a wild rage.

There was an incident in the middle of the afternoon at the Omni, a high-class Miami mall, when Osvaldo was with Marta, Rafa's pretty mistress. A passerby brushed Marta or pinched her bottom. She let out a high-pitched scream and grabbed her behind. Osvaldo went crazy. On the spot, he whipped out his gun and started shooting at the man, who ran for his life through the highly polished marble corridors of the mall. After he fired several shots, Osvaldo took off for the garage and the black Mercedes 450 Rafa had given to Griselda for Christmas. He sped off, chased by the Omni security, and eventually by the police, who finally cornered him in downtown Miami after a long tire-screaming, high-speed chase through the city of Miami.

They found an automatic weapon in the trunk and threw him into jail. He was traveling on false papers, so he was booked under an assumed name. His bail was posted, and he jumped, forfeiting the bond.

Max couldn't believe his ears when he heard about it from Osvaldo and Marta. It was like a story from Chicago in the '30s. There was no question that Osvaldo was definitely his mother's son.

Yet on occasion Max had some fun with the Blanco family. Once he went shooting at a commercial gun range on the Tamiami Trail with Griselda, her three sons, and Jaime Bravo, one of Griselda's shooters. Griselda loved to shoot. She normally carried a Walther PPK, like Dario, but any weapon would do.

Max had never been shooting with her before. He could not believe his eyes as he watched Griselda fire her pistol. It was as if all her anger was concentrated on the barrel of her gun. She brought each shot down from above her forehead until her arms were extended directly in front of her, pumping each shot outward, as if she were slinging the bullets at the target. Firing in wild abandon, with no regard for the target, Griselda unleashed a nonstop volley. She quickly slipped a second clip into her gun, which she slapped tight with the palm of her hand, and resumed firing. The range quieted down as the other shooters began to watch this wild woman as she threw her arms toward the target, her gun blasting nonstop bullets. The bullets tore into the surrounding targets. The attendant ran the length of the range and screamed at her to stop shooting.

Griselda looked at the attendant, bewildered, wondering what his problem was. "That's it, lady, no more shooting for you. You're going to fucking kill somebody before you're through. That's it!"

Max, sensing potential trouble, stepped in to calm things down. The attendant did not know who he was talking to. The sons glared at the attendant, three pairs of deadly eyes; they did not want to listen to their mother being talked to that way.

"No problem, no problem; everybody just take it easy. These are all loaded weapons." That was all Max had to say as he eased the attendant out of the line of fire and defused the situation. The attendant knew about Colombians; he shut up and walked away. Griselda finished shooting the clip.

Altogether, there were four Sepúlveda brothers, Diego, Paco, Dario, and Hugo. Hugo was running the drug importation operations in France. The rest of the brothers were all closely associated with Griselda.

Diego Sepúlveda grew to hate Griselda, and she could feel his hatred. He believed that Griselda was using him, Dario, and Paco for her own purposes, and that it was inevitable she would cause their destruction. Once Griselda's antennae picked up on his real feelings, it was as if Diego had signed his own death warrant.

Diego lived in a motel on the Galt Ocean Mile in Fort Lauderdale. Griselda dispatched Riverito to kill him. Riverito was admitted to the motel room by Edgar Díaz, a close friend of Max's and an employee of Rafa's, who was visiting Diego. Diego sat on the couch with a girl. The three of them were sitting in the room freebasing. They were high. They greeted Riverito as he entered.

Riverito walked over and shot Diego in the head, then told Edgar Díaz and the girl that they would be next if they ever spoke a word of what had happened. Riverito had been surprised to find Edgar Díaz and the girl in the room; he had only been contracted to kill Diego.

Riverito then set up the scene to look like a suicide. And that was the story he stuck with. A few hours later, he told Griselda and Dario that he had entered the motel room to visit Diego and found that Diego had taken his own life, probably because he was despondent about the fights he was having with Dario and Griselda.

Dario broke into tears at the news and collapsed on the couch. Griselda did the same, with rivers of tears flowing down her face. She let out a scream and whined to the heavens like a bereaved sister.

"Toto" was Diego's best friend. Even though Diego was Toto Sepúlveda's uncle, they were the same age. The two had been inseparable since they were both five years old. They did everything together: slept with women together, traveled together, ate together, and they killed together.

Diego had taught Toto how to kill. Diego accompanied Toto on his first hit to make sure that the hit went down without any problems. Toto's grief was inconsolable. He sat on the couch in Max's Florida room and cried for eight solid hours; nobody could get near him. He just wanted to be left alone, and he stayed alone in his grief for three days.

And nobody could claim the body. Everyone was either in the country illegally or there were arrest warrants out against them, and Max was not about to volunteer. So they sent for one of the Sepúlveda sisters, Stella, who was Toto's mother. She came up from Colombia, identified and claimed Diego's body.

Max's house became the mourning house. Never had he seen such grief, especially from Griselda. It wasn't until months later, when they were at war with Griselda, that Edgar Díaz finally confided in him about what had really happened in that motel room. Max sat and listened as Edgar explained. He was almost dizzy when he heard the truth; it was such a shock to him. People had told him that Griselda could have easily won the Academy Award for best actress, and now he knew why.

The tension between Griselda and Dario was building, until it finally exploded in Max's living room. Griselda had suspected Dario of having an affair with a young topless dancer from Fort Lauderdale, but she couldn't prove it.

It was lunchtime and everybody was eating. Griselda put a plate of Colombian stew in front of Michael. Michael didn't want to eat.

Dario looked at his son and said, "You don't want any, you're not hungry, Miguelito? Don't eat, then. Say 'no, thank you.'" He smiled, patting Michael's hand.

"He will eat!" Griselda screamed.

"He doesn't have to eat," Dario said quietly but firmly.

Griselda walked over and sat next to Michael. She squared the bowl of stew in front of Michael, grabbed a spoon, and holding Michael by the back of the neck, she started to force-feed her son. Michael started to scream and cry, trying to squirm away.

Dario rose from his chair and stared down at Griselda. "You've done everything you possibly could do to this kid to destroy him. You won't let him go to school, you treat him like an animal. You want him to be brought up to be a killer. You don't know the first thing about raising a kid. You want to turn out an animal like the other three. It's not going to happen with him. My son will be educated. He will be as normal as he can be with all this around him. I'm going to take him to Colombia." Dario reached over and scooped up Michael from his chair. He nodded at his two shooters, two of the deadliest killers in the Colombian underworld, Carlos Arango, known as *Cumbamba,* "The Chin," and Jaime Bravo. The two hitmen stood and walked over next to Dario. The three of them stared at Griselda for a second with Michael crying and whimpering, his head buried in his father's shoulder. The tears were staining Dario's white silk shirt. No more words were said. The three men turned on their heels and walked quickly out the door.

Max sat in silence, nonplussed.

Griselda cried with deep heartrending sobs; she knew Dario was gone and so was Michael. Her faithful shooter Riverito sat looking off into space, not knowing what to do. In between sobs Griselda stood and shouted, "I will get him back no matter what it takes. For all that's holy, Michael will be back. No one takes my son from me!"

Max had never seen such wild rage. There was no question in his mind that Dario was a dead man. Dario just didn't know it. He feared nothing and would face anything; but Dario had underestimated Griselda's power.

Dario went down to Colombia and began to work secretly with Rafa, sending him coke. Dario's two shooters stayed in Miami and quietly moved over into Rafa's organization. Rafa never mentioned any of this to Griselda.

Two months later, Dario's car was stopped in Colombia by two policemen. They questioned him at length, studied his papers, and finally let him go. Dario knew he had just been fingered. He didn't know why.

Two days later, he was driving with Michael, and he was stopped again by a police car, this time containing four cops. Dario was told to get out of the car. As he stepped out of the car and was being handcuffed, he recognized one of the cops as one of those who had stopped him two days before.

He knew he was a dead man, but he wanted his son to live. He took off running, so none of the bullets would accidentally hit his son. The four cops stood shoulder to shoulder and emptied their guns. A hail of bullets tore into Dario's fleeing form. His bullet-torn body fell in a heap less than ten feet from the car.

Michael had watched it all from the front seat. He screamed, and ran to bury his face in his father's blood-soaked silk shirt.

Max never found out how much Griselda had paid the police to murder Dario, but there was no question in his mind that she had ordered the hit.

Griselda came to Max for help in getting Michael back into the United States. Max had the people who forged the visas and passports for Rafa's organization under his control. Rafa told Max, "Okay, we'll go get the kid and bring him back; why should he suffer?"

Max flew to Panama and made arrangements with Martín Silva, his man in California, who had flown down to meet him. Rafa waited for the phone call in Medellín. "Okay, Rafa, Martín will do it. He'll come and get Michael. It's going to cost $20,000."

"Okay, send Martín to Medellín. I'll pay him here."

"Griselda is waiting in California."

Martín Silva flew to Colombia and picked up Michael. Silva told Max that the flight back to California was awful. Michael was sobbing the entire journey, "The police killed my father, the police killed my father."

Griselda also blamed it on the police. She was not going to admit that she had paid them to do it. She had kept her word: She got Michael back. It had cost her another husband.

* * *

By early 1983, the total line of credit with Griselda's family had crept up from five to fifty kilos, but they were still paying their bills.

Max knew that Griselda had a very bad habit for which she was slowly becoming famous. When she owed somebody money and they started pressing her for it, she'd pay them, but she'd pay them with lead instead of with money.

Marta Ochoa Saldarriaga was a first cousin to the Ochoa family, and Rafa's mistress. Rafa and Marta were deep into freebasing and would often slip away into oblivion for days at a time. Griselda often joined them. Rafa was able to extricate himself from the seductive arms of the freebase, but Marta only sank lower and lower.

Marta lived for the freebase, and she had a means of supporting herself through an unlimited supply of dope from her cousins, the Ochoa brothers. A constant supply of cocaine came into the United States, and a constant supply of cash left. She, like Rafa, was a major supplier. From the proceeds of her sales, she supported her own enormous habit and lived a high lifestyle.

When Marta and Rafa were freebasing together, they were not to be disturbed. Armed bodyguards stood outside their locked door with strict orders that nobody, absolutely nobody, was to disturb them. The freebasing usually went on for two or three days; then they needed two days to come down off the high.

Griselda went to work on Marta's weakness. Rafa was often in Colombia on business trips, and when he was away, Griselda would feed Marta's habit, so that soon Marta began to lean on Griselda as a freebasing partner. When freebasing a person does not want to sit alone; being so paranoid, the person needs company.

Over time, Griselda lulled Marta into a sense of security, until their relationship developed to the point where Marta started supplying coke directly to her, and Marta started to use Griselda's distribution network. Griselda loved the fact that Marta had an unlimited source of supply and unlimited credit with her cousins.

But Marta, even though she was living in a fog much of the time, still kept good accounts and accurate records of all transactions.

Griselda had been through this drill many times. She knew that the best way to get deep credit was to pay her bills promptly at first, then stri g them out slowly over a long period of time until one day the creditor would wake up to find that she owed them big money.

And that's what she did with Marta. Slowly, inexorably, Griselda's credit rose, until one day Marta looked at the account and saw that Griselda owed her $1.8 million.

Marta was livid. She had been conned, taken.

Marta demanded her money from Griselda. Suddenly, Griselda and her organization just dropped from sight. For the better part of a month, Marta and Rafa looked for Griselda to collect the money, with no luck.

Then Marta disappeared, but not for long. Rafa received a call from his cousin that Marta's car had been found parked down near the Southland Mall on 104th Street, right off U.S. 1, and that the entire front seat was covered with fresh blood. Rafa took one look at Max and they moved immediately to a wartime readiness. Stash houses, money houses, and residences were immediately changed. But they still weren't sure who had killed Marta.

The next day Marta's body was found. She had been tortured, badly beaten and shot. The body had been wrapped in plastic and tossed into a canal.

The body had been left out in the open for a reason. It was a signal to Rafa and Max that they were now at war, and they would be next. They knew now that

Griselda had tortured Marta to try to get her to give away their addresses. But Marta didn't know the new addresses.

Rafa was enraged. He and Max prepared for a full-scale war, but before it could begin, Marta's father arrived in Miami to claim the body of his daughter. He was shattered when he learned that she had been beaten and tortured before she was killed, and that Griselda Blanco had done it. Nevertheless, he still asked that no further violence be perpetrated, saying that the Ochoas were willing to forgive and forget.

But Rafa wasn't forgiving anyone. He had loved Marta, and his grief was all-consuming. He vowed secretly to hunt down and kill Griselda. He made war calls the very day Marta's father talked of peace. Rafa called every shooter, dealer, hitman and contact he had. He put a reward of "five kilos" on the head of the Godmother. At that time a kilo was selling for $40,000 wholesale on the streets of Miami. Rafa raged totally out of control. He was worth at least fifty million dollars at the time, and he was prepared to use all his resources to kill Griselda. Rafa's orders were: "Kill her or her sons on sight. It doesn't matter where, who, what, when, or how. You see 'em, you shoot 'em, 'cause they're going to do the same to you."

The Ochoas were smart businessmen. They knew that this war would only bring destruction on them. Griselda was out of their control, and it was inevitable that her conduct would only precipitate destruction. She was making it too hot to do business. It was at this point that the Cartel finally and irrevocably turned against the Godmother and her sons. They sat back and hoped Rafa would do the job for them while they went about their business.

Max and Rafa confirmed that Griselda had kidnapped and tortured Marta, then killed her. Griselda's people had then put Marta's body back into her car, driven her to where they dumped her, and parked the car at a second location. That's why the front seat was covered in blood.

Max believed that Griselda could have been the Chief Inquisitor of the Spanish Inquisition. Of all the deadly Colombians Max met in his illustrious career with the Medellín Cartel, he never met any to match the Godmother for violence and wanton mayhem.

She simply loved it.

CHAPTER 11

The Red Rose

On February 6, 1982 there was a murder in Miami that got to every cop who heard the story, including Bob Palombo. It had been ordered by the Godmother.

According to police informants, Chucho Castro, a former bank robber, was an important dealer and shooter for Griselda Blanco, but they had come apart over money and were at war. Griselda sent Riverito to find and kill Chucho.

On the afternoon of the 6th, Chucho's heavy Cadillac Seville was cruising around downtown Miami. Chucho had no particular destination; he was just out for a drive with his son, Johnny, who was just over one year old. Johnny stood in his car seat bouncing up and down, his little bare toes digging into the plush upholstery.

Chucho eased his Cadillac to a halt at a red light in downtown Miami. A car suddenly pulled up next to him, the brakes squealing in the hot afternoon silence. Chucho knew he was in trouble before he looked. The hairs on the back of his neck were standing up, and his hands gripped the wheel very tightly as he turned his head.

He looked to his left at the grinning face of Riverito and the black muzzle of a deadly Mac-10, the Miami chopper. Riverito had waited for him to look over before he shot, so Chucho could see his death coming.

Chucho Castro suddenly disappeared from Riverito's view, slipping from sight, as the muzzle of the Mac-10 lit up fire-red, spraying the car with bullets. Chucho slid under the wheel and slammed his foot down hard on the accelerator. The Cadillac leapt away from the light, leaving a trail of blue smoke from its screaming tires and the blazing Mac-10.

Seconds later, Chucho climbed up from the floor to situate himself behind the wheel; he kept his foot tight on the accelerator, pressing firmly against the floor with all his might. The air rushed in on him from every side; all the windows had been shot out.

Chucho Castro was afraid to turn his head and look to his right. There was only silence from his son, no crying, no gurgling. He took a deep breath and looked.

His tiny son's body hung limp in the car seat; there were many blotches of red, as if he had squashed grapes against his new clothes. One bullet had passed cleanly through his head.

Chucho forced the terrible image out of his mind.

He was still traveling at high speed. He pressed hard against the accelerator. He wanted the force of the wind to tear him apart. He looked up at the rearview mirror out of habit, but it had fallen to the floor, shot away with the windshield.

Tears formed in his eyes and started to flow down his cheeks. He could not look again at his son. He looked in the sideview mirror, which hung on the door. There was no one behind him. Chucho knew that if he kept on speeding, the Miami police would pull him over and he would be finished.

Chucho seemed to be drifting through a nightmare from which he could not wake up.

He made his way home, where he garaged his bullet-sprayed car. He carried his son into his house and listened to the cries and screams of his wife as she looked at her poor dead son.

Chucho sat stunned in a chair for a while, deciding what to do. Then he went to the garage and got his second car. He drove to a store and bought bags and bags of ice, as many as he could get in the car. He took the bags of ice into the bathroom and slit the plastic, pouring the cubes into the tub. He did this until there was more than a foot of ice in the bathtub. Then he ran the cold water for a few seconds to float the ice.

He went into the room where his son was lying and undressed him, then carried his limp body into the bathroom, where he gently placed him in the tub. Chucho pulled a chair up to the edge of the tub to be near his son. He buried his face in his cold hands and cried as though he were going to die.

He spent the night in the bathroom with Johnny. By dawn Chucho knew what he was going to do. When he saw the morning sun rising through the bathroom window, he plunged his hands into the ice water and lifted Johnny's frigid body out of the tub and took him into the living room. He carefully dried his son and dressed him in his white christening suit. He took a long time doing it. This morning would be the last time he would see his son. He plucked a rose from a vase in the living room on his way out.

Chucho got his car and parked it in front of his house. He came out of the house with his son in his arms and gently placed the body on the front seat. He then drove around the streets of Miami, almost empty in the early morning, trying to find the church where his son had been christened.

But his mind wouldn't function. After about an hour of looking, he gave up and pulled up to the first church he saw.

He walked up the stairs and tried the front doors of the church but they were locked. He walked back and carefully laid the baby on the stone steps. He then took the red rose and placed it on his son's chest. Chucho scurried down the walk and drove off, not looking back.

Minutes later, an anonymous call was placed to the Miami Police Department. Officers immediately drove to the church and found a baby's body, dressed all in white, his small hands folded peacefully on his chest, his fingers closed on a single red rose.

Johnny's death was avenged—whether by design or coincidence, no one knows. Shortly after Chucho's son was killed, one of Griselda's sisters, Olga, was executed in Colombia. She was shot to death in a parking lot in front of a prison. Although she never had proof, Griselda told friends she believed Chucho had ordered the killing.

This murder heralded the beginning of the end for Griselda Blanco.

PART IV

THE SPIDER AND THE FLY

CHAPTER 12

The Handsome Informer

It was late 1982 and Bob Palombo's wife was ecstatic about their transfer to Florida. Bob was thirty-seven years old, and had been working in New York for fourteen years. In that time two sons had been born: Rob, in January 1977; and Richie in September 1980. If Bob wanted to get ahead in the DEA, he had to broaden his base of experience. He could still work on Colombians in Miami, and the change of scenery would do the boys good.

But until he hit Miami, Bob did not realize what an emotional trauma it would be to leave New York. After years of working with Luis Ramos, who was now with the DEA, and Frank Colavito, a kinship closer than he realized had developed. He did not consider himself sentimental, but his roots in New York ran deep.

In Miami, he fell into a strong state of depression. He longed to be back in New York, and to make matters worse, he had been working on so many cases up there that he was constantly being called back to appear in court.

On the very day he moved to Miami, as the moving men were emptying the truck into the Palombos' temporary quarters in Coral Springs—where they would live while they waited for their house to be built—Palombo got a call from the New York office. "Bob, we need you up here for trial."

"When?"

"Tomorrow."

"Tomorrow? Hey, I'm entitled to five days' administrative leave. I'm unloading the damn moving van right now. My wife's going to kill me."

"Tell her not to worry. We'll have you in and out. If you don't get up here and testify, the judge may dismiss the charges; you've got to come up."

"All right, all right," Palombo said.

Bob went in to tell his wife the bad news. He flew to New York the next morning and went straight to the U.S. Attorney's office. On arriving he was told there was a screw-up and he wouldn't be testifying for a while. When he called his wife to tell her, she went all to pieces. While she was away from the house, they had been robbed. The thieves had come in through the patio doors and emptied the house of everything they could sell quickly.

The Palombos had moved to Coral Springs, an affluent middle-class neighborhood half an hour from Miami. Coral Springs, it turned out, was a haven for burglaries.

When Bob returned from New York, Grace said, "I can't believe this place. We move here, and they rob us the first day. They rob you right out in the open. Every night I hear burglar alarms go off. It was safer in New York!" As a result, for the next two years that they lived in Coral Springs, Grace and Bob lived a cloistered life, with the windows shut and the curtains drawn at all times.

In December of 1983, when Bob Palombo was briefed on the Griselda Blanco case in the Miami office of the DEA, he couldn't have been happier. It was as though Griselda was a present to him, to get his mind off leaving New York and entering the strange world of South Florida.

And it was great to work with his old pal Bill Mockler from New York, who had also been transferred to Florida. Mockler was the supervisor of Group 2. He made Palombo the case agent. Palombo had the experience and the desire to catch the Godmother, and Mockler knew it. The case was named *Los Niños,* "The Sons." Griselda's three older sons were now deep into the cocaine trade, and the DEA hoped that the sons would lead them to the mother.

Dan Moritz had begun the case as an intelligence probe in September of 1983. The DEA had received an anonymous tip about Uber Trujillo, Griselda's second son. The caller was able to say that Uber Trujillo was dealing drugs and that he had some relatives who were also dealing drugs. And the caller knew of Uber's mother, who was a very vicious person, so violent that she was the reason for the call. This evil woman had to be put away.

That was enough to get Moritz started, but he had no background information or knowledge of who she really was, and he had no real experience with Colombians. Moritz was a new agent at the time, with only six months' experience, a very hard-working, bright, and energetic agent from Detroit. He went to the computer first with the information he had, and punched it in. The NADDIS (National Narcotic and Dangerous Drug Information System) computer came alive and started spitting out information, reams of it. Moritz just sat there astounded as the computer kicked in and did its thing. By 1983, the DEA had become very sophisticated in the collection and cataloguing of intelligence. All the background popped out, including the other cases cross-referenced with the Blanco case, the outstanding warrants, and the names of the other agents who had worked on the case.

Dan Moritz took what he had to Bill Mockler, the group supervisor. The Miami office was made up of nine groups; each group consisted of a ten-man squad.

They had information that Uber was dating a beautiful model by the name of Suzanne Wilson, aka Sissy, and that he had bought her an $85,000 red Ferrari. The DEA also knew where Uber was living in Turnbury Isle.

Dan Moritz said, "Let's go up and take a look at Turnbury Isle."

On arriving there, Dan slipped into the garage. He saw that Uber was driving a brand new BMW. He ran the plates through the DMV computer, and found out it was registered to Uber Trujillo, Brickell Key, Miami. Moritz then checked the Brickell Key address, its phone, and utilities, and came up with the name Suzanne Wilson. He checked her out and found the red Ferrari registered to her. But all this was leading him nowhere. Dan knew Uber was moving packages, and he was frustrated.

So Bill Mockler introduced Bob Palombo as the senior agent and team leader, and said, "Why don't you work with Dan and see if you can steer the case in the right direction. You know Colombians; let's see if together we can nail the Godmother."

To celebrate the new alliance, Dan Moritz went down to Miami Beach and bought a coconut carved in the shape of a man's head—"Coconut Man." Inside the coconut was a battery-powered device with a string attached; when the string was pulled, Coconut Man laughed in a hysterical high-pitched cackle, its jaw bobbing up and down. Moritz hung the coconut man in the squad room and waited for the right moment to pull the cord.

Palombo couldn't have been happier. He hit it off with Moritz; there was no jealousy as to whose case it was. They just wanted to see how it played out. She was "the big one," the Al Capone of Colombians. Bill Mockler and Bob Palombo had chased her in New York and had kept track of her for years. Now they had a chance to nail her.

As Palombo got deeper and deeper into the case with Moritz, he began to forget about New York, and his depression began to drift away. It was almost as if Griselda Blanco had come back into his life to make him happy, let him practice his skills at the highest level, and provide him with an adversary that was his equal. She was an adversary who had eluded anyone who'd ever hunted for her, including many Colombians who wanted to kill her. Palombo had known in New York that somehow they would meet again.

But it was like 1974 all over again; Griselda was the mystery woman. The agents were always aware of people associated with her, and now they even had one of her sons under surveillance, but she was an elusive shadow. Some intelligence said that she was actually in Miami. Other sources said she was hiding in Colombia, that she would not be foolish enough to leave the safety of Colombia and face American justice.

They couldn't get a fix on her. Palombo was sure that Uber, the son, would lead them to his mother. Maybe she might show up at Uber's apartment.

Slowly, information was starting to build, bits and pieces of information, mostly from other offices, predominantly from Los Angeles and San Francisco. Seizures were being made in those areas, and when the documentary evidence was examined and entered into the NADDIS computer, the same telephone numbers would suddenly appear. The numbers were traced to other apartments in Turnbury Isle, showing that other people were involved. The agents assumed that at least one of these phone numbers belonged to another son of Griselda Blanco.

Further information indicated that Uber was driving a black Porsche, and contact was made with the chief of security, who recognized his picture. "Yeah, that's the guy all right; he lives in apartment 3D, and that's his Porsche over there," he said, pointing at a $40,000 black Porsche Carrera.

Palombo was not used to the "Scarface" attitudes, the "Miami Vice" blatant lifestyles the sons were living. He was used to the invisible, innocuous, low-key lifestyle of the New York Colombians, where the hottest car they drove was a three-year-old Monte Carlo.

Things were going well with the surveillance until late March of '84 when they "took a burn." The head of security made a mistake; he asked one of his guards a question regarding Uber's car. It was a mistake in judgment.

The guard was on Uber's payroll, and he informed Uber immediately that he was under surveillance. Then Uber surprised everyone. He called his lawyer, and his lawyer called the U.S. Attorney's office wanting to know "what the hell is going on?" The surprise call was ignored, but the cat was now out of the bag.

The surveillance continued but nothing happened, no movement. Days went by. The DEA teams sat there with binoculars, watching a dark apartment, drinking coffee and waiting, but there was nothing. Uber had fled; their one thin thread to the Godmother had vanished.

Group 2 was the Centac group. Aside from making drug cases, they also had the responsibility of investigating drug-related homicides. That was Bill Mockler's idea, and the origin of the idea came from New York, where he had organized the DEA to work closely with the NYPD. So when Mockler got down to Miami, he connected many of the homicides that were occurring between New York and Miami, because he knew that in many cases the players were the same in both cities. Centac stands for Central Tactical, and the Miami group was Centac 26, because there had been 25 predecessors in the United States. The special operational plan was written up and approved. Group 2 of the DEA joined forces with the Metro–Dade homicide squad. Centac 26 responded on all drug-related homicides in Dade County. Aside from assembling valuable forensic evidence, they were able to gather books and ledgers that were of tremendous value to the DEA. All assets, cash, and property that were seized were forfeited to the government and shared with the Metro–Dade police. The seized cocaine was used as evidence, then destroyed.

The Centac 26 "family photo album" grew rapidly. In 1983, there was a murder a day, and most of them were drug-related. The album comprised some of the goriest photographs ever taken—a lot of splattered brains and riddled bodies, very hairy stuff, even for veteran cops—as well as photos of shooters and of major players, like Griselda Blanco and her sons.

After they had lost their target, Uber Trujillo, a decision had to be made on whether or not to proceed with the investigation of the Godmother and her family. Palombo and Moritz were frustrated, getting nowhere, and facing possible orders to drop the case, when their luck changed.

In the third week of April, an agent from DEA Group 6 called Palombo. "Hey, Bob, I got this Colombian guy, his name is Gerardo Gómez, and he wants to cooperate. He was a confidential informant once before and got popped a few times, once by us here in Miami for ludes, and once for coke out in Tulsa, Oklahoma. He was just sentenced two weeks ago to ten years; he's out on appeal bond. He wants to do the right thing; he says he can do some big Colombian people. You know Group 6 is a lab group; we have no use for the guy. Are you interested in talking with him?"

"Absolutely," Palombo said.

Moritz and Palombo went over immediately to meet with Gerry Gómez, and they brought the album with them.

Gómez was a well-dressed, debonair man in his midthirties. He was an ex-merchant-marine sailor, a pilot and mechanic who had owned a speed-shop in Medellín that serviced cars and motorcycles.

They debriefed him for an hour, and finally brought out the album. Palombo showed Gómez the Godmother and her family. "What about these people?"

"Oh, yes, I know her," Gómez responded, pointing at a picture of Griselda.

"How do you know her?" Palombo asked.

"I had a speed-shop in Medellín, and she used to come in with her fancy cars and I would fix them. And I knew all her sons; Uber and Osvaldo were motocross nuts. In fact, I believe Osvaldo won the Motocross Championship in 1982."

"What do you know about the boys?"

"Well, I don't know what they've been doing. I've been out of touch with them. I know Dixon is living out in San Jose, because a relative of mine, my cousin Lucía Gómez, is living with Dixon, and her brother, Jorge Gómez, is also with them. We went to school together, and we all know each other very well."

"What do you think Dixon is doing?" Palombo asked.

"What do you think! He's doing cocaine."

"Do you think you could get entrée to him?"

"I could always call up and speak to Lucía, and have her tell him that I'm interested. In fact, I have a scenario that would probably work. I know Harold Rosenthal real well. You know who he is?"

"Yes, of course," Palombo answered. Harold Rosenthal, a former bail bondsman from Atlanta, went to work for Jorge Ochoa and Pablo Escobar, and ran one of the biggest smuggling rings ever organized.

He was arrested in Colombia in 1983, extradicted, and sentenced to life in prison.

"I know him," Gómez continued. "He's in jail right now. He was a major mover of cocaine. I could come up with the story that I inherited Harold's customers, but that I need some help, since I'm not in the cocaine business myself. I'm a transportation person, and I'm also involved in money transfers and money laundering. So it would be logical that I would need some help with the supply side of the business. What do you guys think?"

"It's credible, and if they check, they can confirm you knew Harold, right?" Palombo asked.

"Yeah, and Lucía and her brother know I never dealt cocaine, so it will be logical for me to ask for help from Dixon."

"Hell, let's give it a shot."

"And what about me? What do I get out of this?" Gómez asked.

"Gerry, you're face to face with a ten-year sentence right now. You do the right thing here, and we'll make the amount and significance of your cooperation known to the United States Attorney in Texas; you already know that he will listen to what we tell him. That's the best we can do. You can chip away at your sentence, maybe get it right down to nothing. It will be up to you, but we can't promise an exact deal."

"All right, I'll call Lucía and her brother."

Gómez called and was told that Lucía and Jorge Gómez would be seeing Dixon that night, and that they would be partying with him. They said, "We'll tell him that you're interested in dealing; he'll get back to you."

Within a day Dixon called back. "Tell me what's happening with you, Gerry."

"Harold Rosenthal has been busted."

"I know."

"I've inherited part of his customer list, and I need

some help from you. I'm going to be out in Los Angeles on some related business; maybe that would be a good time for us to get together."

"Okay, no problem," Dixon said. "I'll come down and meet you in Los Angeles."

"Or, when I finish my business in Los Angeles, I'll call you, and we'll set up a meet somewhere near you, maybe San Jose."

"Fine, you're on," Dixon said and hung up the phone.

On May 9, 1984, Palombo and Moritz met Bill Mockler in the squad room and briefed him on the status of the Godmother case. Mockler approved the travel vouchers and said as he left, "This looks good, guys, maybe the first break in this damn case. Try not to fuck it up."

Just as Mockler passed through the squad room portal, Palombo pointed at Coconut Man and nodded to Moritz. "Don't worry, Bill," Palombo shouted, "you can count on us!"

On cue, Moritz pulled Coconut Man's string, and he let off a burst of high-pitched insane laughter, his jaw bouncing up and down. Palombo and Moritz burst out laughing, but Mockler never turned around; he wouldn't give them the satisfaction. He just shook his head and slammed the squad-room door shut behind him.

With the approval for the travel and expense money in hand, Palombo, Moritz, and Gerry Gómez headed for San Francisco. Palombo checked in with the San Francisco DEA office, and the agents there helped. Dixon was located in the Morgan Hills area near San Jose. Gómez checked into the Holiday Inn in San Jose and called up Dixon; he got one of his people. "Dixon is out on the road, taking care of some business; he'll get back to you later."

"I'm at the Holiday Inn."

Dixon called back and said he would be over to

meet Gómez in his room between nine and ten that night. The DEA had wired the adjoining room and asked Annabelle Grimm, who was now stationed in San Francisco, to join them. She spoke perfect Spanish, and they wanted a hands-on immediate translation, just in case something went wrong.

At nine o'clock, Dixon and Lucía showed up at the hotel. Gerry Gómez was very concerned about implicating a relative, knowing it is easy to get involved in a conspiracy. All she would have to do was deliver a package, or money, and she could be arrested. So Gómez suggested, "Lucía, you know, maybe if you want to go get coffee or wait for us in the bar, I'll just have a conversation with Dixon."

"No, I know everything that's going on. No problem, I'll just sit here," Lucía responded.

Gómez and Dixon talked about their experiences for a few minutes and then got down to business. Gómez explained how he had acquired Harold Rosenthal's customer list. Gómez also indicated to Dixon that he was looking for a steady supply for some customers in the Los Angeles area.

"I'm moving more than a thousand kilos a month out here, and I don't deal in anything less than fifty-kilo to hundred-kilo customers," Dixon told Gómez.

"That's too much for me right now. My customers can do volume, but now they only want a few kilos to sample the merchandise."

"Well, for you, Gerry, we can make an exception. We'll do smaller quantities."

"How much?" Gómez asked.

"Per kilo—$23,000. If you like, you can take it with you when you leave."

"I don't want to take it with me. I want to pick it up in Miami."

Gómez had to be careful. He had been thoroughly briefed to avoid having to buy two or three kilos on the spot. The DEA did not have that kind of money to gamble with, and the last thing they wanted was to arrest Dixon with a mere three or four kilos when they could nail the entire family if they played their cards right. Gómez had to be fast on his feet and light on his toes; he had to dance around any traps and pitfalls.

"Osvaldo handles Miami; he travels back and forth from Miami to the West Coast every couple of weeks," Dixon said. "He's here in the San Francisco area right now; you want to talk with him?"

"Yeah, sure."

"Here's his beeper number, call him tomorrow and set up a meeting."

"Where you getting your stuff from?" Gómez asked.

"Brazil, through Mexico directly into California. We don't use Colombia any more."

"What about Uber?"

"He got some heat from the cops in Miami, so he has moved to Los Angeles. Here, I'll give you his beeper number in the L.A. area. You need anything in L.A., you call him."

"What about your mother?" Gómez asked.

"She is living in Hollywood, Florida. She does a few things on her own. Gerry, can you move money out of the country?"

"I have good contacts, legitimate businesses in the Miami area, that are capable of getting money into foreign countries," Gómez answered.

"We are very interested in moving some money. I can give you $150,000 now to be sent to my Panamanian account, and an additional $100,000 to be sent to Colombia and converted to pesos. I will call you in a couple of days. You interested?"

"Yeah."

"Good, call Osvaldo tomorrow and see about delivery of some merchandise in Miami."

"I will, thanks."

The meeting concluded at ten-thirty that evening.

On the next day, May 10th, at noon, Gómez phoned the San Francisco beeper number as instructed by Dixon, and was called back by a man named Gerardo, who indicated that Osvaldo would call back about one o'clock.

So Gómez had an hour to kill. He went to see Jorge Gómez, Lucía's brother and his cousin. Jorge told him he and Lucia were not involved with the drug business, but he had been at a party Osvaldo held a week earlier at his ranch. Osvaldo had had the ranch blanketed with more than $10,000 worth of freshly cut flowers, and all there was to drink was unlimited amounts of Dom Perignon. He had hired a very famous Latin band to play all night. Jorge told Gerry Gómez that Osvaldo's ranch was about ninety miles from San Francisco, between Sonoma and Lake Tahoe. Osvaldo had had a professional motocross track built around his property for personal use.

Gerry Gómez said goodbye to his cousin and hurried back to his hotel to call Osvaldo on his beeper.

"I don't want to meet you in San Jose; drive to San Francisco, then call me back when you arrive there, and arrangements will be made," Osvaldo said.

Gómez met Osvaldo at a quarter of five at a Safeway market in San Francisco. Osvaldo arrived in a gray Ford, accompanied by his girlfriend, Gabriela Santos. They were followed by a second car, obviously Osvaldo's bodyguards. Gerry Gómez had also noticed that there was a third car already parked in the lot when he had arrived. The car was there to do presurveillance for Osvaldo to make sure the area was clean.

Osvaldo jumped out of his car and into Gerry's car so they could talk privately. "Dixon has told me everything, but I do not have any merchandise in Miami for you. I am expecting a large shipment from the Ochoa family, but it has not come in yet. But I do

140

have a five-hundred-kilo shipment coming in this weekend. How much merchandise can you move? I only deal with large-volume customers."

Gómez told the same story he had given to Dixon, that he just wanted a few kilos for samples, then his customers would become heavy clients.

"I don't handle these small orders, but I will do it for you, since you are such an old friend. And one more thing, Gerry."

"Yes?"

"If you find any better merchandise anywhere, I will give you mine for free."

"I'm sure your merchandise will be the best."

"Here, call Eddie; he is my man in Miami; he will handle everything. Use his beeper number, and use the code." Osvaldo explained the code: The first three digits of the number are to be given in English, the last four are to be reversed in Spanish. "The price is very special to you, $16,000 per kilo."

"You are very careful."

"Yes. If you want to contact me in San Francisco, you will have the code 1335; 13 is for your name; it will identify you. 35 is for Miami. Always ask for Johnny. Use the code and you will be put through to me."

Osvaldo and his brothers had been trained well by their mother; they left little to chance. Osvaldo told Gerry that they were doing well: he was moving about eight hundred kilos per month, Uber about two hundred, and Dixon about six hundred. At $16,000 per kilo, they had a monthly income in excess of $25 million. Osvaldo also went on to tell Gómez that he had numerous corporations in Panama and the United States, and that no one could ever find his assets. He said that his aunt Nuri Restrepo had been carrying money orders to Colombia, but he needed an additional method to transfer his money.

"Gerry, if you want to wait a day, I can give you

$300,000 to take back to Miami and arrange for it to be transferred to Colombia. I am moving about $3 million a month."

Osvaldo got out of the car, walked back to the gray Ford, and returned with a bag of money and handed it to Gerry. "I would like you to get this to my aunt Nuri in Colombia; there's $5,000 inside."

Osvaldo opened the bag and withdrew a twenty-dollar bill. "Now there's only $4,980. I don't want to break the Customs laws by sending more than $5,000 out of the country!" He laughed. "Call at the beginning of next week if you can move the money for me, and get hold of Eddie in Miami if you want merchandise. You must keep in touch with me, because we change our beeper numbers every ten days."

And that was the end of the meeting between Osvaldo Trujillo and Gerry Gómez.

Bob Palombo and Dan Moritz were ecstatic; they had made great progress. Now if they could just get the mother involved, they could pull down the entire family.

But it wasn't going to be simple. When Palombo laid it out for the U.S. Attorney's office, the lawyers insisted on "powder on the table" when an arrest was made. "We've got to get dope to prosecute," they stated.

"No, we don't; we can make the arrest on documentary evidence and supporting testimony. There is absolutely no need for dope." Palombo was a master at "conspiracy cases"; he had successfully arrested dopers and prosecuted many cases against the Chileans and the Argentinians without dope.

Palombo knew that Griselda Blanco and her family were too smart to ever get caught handling drugs. Like the Italian Mafia before them, they ordered things done by their minions.

Palombo needed to find a U.S. Attorney who had

the nerve to take on a case like this. The veins on the side of his neck were starting to bulge, and his fellow officers would laugh as he rubbed his bad arm. "Oh-oh, Palombo's rubbing his arm, the shit's going to fly now!"

And it did, as he tried to explain to the lawyers. "Hey, what the fuck are you talking about, we have no case? We have a strong case! What are you telling me, that we don't have anything? We have people and time invested; we can bring her and her family down."

The response was not enthusiastic.

"I'm willing to stick my neck out, and you should be willing to stick your neck out. This is just the beginning of taking her down. We can do it, goddammit, we can do it. You can't leave a criminal of this magnitude on the fucking streets!"

"We need physical evidence, we need powder on the table," was always the response, even though it was phrased in many different ways.

Palombo and Moritz had to figure out how to approach the case, and they needed to do it fast. They reviewed the information they had. The sons were now all based in California: Dixon in Morgan Hills, Osvaldo in San Francisco, and Uber, who after he had caught on that he was being followed in Miami, was now settling in L.A. But Griselda was still in the Miami area, in Hollywood, Florida. In Gómez, they had an informant who had obviously penetrated the veil of the sons' security and was "inside" now. They could easily set up the boys for a buy and nail them, but it would be fragmentary and unreliable. To set them up, it would also mean that the DEA might actually have to buy the dope, something it was not prepared to do without a straight line to Griselda. Palombo and Moritz decided to play it out to see if it would lead to the mother lode—a major bust and the destruction of this cancerous cocaine crime family.

Then things got even more complicated. The San

Francisco office of the FBI was investigating Gabriela Santos, Osvaldo's girlfriend. She was a beautiful Nicaraguan girl allegedly involved in gunrunning for the Sandinistas.

Palombo got a call from the FBI and was told that they were making a major case on Santos, and that the DEA would only "fuck things up" if they started working on Osvaldo.

"Tell you what," Palombo said. "You work your case, and we'll work ours. We are not going to interfere with your case." Palombo did not think much of their case against Santos, but he said nothing.

"Let's share information," the FBI agent suggested.

"Okay," Palombo responded, and he sent them the file.

What happened next was a perfect example of interagency exchange of information. The FBI got all the DEA information, and sent over nothing in return. But Palombo didn't care. "If it gets to a point where they try to steal our case, we'll deal with it," he told the other agents. "Till then, let them have what they want. I won't play their games."

Palombo thought he could lure the family back to Miami. He didn't realize that California was now the family's permanent home. They had done New York, and then Miami. California was the perfect new place of business for them: There was virtually no competition there, and a huge market was just opening up. In Miami, it was one Colombian against another, with price-cutting, wars, and murder devastating their treasuries. And the Marielitos—the Cubans from Mariel—were constantly ripping off and killing the Colombians. Profit margins were falling rapidly; it made good business sense to move to the West.

The Colombians were also moving their transit routes from Florida to Mexico, and then into Southern California, Arizona, and Texas. That was because the DEA was intensifying interdiction efforts in the Bahamas and Florida. The dopers were feeling the pinch. More loads than ever before were getting busted. But Palombo didn't know that at the time. He was still looking at Miami in South Florida as the main port of entry.

Since he couldn't locate the Godmother, Palombo decided to locate Uber by checking out Carlico Tavera, Uber's neighbor in Turnbury Isle. Carlico had moved to Newport Beach, California, and married Billie, the sister of the beautiful Sissy, Uber's girlfriend. They had to be in touch with each other, if only for the women to talk.

From the Miami phone records, they knew Carlico's residence was on Jasmine Circle. Moritz and Palombo decided to do a trap-and-trace on Carlico's line: trap the calls coming in and trace the ones going out.

Palombo and Moritz got the okay, and headed out for the Newport Beach DEA office in Santa Ana. Frank Briggs was the Resident-Agent-in-Charge. He was very cooperative. "Hey, knock yourselves out. If my office can help, just give us a holler. We're small and overworked, but always ready to help."

Briggs connected Palombo and Moritz with the Newport Beach Police, who were coincidentally getting intelligence of their own. The Newport Police had been monitoring Tavera's house. They kept the house under surveillance, although they never charged him. The Newport Police told Palombo and Moritz, "Ever since this little Colombian named Carlico moved into Newport Beach, there are dopers visiting him at all hours of the night and day. We're getting license plate numbers from concerned citizens. We've checked the plates and most of them are connected to known or suspected dopers. We don't like it."

Palombo and Moritz shared some information with

the Newport Police, surveilled the house, checked out the Jeep Wagoneer that Carlico was driving, took some pictures, had the phone company install the trap-and-trace, and then returned to Miami and waited. They had almost begun to wonder if there really *was* a Godmother.

CHAPTER 13

Betty's Bagboy

On May 28, 1984, Gerry Gómez called his cousin Jorge Gómez in San Jose, and was told, "I'm glad you called, Gerry. The Godmother wants to speak with you; it's very important. You're to call her in Los Angeles on her beeper."

With a shaking hand, and with Palombo and Moritz listening, Gerry Gómez called Griselda Blanco as he had been instructed. The call went well, but it was general in nature. Griselda said she wanted Gómez to transfer money from the United States to Colombia, but she didn't say when. She did say she would call back, but Gómez was not sure she would follow through. When he hung up, all three of them looked at each other in wonderment. It was the first time the agents had ever heard her voice. She did exist! The Godmother was real, and she was in California.

On May 29th, Griselda Blanco called back as she had said she would. "Gerry, a man called David will contact you and make exact arrangements to deliver the money in Miami. Once the money has been delivered, you will have to travel to Los Angeles to pick up an additional quantity of money. Is all this okay with you?"

"Yes."

"Good; we will talk again tomorrow."

On May 30th, at approximately twelve-thirty in the afternoon, Griselda called Gómez again. "David, my man, will call you this afternoon. I will call with the exact bank in Panama where the money is to be deposited."

At one-thirty, David telephoned Gómez, and arrangements were made for a meeting at Midway Mall in front of the Jefferson Department Store at two-thirty.

At two-fifteen, Gómez met with Palombo and Moritz and submitted to a body search. Every time a confidential informant received money, they did a body search before and after, to ensure that no money was kept by the informant. "I got another beeper call from Griselda. She asked me to call her back on a 714 number."

Palombo and Moritz looked at the number. The fourth digit was a 9, which meant it was a public phone. They made a special note; maybe it would help in tracking her later.

Gómez made the call. "Gerry, I want you to transfer the money you receive from David to the account of José Ali Parada. Have you got a pen?"

"Yes."

"Good; it is at the Banco Ganadero in Panama City, Panama. You got it?"

"Yes."

The call was concluded, and at two-thirty, Gómez was at the Jefferson Department Store. Palombo and Moritz watched as David got out of a Volkswagen and walked up to meet Gómez. The two walked back and got into the Volkswagen; Gómez emerged some minutes later with a package in his hands. As David disappeared in the Volkswagen, Palombo and Moritz gave each other the thumbs-up sign and big grins. They let David go. After the experience with Uber, they were reluctant to risk another burn by trailing the car. They had what they wanted. They were close to Griselda now, so close they could feel her presence.

Palombo and Moritz followed Gerry back to a Denny's restaurant and climbed into his car. According to DEA procedure, they searched him again, and took possession of the money.

"What happened?" Palombo asked.

"'Betty' is Griselda's new code name. David told me to tell her that the amount is $40,000; to tell her that's all there is, because Uber took the remainder of the original amount."

"What else?" Moritz asked.

"He made me count it in the car. I counted $39,900 and he told me that a hundred dollars over or under doesn't matter."

Back in the office, they had the money serialized, photographed and deposited. It came out to $39,900 just as Gómez had said. Palombo, Moritz, and Gómez left for California that same day.

When they arrived in California, they picked up two agents from the San Francisco office—Monier and Yang—and headed for Newport Beach. After registering in a hotel, Gómez called Griselda, and was told to recontact her.

On May 30th, Gómez and the DEA agents registered in the Marriott Hotel in Newport Beach. Gómez called the Godmother again. "I will meet you in front of the hotel in a short while. Wait for me in front," she instructed him.

Palombo and Moritz checked the listening device Gómez was to carry when he met Griselda. They did not have time to bug the room, and they didn't know where the final meeting would take place. Gómez was given a leather attaché case with a slim tape recorder buried in the base. The brass studs on the bottom of the case acted as microphones, and the locks on the top activated the machine. If the left lock was snapped open, the machine was working.

At quarter to twelve that night, Griselda and her entourage of bodyguards in two trailing cars arrived in front of the hotel. Griselda got out of a white Jeep that the agents had seen before in front of Carlico Tavera's house.

Griselda hugged and kissed Gerry Gómez, greeting him like a long-lost relative, as one of the bodyguards got out of a trailing car to join them. He was carrying a maroon shoulder bag. Griselda, Gómez, and the bodyguard carrying the shoulder bag walked through the lobby and headed for Gómez's room in the Marriott.

Palombo and Moritz were sitting together in the lobby on one of the many couches, reading a newspaper and talking, when Palombo first laid eyes on Griselda. The first thing he saw was the cleft in her chin. Maybe it was the light, maybe it was her makeup, but the cleft in her chin was the first thing Palombo noticed. Second, he noticed her dimples.

Griselda was wearing a fashionable dress, a wig, and a tunic as she walked past them with Gómez and her bodyguard. Palombo and Moritz had all they could do not to whistle and give a high five. There she was walking past them, big and bold as life. Instead, they sat there sedately reading their papers, appearing disinterested.

For Palombo and Moritz, seeing Griselda Blanco, the Godmother, and having her within arm's length, was a great event. They believed this would be the beginning of the culmination of a tremendous amount of work.

Gómez was well-dressed. He wore a freshly pressed pair of slacks, a sport coat, and an open shirt. Griselda clutched his arm, smiling and chatting. Gómez kept his eyes straight ahead, not noticing Palombo or

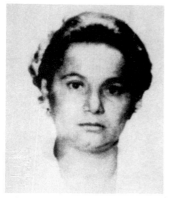

The Godmother's passport photo as a young woman. A master of disguise, she always carried at least two passports. (Metro Dade Police Department photo)

Dario Sepúlveda, famous Colombian bandit and bank robber; Griselda's third husband. (Metro Dade Police Department photo)

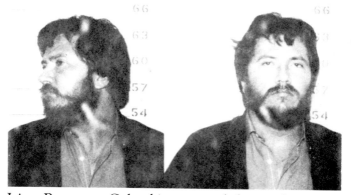

Jaime Bravo, ex–Colombian cop and shooter for Griselda. Shot seventeen times by Colombian police death squads, his body looked like a cheese grater, but he lived. (DEA photo)

Marta Ochoa Saldarriaga, a cousin to the famous Ochoa Cartel clan. She was tortured and killed on the Godmother's orders. Her death initiated another Miami cocaine war. (Metro Dade Police Department photo)

Diego Sepúlveda, a vicious shooter for Griselda's organization. He was shot to death in a Fort Lauderdale motel room. He made the mistake of coming between the Godmother and Dario Sepúlveda, his brother. (Metro Dade Police Department photo)

The Godmother attends a christening.

The Godmother
at Max
Mermelstein's
Miami house, in
Christmas of
1983, with two
of her sons.
From left: Dixon,
Griselda, and
Osvaldo. (photo
by Max Mermelstein)

The Godmother strikes a slinky pose.

Griselda gives Dixon a motherly kiss.

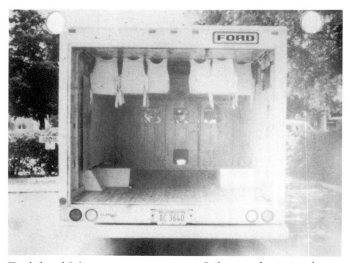

Dadeland Massacre war wagon: Like cowboys in the days of the Old West, Griselda's shooters jumped out of this war wagon and opened fire in an upper-class Miami mall, in broad daylight. (Metro Dade Police Department photo)

Dario Sepúlveda and little Michael Corleone Sepúlveda watch the Miami inland waterway drift by. (Metro Dade Police Department photo)

From left: Dario Sepúlveda, an unknown, Paco Sepúlveda, and Chucho Castro holding his one-year-old son Johnny, who was later shot to death. (Metro Dade Police Department photo)

Griselda with her four
sons. From left:
Griselda, Michael,
Osvaldo, Uber, and
Dixon. (DEA photo)

Christmas in Miami,
with Griselda's
nephew, a hit man.
(photo by Charlie Cecil)

Michael Corleone Sepúlveda, the Godmother's youngest son. He witnessed the death of his father, Dario Sepúlveda, who was shot to death by four Colombian police. (photo by Max Mermelstein)

El Duque, a money launderer for the Godmother. He had a hit list from the Godmother which included eight DEA agents. He was killed by the Godmother when he was short on a money count. (photo by Charlie Cecil)

A mug shot of Riverito, a shooter who loved his job. He killed on the slightest whim, and by order of the Godmother. According to witnesses, he killed Diego Sepúlveda and Chucho Castro's baby. "Rivi" also ran the Marielito hitmen for Griselda. (DEA photo)

Charlie Cecil and other DEA agents count over $250,000 in confiscated cash. (photo by Charlie Cecil)

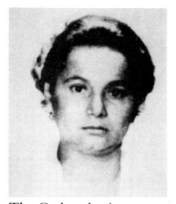

The Godmother's passport photo as a young woman. A master of disguise, she always carried at least two passports. (Metro Dade Police Department photo)

Dario Sepúlveda, famous Colombian bandit and bank robber; Griselda's third husband. (Metro Dade Police Department photo)

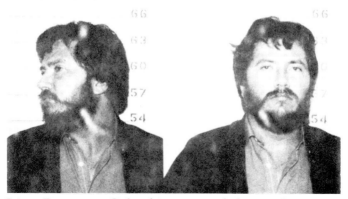

Jaime Bravo, ex–Colombian cop and shooter for Griselda. Shot seventeen times by Colombian police death squads, his body looked like a cheese grater, but he lived. (DEA photo)

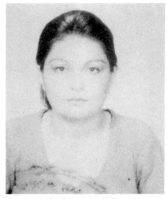

Marta Ochoa Saldarriaga, a cousin to the famous Ochoa Cartel clan. She was tortured and killed on the Godmother's orders. Her death initiated another Miami cocaine war. (Metro Dade Police Department photo)

Diego Sepúlveda, a vicious shooter for Griselda's organization. He was shot to death in a Fort Lauderdale motel room. He made the mistake of coming between the Godmother and Dario Sepúlveda, his brother. (Metro Dade Police Department photo)

The Godmother attends a christening.

The Godmother at Max Mermelstein's Miami house, in Christmas of 1983, with two of her sons. From left: Dixon, Griselda, and Osvaldo. (photo by Max Mermelstein)

The Godmother strikes a slinky pose.

Griselda gives Dixon a motherly kiss.

Dadeland Massacre war wagon: Like cowboys in the days of the Old West, Griselda's shooters jumped out of this war wagon and opened fire in an upper-class Miami mall, in broad daylight. (Metro Dade Police Department photo)

Dario Sepúlveda and little Michael Corleone Sepúlveda watch the Miami inland waterway drift by. (Metro Dade Police Department photo)

From left: Dario Sepúlveda, an unknown, Paco Sepúlveda, and Chucho Castro holding his one-year-old son Johnny, who was later shot to death. (Metro Dade Police Department photo)

Griselda with her four sons. From left: Griselda, Michael, Osvaldo, Uber, and Dixon. (DEA photo)

Christmas in Miami, with Griselda's nephew, a hit man.
(photo by Charlie Cecil)

Michael Corleone Sepúlveda, the Godmother's youngest son. He witnessed the death of his father, Dario Sepúlveda, who was shot to death by four Colombian police. (photo by Max Mermelstein)

El Duque, a money launderer for the Godmother. He had a hit list from the Godmother which included eight DEA agents. He was killed by the Godmother when he was short on a money count. (photo by Charlie Cecil)

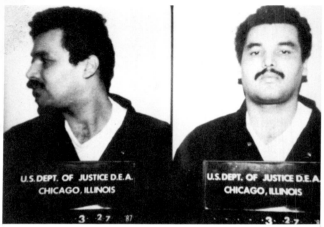

A mug shot of Riverito, a shooter who loved his job. He killed on the slightest whim, and by order of the Godmother. According to witnesses, he killed Diego Sepúlveda and Chucho Castro's baby. "Rivi" also ran the Marielito hitmen for Griselda. (DEA photo)

Charlie Cecil and other DEA agents count over $250,000 in confiscated cash. (photo by Charlie Cecil)

Moritz as he walked by them. The agents watched the three of them disappear into the elevator.

The agents sat waiting in the lobby for twenty minutes, until Gómez reappeared with Griselda and her bodyguard. He gave her a hug and a kiss as she entered the Jeep, her bodyguard entered the trailing car, and they disappeared. There was no surveillance planned for the cars. The bodyguards would be too wary, and the agents couldn't take a chance of exposing Gerry as an informer.

It was a big gamble, but one that the Miami U.S. Attorney's office agreed with, not being eager to get her back on the old "Banshee" warrant and try a case that was ten years old. That was yesterday's news, and it would be a tough case to reconstruct. But then again, she could slip away to Colombia, and they might never see her again. They all agreed to take the chance.

Gómez had been instructed to return to his room and wait for the agents, but after he waved goodbye to Griselda, he took a straight line direct to the bar and ordered a double scotch. His hands were shaking so badly that Palombo thought he might have to hold the glass for him. Gómez was in now, up to his ears. Before, it had only been talk with the agents, and talk with the sons, who were full of bravado and stupid macho attitude; but with Griselda, the Godmother, it was a different story: she was deadly. The maroon bag was lying on the bar. Gómez unzipped it slightly, and pointed for the agents to peek. The bag was packed solid with cash. Palombo and Moritz knew the bar was clean, so they let Gómez have another drink and compose himself before they hauled him off to his room.

Inside the room, Gómez opened up. "Griselda said that this maroon bag contains $460,000, and the plastic bag inside contains $25,000. I'm supposed to deposit the $460,000 in the same account in Panama that we sent the $40,000 to. The $25,000 is to be sent to her sister Nuri Restrepo in Medellín."

"What's your cut, Gerry?" Palombo asked.

"Five grand."

"Did you get everything on tape?" Moritz asked.

"Yeah, if that thing worked, we got it."

It had worked. Griselda acknowledged the death of Marta Ochoa Saldarriaga as the reason she had not returned Gómez's calls. Griselda went on to tell Gómez that she had a big problem with Jaime Bravo, her ex-shooter. The agents all listened to the tapes. "I have a problem with that son of a bitch Jaime Bravo. He stole forty kilos from me."

"Who is he? I don't remember."

"The one with the blue eyes. He used to be a gunman who hung around with Dario, the father of Michael, my youngest son. The death squads, the F-2, shot Jaime in Colombia. They shot him many times, but he lived."

"Is he in Miami?" Gómez asked.

"Yes. I have people on top of him trying to find him. And Osvaldo is completely obsessed with trying to find him; he and Uber are constantly in Miami, looking for him. Jaime is a complete bastard."

Gómez shifted the conversation to the death of Marta. "What was it that happened in Miami?"

"A young girl, a very good friend of mine, was killed. She was the first cousin to the Ochoas. Her lover killed her, and Jaime Bravo was involved."

She rose. "All right, Gerardo, may the mother of God accompany you. I must go. It has been a great pleasure seeing you after such a long time."

"The same for me, Griselda."

The next day Gerry Gómez met with Osvaldo. But instead of Gerry getting out of the car to meet Osvaldo, Osvaldo jumped into Gerry's car. And all Gómez could think of was what Palombo had told him: "You make sure you record that conversation, Gerry. I don't want to hear any bullshit from you."

To record, Gerry's special attaché case had to be open. But it was closed and in the backseat. The case was the first thing Osvaldo noticed. "Hey, Gerry, what's that?" Osvaldo said, pointing at the case.

Gerry took his cue, thought fast, and grabbed the case from the backseat, immediately flipping both locks open. He pulled out some plane magazines. "Yeah, I'm glad you asked. I was thinking about doing some aircraft brokering, and I want to show you . . ." Gómez showed Osvaldo his plane magazines.

"Nice case you got here, Gerry," Osvaldo said, fingering the open case, not interested in the magazines.

"Yeah, right," Gómez said, flipping the magazines back into the case and tossing the case onto the backseat, unlocked.

Osvaldo looked back at the open case, feeling content that it was empty, not knowing that it was recording every word they said. Gómez and Osvaldo finished their business in the car. Osvaldo gave Gómez $15,000 to launder for him.

Osvaldo's last words to Gómez were, "Don't forget, if you want to get a sample of the merchandise, call Eddie in Miami."

"I won't forget, believe me," Gómez responded.

Gómez and the agents then traveled to San Francisco and checked into a hotel. There, they transferred the money to U.S. Customs; a dog handler was there with Rodney, a black Labrador, who reacted to the presence of cocaine on the money. Usually, cash handled by dopers picks up cocaine that can be detected by trained dogs. The money was then taken to the district office and photographed, then transported to a large commercial bank, where it was counted. A cashier's check in the amount of $500,000 was issued in the name of undercover DEA agent Michael Hanson. The agents flew back to Miami and delivered the check to Hanson, who tried to deposit it in an undercover account in a bank in Miami. The transaction was refused for technical reasons and the money was returned to the original bank, which wired the money to Panama into the account of José Ali Parada.

As soon as Gómez got back to Miami, he called Eddie, but his calls were never returned.

On June 14th and 19th, U.S. Customs seized 860 kilos in Miami. Bob Palombo watched on his TV at home as the Customs agents held up kilos for the cameras. Written across several kilos was the name Eddie. Was it the "Eddie" that Gómez was supposed to contact? It was a long shot, but it was worth a try. Palombo called Gómez and told him what to do the next time he spoke to the Godmother's organization.

Contact was made on July 2nd. The Godmother called Gómez.

"How are you?" Gerry asked. It was well known to Gómez that Griselda was thought of as a hypochondriac by the people who knew her. So it was with some trepidation that he asked after her health.

"I have this horrible virus, along with a cold, which I can't stand. The doctor says that I have very few defenses. I'm going into a clinic; I'm going to have a total executive checkup."

Finally, Gómez got to the part that Palombo was most interested in. They spoke in code. "Did an Eddie mark come in?" Gómez asked.

"Uh-huh."

"Was that yours?" Gómez persisted, referring to the bust. "I saw it on television."

"Umm-hmm."

"Oh damn! I thought that was yours, because of the name. How many apartments were lost?" Gómez kept inquiring.

"Well, imagine, we were constructing the building.

It seems the engineers wanted to steal the money. They let it collapse, and it will be difficult to raise again. It was a large amount of money. The site was quicksand."

"Oh, my God, no! Well, I saw that and because of the name Eddie, that's what I imagined." Gómez concluded the discussion of the seized kilos of cocaine and moved on.

"Riverito called me today; what's he like?" Gómez asked.

"He's tall, very good-looking, with a mustache, young . . ."

"Does he have a very high thin voice?"

"Yes. You tell Rivi that I told you that you could talk to him as if you were talking to me. You just explain to him what you want." It was unclear to Gómez what Griselda was talking about. In a previous conversation with her, he had said, "I'm having a party and I need to take care of a couple of guys." Gómez was looking to get a sample of coke. The U.S. Attorney's office wanted to see some powder on the table, so Gómez was fishing for some.

But that's not how Griselda interpreted the phrase, "take care of a couple of guys." She thought Gómez wanted a couple of guys killed. So she put Gómez in contact with her number-one killer, Jorge Rivera—"Rivi"—and told him, "I got this guy Gómez back in Miami; he needs a couple of guys whacked, so meet with him and take care of him."

And those were the circumstances that led up to the strange, almost comical meeting on July 3rd between Gerry Gómez and Riverito. The meeting was held at the Victoria Station restaurant in Miami near the airport. Palombo and Moritz were sitting in the parking lot of the restaurant and Bob recognized Riverito immediately as he climbed out of his car. He left a woman and a child sitting in the Jeep as he entered the restaurant.

"Holy shit, look at that guy," Palombo said to Dan Moritz. "What a wild-looking son of a bitch. Just look at the way he moves. Weird." Riverito was tall and well-built, with beady eyes and a loose-fitting shirt that clearly outlined the piece he was carrying. The gun almost hung out of his shirt. Gómez was waiting for him in front of the restaurant; he too recognized Riverito immediately. Together, they walked into the restaurant. As they did, a second car pulled into the parking lot. Palombo recognized the occupants as Marielitos, Cuban *pistoleros,* who came in during the Mariel boatlift in 1980—when 125,000 Cuban criminals and insane were sent to Florida's shores. They parked and waited in the parking lot to make sure everything went okay for Riverito.

The meeting lasted around forty minutes. Riverito was the first to leave, followed by the Marielitos. Minutes later, Gómez wandered out with a bewildered look on his face.

He climbed into Palombo's car and said, "Fucking strange, that guy scared the hell out of me. I knew he was packing a piece, and those eyes! Holy shit, what weird eyes."

"Yeah, we saw him go in," Palombo said.

Gómez continued, "When we got to talking, he says to me, 'Yeah, I used to be out in California, but I had to leave there in a hurry. I was a bad boy, a cowboy; I got into a shooting out there and had to leave fast.' He also said that he'd had a problem recently up in Pompano. 'I was in the middle of whacking some Cuban in a Shell gas station, when the cops came on the scene, and I was chased by the police car, and shots were fired.'"

"We'll check it out," Palombo said.

"This guy wouldn't talk about dope; I'm talking about dope and this guy won't talk to me about dope. Finally, he says, 'I don't have no dope, what the hell are you talking about dope for?' So that was the end of the meeting; we both walked away shaking our heads."

Palombo and Moritz did not believe the story of the shooting in Pompano, so they decided to check it out. The next day they went to the Broward County Sheriff's office and talked to homicide detective Nick Argentine. Palombo asked, "Listen, did you guys have any shoot-outs recently, say in the last couple of weeks?"

"Yes," Detective Argentine said. "Only a couple of weeks ago, a patrol car happened to pull into a Shell station at Pompano Beach, purely by chance, and some crazy Latin was pumping rounds from a Mac-10 into this guy who was sitting in the car with his girlfriend." Argentine read silently from his report for a second and then continued, "The girlfriend was untouched, but the driver got drilled. He lived, but he's a vegetable. The shooter was plugging him when a marked unit pulled into the Shell station. The shooter threw one gun away and jumped back into his car, and the patrol car chased them. But once the shooters started pegging shots at him, the patrol car driver backed off a little and called for backup, which is exactly what he should have done, but the shooters got away."

Argentine presented them with an artist's composite drawing of the two shooters, a Puerto Rican and a face that matched Riverito's. They showed the montage to Gerry Gómez, who said, "That's Jorge Rivera; it's him." But it wasn't enough for the Broward-County Sheriff's department to be able to issue a warrant for Riverito.

More information was sifting through to Palombo. On July 6, 1984, Rodrigo Arturo was shot fourteen times with a Mac-10 automatic pistol, and an additional three times in the head with a .22 revolver, in his residence in Hollywood. Arturo's 15-year-old stepson, John Henry García, was killed the following day and dumped in the Palm Beach area. During interviews after the shootings, the mother, Melda, told homicide and Centac 26 agents that she felt Griselda Blanco was responsible for the shootings. She thought Griselda was trying to find the whereabouts of Jaime Bravo. Melda García also said that she was present and overheard a conversation between Jaime Bravo and one of Griselda's sons. There had been a wild argument and when Bravo got off the phone, he stated that there was going to be another war.

Melda García also said that Griselda had called her husband, Rodrigo Arturo. Griselda had said that he was the only one who knew where Bravo was, and that he had "better turn the information over to her." The speculation was that it was Griselda's gang who whacked Rodrigo and his stepson, trying to locate Jaime Bravo.

There was also a rumor that Jaime Bravo had imported some *pistoleros* from Colombia to help him kill Griselda. Both sides were actively hunting each other, and the word was that they were barely missing each other. The DEA feared a bloodbath in a public place. Informants had stated that they had come close to a fight on two occasions, once in the Broward Mall, and once in the Galleria in Fort Lauderdale, a place where Griselda loved to shop. Informants told Palombo that on one occasion, Riverito's henchmen had spotted Jaime Bravo in a mall and called Riverito, who immediately jumped in his car, ready to do battle in broad daylight, but by the time he got to the mall Bravo had left.

Palombo figured that the only reason Griselda and her boys weren't in Miami was that Bravo was hunting them. And if he did find them, there would be an incredible bloodbath. Palombo had to take Jaime Bravo off the streets, but where was he? No one was talking.

Another informant told them that Uber had been in

a gas station when another Colombian recognized his car and called up Jaime Bravo. Jaime sped to the gas station to blow him away, and only missed him by minutes.

Jaime Bravo was hunting Griselda; Griselda's people were hunting Jaime. And Palombo was hunting them all.

Palombo was getting nervous now; he had had her right in the palm of his hand, so close he could have reached out and touched her, arrested her on the old New York warrant if he wished. But he had done nothing, hoping to bust her entire empire.

Had he done the right thing?

CHAPTER 14

The Brazilian Link

In early August, Gómez called his cousin Lucía, Dixon's girlfriend. "Where the hell's Griselda?" he asked.

"She's in Hawaii with Little Michael, recovering from an illness," Lucía said.

"She's a hypochondriac, always pissing and moaning about something. How are you and Dixon doing?"

"Bad. We have broken up. I am going to live with my brother Jorge, and attend UCLA. Dixon put the Morgan Hills house in my name and gave me the BMW and the pickup truck. Dixon says he is going to live with Osvaldo."

"Have you heard of a man called Riverito?" Gómez asked.

"Yes, he is very crazy. Stay away from him. I must go now; good luck, Gerry," she said, and hung up.

Everything was quiet until August 24th, when Gómez received telephone calls from both Osvaldo and Dixon. They told him they were having big problems, but they were not specific. Osvaldo said that things were so bad he'd had to dismantle the motocross track that circled his ranch house. It was unclear to Gómez whom Osvaldo feared most, the police or other dopers. Osvaldo told Gómez that he wanted to send more money to Colombia. Both brothers told Gómez that their mother was in New York on business.

In an attempt to make contact with the Godmother, Gómez played his trump card, based on information he had been given by Palombo. "It's important that I speak to your mother. There have been recent raids in Bolivia at the ranch of her main supplier, José Ali Parada."

"We'll tell her," was all the boys said, and they hung up.

The Bolivian police had raided Parada's ranch and seized some cocaine base and finished product. But most important for Palombo and the DEA, they had seized a checkbook at the ranch that had the same account number as the one in Panama where the DEA had sent the first $500,000.

Palombo and Moritz were ecstatic. What a piece of luck: It tied Griselda Blanco directly into an international drug conspiracy. With just a little more evidence, they could get her on a CCE, a "continuing criminal enterprise," which meant life with no parole. If they got a conviction, they could take her off the streets forever. They believed the U.S. Attorneys in both California and Florida would be thrilled; but they were wrong. The U.S. Attorneys weren't interested. They still wanted "powder on the table." This other stuff was just a bunch of "complicated shit."

So Palombo and Moritz carried on. They were nervous; the Trujillo boys did not call back until September 7th. It was Uber who called for a brief chat, and once again Gómez asked to speak to Griselda. She wasn't available.

On September 8th, Palombo was relaxing, watching "Miami Vice" while he spoke to Gómez on the phone. The call was interrupted and Palombo was left holding the line. Gómez never came back on, so Palombo hung up. Twenty minutes later, Gómez called back. "Holy shit, Bob, that was Griselda. I just took her call; sorry to leave you hanging like that." Gómez's voice was trembling.

"What happened?" Palombo asked.

"She called from Southern California, and she told me she wanted to move $500,000 from California to New York. She needs it in New York in two days, by the 10th."

"What did you say?"

"I told her I wasn't accustomed to physically transporting money but I would do it as a favor to her."

"Did you ask her about Jaime Bravo?" Palombo had asked Gómez to probe to find out how deep the rift between them had become. The rumor on the street was that they were out to kill each other.

"Yes, and it almost blew the deal. The mention of his name scared the shit out of her. I had a hard time convincing her there was nothing to worry about. Finally she agreed to go ahead with her original plan."

Gómez had told Griselda he would go to California to see her. "Are you able to pick me up," Gómez asked, "or shall I stay in a hotel?"

"No, arrive and park yourself in a hotel, then call me."

"Okay, just be attentive to your beeper tonight and tomorrow morning," Gómez said.

"Fine. There is much we have to talk about."

On September 9th, Gómez met with Griselda at the Los Angeles Airport Hilton. She told him she would be there at five o'clock, but showed up at six-thirty. She asked him to launder another $500,000 for her. Gómez asked for a commission of $10,000 for his efforts.

Griselda didn't agree. "You told me you were going to charge 1 percent; 1 percent of $500,000 is $5,000. You're now saying you want 2 percent. Don't be such a thief with me."

"Okay, the $5,000 will be fine," Gómez said, giving in.

Gómez looked tired; he hadn't slept in twenty-four hours. "Haven't you slept yet?" Griselda asked. "Go to the bathroom and wash your face with cold water."

"For me it is almost midnight. I have just had five hours of travel and I got up at five this morning," Gómez whined.

After Gómez returned from the bathroom, Griselda said, "Take my small suitcase to carry the money." She also made arrangements with Gómez to deposit $30,000 in her sister's account in Colombia.

Gómez talked to her about buying some dope for his clients, the ex-clients of Harold Rosenthal. "Can we pick up whatever we want in Miami?" Gómez asked.

"I will send you a very nice boy, a good person who has all my trust. He is used to dealing with people. His name is Henry. He speaks English, but his parents are Cuban. All his working life Henry has worked with us, over eight years now. He will take care of you."

"I'm going to call him in Miami," Gómez said.

Gerry Gómez spoke about the meeting in the Victoria Station restaurant. "This Riverito guy is nuts. I'm over there taking care of business like you told me, and he's talking about something else. I don't know what's the matter with him."

"It was a misunderstanding," Griselda responded. "I told him you wanted to take two people off your back."

"I didn't have any idea . . ."

"It's a misunderstanding that I must speak directly to you about," Griselda said. "And the truth is, when Riverito came to me so scared and asked me 'what does Gerardo want?' I also got scared."

"What I was saying was that I needed the two things for a party. Well, I did notice that he was very nervous."

"Nervous! He called me later, the poor thing, and

when he came to me so scared and confused, well, I also got scared. I understood what he told me. What was it that Gerardo wanted? Just imagine, since he told me like that. What was I to think? He was there to break two guys' asses."

"If he had told me that at the restaurant, then I would have peed in my pants," Gómez answered.

"No, I sent him for that! I sent him for that!" Griselda said, meaning she had sent Riverito to Gerry to kill two people for him.

But the damage had been done. Griselda was permanently paranoid, and she wasn't going to take any chances. She didn't understand what was going on, and her standing rule of operation was "when in doubt, drop out."

But that didn't stop Griselda from flirting with the handsome Gerry Gómez. "All right, you hunk. Prepare yourself, so that we can go out and get drunk. Don't make me wait or I'll kill you," she joked, and continued, "The next time we meet, I'll be single, so prepare yourself to invite me out drinking in Miami. Say to your wife that you have to go on a trip, because with me it has to be all night long."

Gómez just laughed it off.

"Gerardo, don't put it in one ear and out the other. I'm serious."

"I'll be waiting," Gómez said, not meaning it.

Griselda and her entourage left in two vehicles and were not followed. At nine twenty-five, both vehicles returned to the hotel. Gómez had a conversation with Griselda and J. D. Mario, one of her bodyguards. Mario handed Gómez a maroon plastic bag containing $30,000, and instructed Gómez to send the money to Griselda's sister Nuri Restrepo in Medellín, who in turn would give it to Mario's mother. Griselda told Gómez she would return shortly with the $500,000.

Griselda also told Gómez that Isaac Pessoa was her Brazilian partner and that Gómez should meet him in New York the following day. Pessoa was to take the money and transfer it to Brazil. "This $500,000 is the second and final payment for a shipment of cocaine from Brazil that I ordered from José Ali Parada. The first payment was the money you sent on May 30th."

At the conclusion of this conversation, Gómez walked them to the lobby, and after they had left, he made a straight line for the bar, where Palombo joined him. He quickly filled Palombo in on what had happened in the room. He began with a fast drink to calm his nerves. When he had finished it, Palombo sent him back to the room to wait for Griselda.

At ten twenty-five, Griselda appeared for the third time and went to Gómez's room. Minutes later, a silver Mazda arrived at the hotel and J. D. Mario emerged, opened the trunk, removed a brown duffel bag, and went to Gómez's room. Finally, a gray Mercury Marquis pulled up and Jaime Arroyave, another bodyguard of Griselda's, arrived.

Once everyone had gathered, Arroyave and Mario did a security sweep of the room. They checked the bathroom, the closets, beneath the bed, and examined the television carefully for a bug. Satisfied, they turned up the TV, blasting the volume. The brown duffel bag was tossed onto the bed. "Open it," Griselda said to Gómez.

Gómez did as he was told.

"There's $505,000 inside; $5,000 is for your commission," Griselda said.

"I may come into possession of a hundred kilos as payment for a transportation deal that I arranged. Know anybody who might be interested?" Gómez said, as he had been instructed by the DEA.

"I will buy the hundred kilos and any more you might come up with. We're dry right now, waiting on a shipment from Colombia," Griselda said. She gave Henry's Miami beeper number to Gómez. "Henry will inspect the merchandise. You can also contact Riverito through Henry if you want anyone killed; they are roommates." Griselda winked and laughed.

The conversation switched to a more serious note, about her enemy Jaime Bravo. "I have twenty people on the streets of Miami night and day, looking for Jaime Bravo in order to waste him. I will pay big money to anyone who can provide me with his whereabouts. Can I use your phone?" she asked.

Griselda made two calls to Miami on Gómez's phone and then said goodbye. She exited with her two bodyguards in tow.

Gómez waited ten minutes, and at eleven-fifteen he headed for the bar and restaurant. This time nobody joined him. He had a drink, then ate a meal. On his way back to the elevator, he spotted Griselda and J. D. Mario at a bank of phones, just completing numerous phone calls. Gómez walked them back to the bar where they sat around until quarter after one in the morning drinking. Gómez went to his room as Griselda and J. D. Mario headed for the front door.

Palombo watched as three men rose who were sitting by the bar. They made their way out of the bar and were almost immediately joined by four other men. For this meeting there had been seven bodyguards positioned in the hotel, not counting Arroyave and Mario. Three bodyguards left in a green Mercedes, the other four headed for the rear of the hotel and disappeared into the warm California night.

When it was clear, the agents debriefed Gómez. He turned over the $30,000 and the $505,000. The cash was transferred to Palombo's suitcase, which was sealed with evidence stickers.

The next morning, Gómez, Palombo and Special Agent Jeff Behrman flew to New York's JFK Airport and were met by officers of the New York Enforcement Task Force—Centac 5—which included NYPD and DEA people. They all went to the Airport Plaza Hotel, where they met additional personnel. One room, designated as the undercover room, was bugged with audio and visual equipment.

The money was removed from Palombo's suitcase

and counted for the first time. The amount was $534,000. Gómez, as instructed, called Isaac Pessoa at the Banco do Brasil loan department on Fifth Avenue. Pessoa said he was having a few problems and asked Gómez to call him back the following day.

Gómez called the next morning, and a meeting was set for twelve-thirty.

As an extra precaution, the DEA had decided to include Yvette Torres, a very pretty Hispanic agent, in the meeting to act as an undercover. Pessoa showed up at the hotel room at ten to one.

"I have a serious problem," Pessoa said. "I have been at the bank for over an hour. If I transfer the money by wire, I must fill out two documents, which I cannot legally do."

"So what are you going to do with the money?"

"I'm going to talk to Griselda, and if she authorizes me, I will take it by briefcase. I have no problem when I arrive in Brazil. My problem is when I board the plane here, getting through the machines. I do not like to carry other people's money. I could get burned."

"Perhaps your brother can take it. He's the manager of the New York Banco do Brasil, isn't he?" Gómez asked, to confirm that the brother was not involved.

"Yes, but he has refused to help me. He does not want to get into trouble."

"Perhaps Yvette here can help you. She is a stewardess. She goes to work in her uniform and passes through the machines with no trouble," Gómez offered. Yvette smiled at Pessoa.

"That might be good. Why don't you set it up?"

"Maybe I could." Gómez had also been instructed to try to infiltrate the José Ali Parada organization. "Would there be any possibility of some friends investing with you? I have some clients who have money to invest. They want to buy from Parada."

"Yes, of course we can do business."

"How can we communicate?" Gómez asked. Isaac Pessoa gave him his telephone number in Brazil and told him to call him there. "If they catch you here with the money, you go to jail, you know. What about in Brazil?"

"I have no problem in Brazil. Members of the Chamber of Representatives will meet me at the airport, and I will not have to clear Customs."

"I have to ask Griselda. My responsibility really ends here in this room. I have transported the money to you."

"Tonight, it must be tonight!" Pessoa said.

"I do not know if it can be tonight," Yvette said. "I will have to adjust my schedule."

"Anytime today, even late tonight; anytime there is a flight to Brazil. I can go anytime," Pessoa pleaded.

"The other possibility is for me to take it to Miami and send it through Panama, as I did last time," Gómez offered.

"It must be done now; Panama takes too long," Pessoa said. "This matter needs to be settled immediately with Parada."

"Are you going to call Griselda on her beeper or at home?" Gómez asked.

"At home."

"Why don't you call her from here?" Gómez asked.

"Wait, I didn't bring her number. I left my documents hidden in New York," Pessoa said, searching his briefcase and wallet. "Oh no, here it is. This is not the beeper; this is the number of the house."

Inside the next room where the surveillance equipment was recording and filming the conversation, Palombo turned to the other agents; they all broke into smiles. They finally would have the Godmother's home phone number.

"I'm going to go downstairs and use the public phone to call the lady," Pessoa said. "Gerry, you should come with me, in case she wants to talk to you." They excused themselves to make the call.

While they were downstairs, Agent Yvette Torres

immediately got on the hotel phone to ask Palombo if she should make the switch.

"Yes," Palombo said, "agree to carry the money through airport security, providing it's done tonight."

Meanwhile, Pessoa and Gómez were calling Griselda at home. They were told that Griselda was asleep and could not come to the phone. They both assumed she was drugged out on something, probably pills. They decided to proceed with the delivery anyway. Pessoa called Varig Airlines and confirmed a seat on a flight that night. Then they returned to the room.

They decided that Yvette would meet Pessoa at the airline gate for Rio de Janeiro by seven-thirty, after she had cleared the security electronic scanner machine.

"If I arrive first, I will be looking in the shop windows," Pessoa said nervously. "I will be wearing what I have on now."

"Don't worry, I'll recognize you," Yvette said with a smile. "But if I have to kiss you on both cheeks and help you on the plane, it's going to cost you a lot more."

They all laughed and Pessoa left.

At six-thirty, Yvette Torres, Palombo, and the other agents met at the DEA office inside JFK Airport. Torres was carrying the brown sport bag containing $499,000. The $5,000 for Gómez's commission had been removed and the $30,000 had been sent by the DEA to J. D. Mario's mother in Colombia.

Yvette Torres moved out to the airline gate at seven-fifteen.

Palombo had asked Customs to provide an inspector at the gate to make an announcement. His voice boomed out in the waiting area: "It is illegal to leave the United States with currency in excess of $5,000." This was done to ensure that later they would at least be able to arrest Pessoa on a currency violation.

Yvette Torres slipped Isaac Pessoa the brown bag with the half million. Pessoa then stuffed the brown bag inside a shoulder bag he was carrying and walked with the attractive Torres to the duty-free shop, where he handed Torres an envelope containing $2,000. This was her fee for carrying the money. Next he handed her a fifty-dollar bill and his business card with several South American telephone numbers, and told her to call him whenever she wanted.

Palombo stood at the entrance to the plane next to the Customs Inspector and watched. At seven thirty-five, Pessoa and Torres exchanged goodbyes. As Pessoa started to walk down the narrow corridor to enter the plane he was asked directly by the Customs Inspector, "Do you have in excess of $5,000?"

"No," Pessoa blurted, his voice cracking.

Palombo watched him with steely eyes. Pessoa never broke stride as he spoke. He kept right on moving, clutching his shoulder bag to his side.

CHAPTER 15

The Reverse Sting

They had established Gómez's credibility; now they wanted to try the reverse sting: sell the hundred kilos Gerry had said he had to Griselda. They would try to get the family to show up with the cash, and then nail them. It was a long shot, but worth a try.

But first, they wanted to establish the residences of Griselda Blanco and her organization. They started with the address of the phone number they had gotten from Isaac Pessoa. The residence was in the vicinity of Newport Beach. On September 24th, Moritz and Palombo set up a surveillance at an apartment building on Clearwater Avenue in Irvine.

In addition to the number from Pessoa, Palombo also had a list of all the 714 numbers checked by the Newport Police. He had assembled these numbers from the many times that Gómez had called Griselda back after she had beeped him. They were all at phone booths. Palombo had asked the police to supply a map of Orange County showing dots where the phone booths were located. From this he had been able to lay out an interlocking grid. The grid checked out with all the other addresses and phone numbers they had put together on the case, including the new one from Isaac Pessoa.

That evening, they saw an Hispanic male leave the residence on Clearwater Avenue. It was Jaime Arroyave, the same bodyguard who had showed up at the L.A. Airport Hilton with Griselda. He was walking a dog, a rottweiler.

"Could it be Griselda's dog, the one she had in Turnbury Isle?" Palombo thought. He decided to check with security.

"Yeah," the security guard said, "she stands out on her balcony sometimes, and she owns that big asshole rottweiler, a mean-looking bastard. She always looks like shit standing there in a muu-muu or whatever the hell it is she wears. She don't look like no criminal big-time enough to have you two guys after her. She looks like shit, like she ain't never seen the inside of a beauty parlor. I thought she was a maid or something."

Arroyave drove a Mercury Marquis; Palombo and Moritz followed it. They arranged for a vehicle stop by the Irvine PD, who established that the driver's name was indeed Jaime Arroyave. The car registration showed a fictitious name and address. The officer let Jaime go; Palombo tailed him until Arroyave parked in a driveway next to a gray Mazda, the car they had seen at the Airport Hilton carrying bodyguards. Slowly, the picture was starting to fill in.

The next day, Uber showed up, and Palombo saw him for the first time. He was carrying two large suitcases. Palombo and Moritz looked at each other and shrugged. They didn't know what to make of it. Were the suitcases filled with money or dope? It was a frustrating situation. Palombo, the "jump collar" expert, had to sit on his hands and watch as packages and money changed hands. These people were crying out to him, please jump me, please jump me, and he couldn't do it! He was dying to move, but he just sat there. At almost any time of the day or night, he was positive he could have come up with a seizure, but he had to keep the entire case together; he had bigger fish to fry. He wanted to take Griselda and her whole family down. Any wrong move now, and they would go underground and never be found. He almost had the core organization in his hands.

And there were politics to deal with. They hadn't actually seen Griselda herself; what if she wasn't here? What if she had gone back to Colombia? Then they would face the usual Monday-morning-quarterback questions from their superiors: "You had her. Why didn't you just grab her on that old warrant of ten years ago? She's been a fugitive for ten years. You guys fucked up here!" Should-they, could-they, why-didn't-they, if-only-they-had—there were so many scenarios. There were many sleepless nights for Palombo. He was calling the shots and making the recommendations, and right now they were way out of their jurisdiction. They were Florida agents; they were supposed to stay in Florida.

Palombo and Moritz returned to the house on Clearwater Avenue and waited. They followed Uber to Carlico Tavera's house in Newport Beach. The agents found a secluded spot to watch from. The homes under surveillance were all million-dollar-or-more rented properties that overlooked the entire valley at night. From their vantage point, Palombo and Moritz could see lights twinkling in the canyons as far as the eye could see. Boat lights glistened and blinked in the moonlight as they moved across the Bay of Balboa; it was beautiful California at its best.

The driveways were packed with Mercedeses, Rolls-Royces and BMWs. Unbelievable wealth, Palombo thought; white wealth. These Colombians stood out like dark cherries in the sand. They made the residents nervous. The Newport Police were happy to cooperate with the DEA. They had received many calls about suspicious characters starting to appear in the neighborhood.

Palombo kept in constant contact with Gerry Gómez in Miami. On September 26th, Palombo asked him to call Griselda on her beeper number to see if they could flush her out that way. "If she's in the house, maybe your call will bring her out," he told Gómez.

The call was made, and almost immediately a Latin male exited the house. He drove to the closest shopping center, followed by Palombo and Moritz, where he used the phone booth to place a call to Gerry Gómez. Later Gómez talked to Palombo. "I spoke to a guy who said he was Griselda's nephew. He said Griselda was unavailable at the time, that she was about to leave for Dallas, but she'd call me before she left."

"Well, at least we now know that her beeper is in the house," Palombo said.

That same day, the white Jeep appeared, with Uber driving. He entered the house, stayed awhile, then left. Palombo followed him to Carlico's house.

When he came out, Griselda was with him; she slipped into the back of the gray Mazda, which a young man was driving. Palombo and Moritz followed it. Suddenly the car lurched ahead and the driver threw a fast U-turn. He then went through a series of evasive techniques to shake any possible tails, including suddenly stopping dead on the side of the road.

The evasive tactics were the standard rule of operation for Griselda. She was a careful woman. She always assumed she was being followed. It was impossible, even for Palombo and Moritz—who were experts—to follow her. It would have taken at least a four-car team. They dropped out rather than burn the entire surveillance.

The next day they picked up the surveillance again. At ten-thirty, Arroyave, Griselda and her dog walked out of the house. At first, Palombo and Moritz did not recognize Griselda. "I think she must have combed her hair with an eggbeater this morning," Palombo said. "Look at those colors." Her hair was several different shades. She walked to a nearby drugstore and then returned to her house.

In the afternoon, Uber and one of the bodyguards put some luggage into the Mazda. Shortly after, Griselda walked out, this time looking good: her hair had been curled, her dress was designer quality, her makeup perfect. She looked like a different woman. They lost her on the Pacific Coast Highway.

She was headed for LAX to catch a plane to Dallas. Before she boarded her plane, she called Gómez in Miami. She spoke to him in code.

"How are you?" Gómez asked.

"Fine. What's happened with my apartments?" Griselda asked, meaning the hundred kilos of coke.

"They were supposed to arrive yesterday, and they didn't manage to get here. They may come in two lots."

"Speak to Henry."

"Can't we see each other personally so that we can finish our discussion?" Gómez asked.

"Well, I would have to travel to where you are. It would be impossible for me to leave today; I am going to Dallas. I don't know if I will be able to see you."

"Must you go to Dallas?"

"Yes, I must run a little errand," Griselda said.

"So, then why don't you continue on from Dallas and come here?" Gómez was trying everything to draw her to Miami and get her close to the dope.

"Okay, I will try, but you should pretend that you rented the apartment to Henry as if it had been to me."

"To Henry?"

"Yes, to Henry," Griselda said firmly. She wanted Henry to do the deal in Miami for the hundred kilos. "Make a lease with him. Can you tell me the price of the apartment?"

"Between 23 and 25 points," Gómez said, indicating that the price would be between $23,000 and $25,000 per kilo.

"Okay, that's correct for both of us."

"Okay, perfect," Gómez confirmed.

"You just rent it to him, and tell him to discuss the price with me," Griselda said, referring to Henry.

"All right. How are they going to pay?"

"Cash."

"Perfect."

"But it's very, very difficult; right now, it is from check to check for us. I think I'm going to need you this week for an errand similar to the one that you did for me before," Griselda said.

"Hopefully it won't be as complicated as the last one I did for you."

"Tell me, what have you heard about that bastard?" Griselda asked, referring to Jaime Bravo, her hated enemy.

"It seems that there was some new information around here, but I was unable to confirm it."

"Be careful, because you already scared me with the Riverito business. Could it be that you already spoke to him, and that he's got you on his side?" Griselda asked, challenging Gómez, her paranoia ever-present.

"No!" Gómez snapped back angrily. "How could you ever think of saying such a thing to me?"

"I'm just pulling your leg, Gerardo," Griselda laughed. "But I don't want that man to ever find out that we're friends or anything!"

"I didn't see him directly, just one of his men."

"No one must know that the two of us talk, not even your friends. I don't want problems," Griselda said.

"There will be no problems."

"Good. So, do you think that tomorrow this fellow will take possession of the apartment?"

"I think so."

"All right then, my love, I will try to call you tomorrow."

"Ciao."

"Ciao, farewell," Griselda ended the conversation.

For the next few days the agents kept the California houses under surveillance. The only major event was that Osvaldo showed up; now they had two brothers together. The agents were able to compile all the addresses and locations that the Trujillos were using at the time. The problem, as Palombo knew only too well, was that a hot address today could be a cold one tomorrow. He could feel in his bones that this hunt was cooling off.

But Griselda had taken the bait on the hundred kilos.

Palombo decided to bring Gómez to the coast to stir things up. On October 2nd, Gómez arrived in California. He immediately placed a call to Griselda's beeper. It was answered by Dixon, who said he was taking some classes at UCLA. He said he was very interested in the hundred-kilo deal. Unfortunately, he was on his way to San Francisco, so he couldn't travel down to Newport Beach to meet with Gómez. But someone would be in touch.

The next day, Uber called Gómez and said that he would be at his hotel in fifteen minutes.

"How have you been doing? They told me you were studying," Gómez said to Uber when he arrived.

"I was studying, but I dropped out."

"Were you living in Miami?" Gómez asked, trying to pinpoint his location.

"I was, but I came to California. I still spend a lot of time in Miami."

"There are a lot of problems in Miami. How is it over here?" Gómez probed.

"Fine; we work only with Mexicans," Uber answered.

"In other words, you're working through Mexico, no?"

"Yes. I have some airplanes, company airplanes."

"Right," Gómez said.

"I also use older men, who already fly all over South America," Uber said.

"A cargo company?"

"Yes, and also passengers."

"Are they charter flights?"

"They are commercial pilots for Eastern."

"Really?" Gómez asked.

"Yes. They are over fifty years old, and they know their way around. They fly the big planes, the DC-9s, the 10s, the 1011s."

"Have you raced again?" Gómez asked, changing the subject.

"No, I don't race anymore. I have to go pick a friend up. If you want to come in the car with us, we'll bring you back over here later."

"I wanted to do some business," Gómez said.

"What's happening with that business?" Uber asked.

"I also have a second load now. They made another trip and paid for it in merchandise."

"Yes?"

"They are anxious—going crazy—they have to get the money to pay the pilots," Gómez lied as instructed.

"Are they Americans, your friends?"

"Yes. They are all Americans—a Jew and some other guys. Haven't you ever heard of Harold Rosenthal? He was kidnapped in Medellín, and brought over here."

"Who kidnapped him?" Uber asked.

"The police."

"Why?"

178

"Because the man was wanted. He used to live near the Inter-Continental. They called him "Humberto," the same as my brother. It was my brother who first met Rosenthal in Cali, and he introduced him to me."

"So, you are the one who handles the pilots for them?" Uber asked.

"Yes, I handle the pilots. I don't get involved with anything else. That's why I said that to your mother, Osvaldo, and Dixon, but they didn't pay any attention to me."

"The thing is that now I'm the one who controls everything. My mother is the one who knows all the people from down there; my mother has all the connections to purchase the merchandise. But I'm the one who knows everything up here. You understand me? I'm the one who has all the pilots . . . I have everything," Uber bragged to Gómez. "What is it your people want?"

"They asked me to do a favor for them. But the thing is I don't like to get involved with these things; it just makes for risks and problems. I normally only organize the trips and handle some money, but this time I said to them, 'All right, let's do this deal in partnership,' and we did. Now I'll go to them and say that you have recommended that I speak to a young man named Henry. Then they will ask me, 'Do you know him?' I'll have to say no. They will ask, 'Why don't you have one of them come here?' They will put me on the spot, Uber."

"Who do I have to speak to?" Uber asked.

"I'll connect you with them, and we'll do the deal."

"Where are these people from?"

"The Jew is from Atlanta, and the others are from around here. It was my brother who met them many years ago in Cali. I don't like to get involved with Cubans or Colombians; I don't know, all they do is fuck you over."

"You are right," Uber agreed.

"How is your mother doing, man?"

"Very well."

"But the last time, she was quite ill, isn't that true?"

"She's always very nervous. She always has a lot of shit in her head," Uber added, disgusted.

"You can see that there's more to it. She complains about everything all the time. What is that called?" Gómez asked.

"She's always very nervous, brother; she takes a lot of pills, and she can't stop taking them because she's so nervous all the time. We're going to be left in charge of doing everything around here."

"Yeah, you're probably right," Gómez agreed.

"She complains a lot that she can't handle it anymore. She gets very upset. Her head gets full of a lot of shit: she has a lot of things in her mind. It's better for her to be quiet."

"I think it was a mistake to tell her about what my neighbor said about Jaime Bravo. I just bumped into him, and since your mother had talked to me about Jaime, I pursued the conversation with my neighbor. 'Where does he live?' I asked him, and he told me that Jaime and three guys live around North Miami Beach and that they play a lot of football. So then your mother told me that I should tell her where they are and that she would give me a reward. I haven't been able to find out where they are."

"Those assholes, they have guns and they think they are going to rule Miami," Uber said angrily.

"Is Osvaldo in New York?" Gómez asked.

"Osvaldo has been very crazy."

"He screwed up, your brother?" Gómez asked.

"No, but he's crazy with anger. He gave a lot of money to Jaime, who used to be a cop, and cops are not used to seeing much money," Uber said.

"Jaime Bravo was a cop in Colombia?"

"Yes, and you know, with policemen if you are careless, they will take you to the limit, the thieving bastards. Once a thief, always a thief. Jaime stole twenty kilos from us."

The telephone rang and Gómez picked up the receiver. It was Dixon, whose nickname was *El Negro,* "the dark one." Gómez said, "Hello. How are you doing? I am here with Uber. All right, I will call you back from an outside line. Wait a moment, Uber wants to say hello." Gómez gave Uber the phone. They talked for a second and hung up.

Uber spoke of the past. "It was when my mother got pregnant that the shit hit the fan. I was the one who received the goods in Miami. They just showed it to her and no one checked it again. They didn't even pay close attention to the cooking anymore, and that's when all these sons of bitches started to take advantage: the ones who were packing it, the ones who were storing it; everyone was stepping on it. The problem was that it was *everyone* who turned against us, and it was when you least thought it would happen."

"Madre de Dios," Gómez exclaimed.

"The only thing we want to do now is to work and be calm," Uber said quietly.

"Do you want to take this deal?" Gómez asked, getting back on the subject.

"Who are your friends bringing the merchandise in for?" Uber asked suspiciously.

Gómez was ready for the question. "A man called Posada, and the Arangos."

"The pilots are theirs?"

"Yes, there's a group of them. They've worked together a long time."

"But they are friends of yours offering it to you?"

"Just this one time, because they have the merchandise, and they think I can sell it for them, for cash. And I will make a few bucks as well," Gómez replied, knowing he was being put on the defensive; he had to make a move. "I spoke to them about you, and even though they don't know you directly, I told them you were friends of mine for many years. But I have never done business like this with them before, directly with merchandise. They told me to take all precautions, and since I don't know Henry directly, I was worried. Your mother told me that it's no problem to do business with him and to treat Henry as if I were doing business with you. But it is not the same."

"Well, I had a situation to deal with because of the shitty fact that Bravo is in Miami; one shouldn't have to die to do business."

"No, of course not," Gómez added.

"Sometimes innocent people get killed. It isn't worth it for the money you make," Uber added.

"Your mother's in Dallas for the time being. She's not going to do it directly, the transaction?" Gómez asked, hoping Griselda could still be drawn in.

"No, Henry will do it. He will call me."

"I have a couple of messages that he has called my house," Gómez said.

"Henry picks up the merchandise at five o'clock in the morning; then he picks up the money and delivers it in the afternoon. That's how we do it. We pick up the merchandise first," Uber stated.

"The problem is that my people are not used to doing business this way. They want you to look at the merchandise and hand over the money."

"Maybe if we just took twenty at a time they would feel safer."

"Could be. Do you think you or *El Negro* could go? That might make us feel safer." Gómez was doing his best to at least get one of the boys at the scene for a bust.

"With Henry, it's exactly as if you were dealing with us; don't worry."

"Good," Gómez said, frustrated. He felt like screaming.

"My mother had a route like this," Uber said, referring to Gómez's pilots.

"Really!"

"But no more. Now we are working for people and moving it for them, but what the hell."

"Like you have twenty bosses, huh? Everyone's a chief and no one is an Indian. Just remember, it's better to be the head of a mouse than the tail of a lion," Gómez offered in jest.

"We still move a lot. There are months in which three hundred to four hundred kilos are moved. Osvaldo, he moves it hard, and I move it hard, and *El Negro* . . ."

"*El Negro* seems to be the quietest of all, no?" Gómez interrupted.

"He has been doing it the longest time. And me, I do everything around here. I go to New York, San Francisco, Miami . . ."

"What area of Miami di you live in?"

"On Brickell, and afterward I lived around Hallandale. I do nothing with marijuana. *El Negro* almost got killed there on the coast. That famous train that got busted on the Colombian coast two years ago?"

"The one in Ciénega?"

"That one was mine."

"How many pounds?"

"The shipment was fifty thousand. They screwed up, they made the shipment without telling us. *El Negro* was there with the boat, waiting for the canoes and signaling to the train and all that. Then the shooting started, and they had to throw themselves on the deck of the boat to escape. That boat train was a shipment I was making," Uber boasted.

"I had agreed with your mother on a price of twenty-five," Gómez said, getting back to the cocaine deal. "If I start moving it myself, little by little with other people, I can make more, but I prefer to take smaller risks."

"That's what I'm telling you, Gerardo; do it with Henry. He comes, takes the twenty and brings the money, you give him another twenty, and that way you can get rid of the hundred in a day. That way they will get confidence in us."

"All right; let's see what can be worked out. The problem is that I cannot give the okay."

"Okay, but let's at least do it twenty by twenty."

"Maybe they can get more, up to 190 packages," Gómez said.

"Whatever comes in from three hundred to a thousand doesn't last, man; it goes in a week."

"Is that true?" Gómez asked.

"Osvaldo alone moves three hundred to four hundred a month."

"My God."

"And me, I can move up to the same quantity, and *El Negro* can move another good quantity."

"You'll be rich."

"The thing is that as the money increases I want to be able to enjoy myself and stay calm."

"Or you'll end up like your mother, always afraid, or drinking," Gómez added.

"No, I will not become like her; if she does not stop, she will die, unless she retires. I must learn from her experience."

"You're right."

"Even though I'm young I have already seen the problems with these other people. And most of all my mother, who is one of the founders of this shit."

"Yes."

"So, I already know from my experience, you understand me? And, God willing, if it starts to go well for me and I get some money, I'll get out."

"Yes, before it is too late."

Uber continued, "The business is like this: It goes

around and around, spinning; one day it's one way, and one day it's the other way; the one who was on top is gone, and then another person is on top. The people must live in decadence; if not, the one that is on top will become your worst enemy. It is easy come, easy go."

"It's crazy."

"The thing is that they are stupid, you see?"

"Your mother . . ."

"Yes?"

"Your mother told me that she had to send something. She still has it, right?" Gómez wanted to get to the second reason for the meeting, the money that Griselda said she wanted laundered.

"I don't know whether she has already sent it."

"She told me to be here. I don't want to waste this trip completely."

"You went with that man up to New York?" Uber asked, referring to the trip to meet Isaac Pessoa.

"I wish you could tell your mother that she put me in an impossible situation."

"That man is touched in the head, very nervous."

"He's an asshole. I was supposed to deliver the money to the New York Branch of the Bank of Brazil and he says 'No, no, no, the bank will not take it from me. Take it to Miami,' he says." Gómez was working himself up. "What a bitch! She didn't tell me anything about that, and when I tried to call, your mother was sleeping, and I was told that no one could wake her up."

"It's the pills," Uber offered.

"Finally, I got a girl, a stewardess, to deliver the cash to him right at the gate. Can you believe that?"

"Yes."

"So listen, man, will you call *El Negro?*" Gómez asked.

"Yes. You'll talk to him then?"

"Yes, I will."

RICHARD SMITTEN

The conversation ended and Gómez later told Palombo, "This reverse sting isn't going to work."

Palombo responded, "It's your job to make it work, Gerry. They're afraid of Jaime Bravo; I'll try to take him out of the picture. Maybe that will help."

"Maybe it will," Gómez said halfheartedly.

PART V

THE SPIDER
GROWS
WINGS

CHAPTER 16

The Cop
They Couldn't Kill

Palombo was concerned. In every meeting with the Blanco clan, the name Jaime Bravo came up. There was no question that as long as Jaime wandered the streets of Miami with his Mac-10 cocked and murder in his eyes, Griselda's family risked instant death. But Palombo wanted them back in Miami, back in his jurisdiction. He had to take Jaime off the streets.

Jaime Bravo had been a policeman in Colombia, assigned to the secret "death squads," bands of cops who dispensed vigilante justice. If they didn't agree with a verdict of a judge, they simply went out and administered their own punishment. Often it was death.

These death squads were finally eliminated by other death squads who were set up to assassinate the *original* death squad members.

Jaime was put on the death list.

One night in Colombia his car was stopped by four police assassins who opened fire on Jaime as he got out of his car. Jaime shot back and killed them all. In the process, he was shot seventeen times. He was taken to a hospital where the doctor who worked on him said that his body looked like a cheese grater when they carried him in. But he lived.

After this shooting, Jaime decided to change sides. A cop no longer, he came to the United States where he was steadily employed as a shooter. Originally he was employed by Dario and Griselda, then by Rafa. He was feared by all Colombians in the drug business, and was well-known to the DEA.

Finally, in September, Palombo got a break in the hunt for Jaime. He and Moritz had put out feelers to other DEA offices, and the Tampa office had called. They had an informant who said he had information on Bravo. Palombo and Moritz went to question the informant.

He was a former member of the Bravo organization who told the agents that Bravo received between sixty and a hundred kilos of cocaine per month from a man named Mario Betancourt. Betancourt was Bravo's only source of supply. Bravo stored the cocaine at Mario Betancourt's home. The informant told the agents that on one occasion he had seen six kilos in the house.

He told them that while he was still an associate of Bravo's, he had been asked to accompany Bravo and Marta Saldarriaga to pick up $800,000 from Griselda, but a few days later Bravo told him he found someone else to help him and didn't need him. Bravo called back later and said that he hadn't gone to pick up the money, and that Marta had been shot and killed. Bravo was careful to assure the informant that he'd had nothing to do with her death.

Bravo had told the informant how dangerous Riverito was, and that he was Griselda's main hitman. Bravo had said, "Riverito always travels with at least three bodyguards," and had added that Riverito had shot a person at a gas station in Pompano Beach. That statement corroborated the story Gómez had heard directly from Riverito.

Bravo had had more to say. He'd told the informant that Riverito and Dixon were responsible for the shooting murder at Penrod's discotheque in Fort Lauderdale. There had been an argument at the door, and Dixon and Riverito had been refused entry. They later drove by and shot into the disco, killing the doorman, but weren't apprehended.

Bravo had gone on to tell the informant how he and Hector Orlando, the man who had introduced the informant to Bravo, had murdered a man two years earlier in Miami Beach, on Griselda's orders.

One of Griselda's sons had been going out with a beautiful Anglo girl from a prominent Miami family. The father of the girl did not approve of the relationship and told his daughter that he did not want her dating a "Spic."

The girl followed her father's wishes and broke up with Griselda's son, telling him what her father had said. Griselda was enraged when she heard this, and that night she dispatched Jaime and Hugo Osorio to kill the father. The two shooters went immediately to his address and shot him. They returned to Griselda and told her they'd sent the "Spic hater" on his way to a world where he wouldn't have to worry about any "Spics" bothering his beautiful daughter again. They'd all had a good laugh over that.

Bravo had also bragged about how he had once killed a man in a van so quickly and smoothly that the other person with him was unaware that the murder had taken place.

Jaime hated Osvaldo, Griselda's son. Jaime had been an important hitman for the family for a long time. Their relationship started to fall apart when the Godmother put Osvaldo over Jaime. Osvaldo was not yet twenty, and he was now giving the orders.

In January of 1984, Bravo had met with Osvaldo at his apartment in Turnbury Isle. Osvaldo had told Jaime that he should obey orders, since Osvaldo was wealthy and powerful as a result of the cocaine business. "Fuck you, Osvaldo," had been Jaime's response. "You may have the money, but I've got the balls."

Shortly after this, Jaime split from Griselda's organization. Jaime had found out that Griselda had given the order to kill Alberto Bravo, or had killed him herself, more likely. As she had bragged to Max Mermelstein, she had done it "by sticking a gun in Alberto's mouth and blowing the back of his head off." Alberto Bravo was Jaime's uncle, and they had been close.

Finally, Griselda had accused Jaime of stealing thirty to forty kilos of coke from her. After this accusation, Jaime and Griselda had become blood enemies, swearing to kill each other on sight.

The informant had wound up fearing for his own life. During the month of July, Bravo had told the informant that Jairo, a man who worked for him, knew too much. He had told the informant how he had been secretly killing off Jairo's family in Colombia and that Jairo had no idea that he was doing it. Jaime had then told the informant, "I want you to fly down to Mexico and kill Jairo."

The informant had been dumbfounded and scared. He'd decided to terminate his association with Bravo instead, believing that Bravo would kill him next, because he knew more than Jairo.

The informant told Palombo and Moritz that Bravo had recently imported three gunmen from Colombia. Their sole job: to hunt down and kill Griselda and her sons. He gave the informant the gunmen's address in Lauderhill. He didn't know Bravo's address.

This was good information; they were getting close to Jaime. Meanwhile, Palombo activated Gómez to continue the reverse sting. He was to meet with Henry in Miami and tell him he had the hundred kilos. "Okay," Henry said. "I'll come and pick it up."

"What about the money?" Gómez asked.

"I'll just come and pick it up. You work it out with Griselda; that's not my business. I'll just come and get the dope."

Gómez suddenly got the chills. He knew that Henry was very close to Riverito; they were roommates. Gómez got very nervous; suppose they paid him, as Griselda had done so many times before, by putting a bullet in his brain? No, this would never happen, because the DEA had no intention of turning over a hundred kilos to her. It was only a ruse to draw out some players and cash.

"Holy Mother of God!" Gómez said angrily to Henry. "I told Betty [Griselda], I said my clients will not stand for that. The money must be up front."

"Maybe I could take five or ten," Henry said.

"I asked for one of Betty's sons to be here to meet with me. But they can't; they've got this problem with this guy Jaime Bravo," Gómez said.

"Oh yeah. One of Betty's men saw Bravo the other day in the Broward Mall, and they're nervous. I can speak only for my people, not about the money."

"It's not your thing nor is it mine. I cannot set the conditions. It has to be the way they want," Gómez said. "I cannot dispose of something that is not mine."

"Yes, I see."

"And how do I go after them later if there is a problem? They will just tell me to go see Henry. I must speak to them directly," Gómez added.

Henry continued, "Osvaldo told me precisely, 'Take five or what you need . . .'"

"Osvaldo?"

"Yes, he said, 'Distribute it and then pay the money right away.' But right away is two or three days minimum."

"I told Betty from the start, I have a hundred to get rid of. She said, 'Okay, I have the client for them in

Miami.' And because of this, my clients have been holding the merchandise for more than a month. They don't want to distribute just five or ten; they want to get rid of the whole amount. That's why they are working on low points. She told me they could have moved two or three hundred for me very easily, or isn't that true either?"

"It can be done," Henry answered.

"I've called Betty at least twenty times and she hasn't answered."

"She's someplace else these days, New York or Dallas."

"I told her I'll deliver the merchandise in a car. You can take the keys and the car and examine the merchandise, then you bring back a second car with the money and you give me the keys. That's how far we can go, no further. The people I am dealing with are very wicked. If I make a mistake, they will kill me," Gómez said.

"All right, I will call you. Thank you, Gerardo."

"I hope you do well. *Ciao.*"

After Gómez had filled him in, Palombo concluded that the hundred-kilo "reverse" with Henry was a dead deal. Griselda's sons would never show in Miami if Jaime was hunting for them.

He turned up the heat on his hunt for Jaime. In October, Palombo and Mockler set up a surveillance at the gunmen's house. They followed a Grand Prix from the house for a while, but it pulled into a Shell station and disappeared. Mockler and Palombo couldn't figure out where it went; behind the station there was only a golf course.

The next day, they saw a Malibu parked outside the house, registered to Jaime Contraras, an "aka" for Bravo.

Palombo looked at Mockler and grinned. They loved it, assembling the puzzle piece by piece. The big scores, the giant busts, always came out of the tedium of constant surveillance work and small details. Palombo knew that the only way to put Colombians away was to watch them, stay with them, and grab them as soon as they made a mistake.

At seven that night, Palombo and Mockler followed the Malibu to another address. Bingo, they both knew immediately that they had found Jaime Bravo's actual residence. The house was on a canal; on the other side of the canal was the golf course that was behind the Shell station.

Palombo and Mockler sat on the far side of the canal, and were able to look across right into the back of the house using their binoculars. They spotted two women and three men, one cleaning an automatic handgun. In addition to Palombo's car, there was a second DEA car hidden at the end of the block to follow anyone who left.

The people in the house left around eight-thirty and were followed by the second car, but the group only went out to a local theater. For the next thirty days, the surveillance yielded little. The Colombians moved around constantly in different cars between the locations, but Palombo started to see a pattern develop.

Bravo and the three hitmen were constantly moving from mall to mall. Bravo carried with him at all times a soft-sided leather attaché case. It had a zipper and two small handles, almost like a schoolbag. In the bag was a Browning high-powered pistol and two clips; Palombo had seen them with the binoculars.

Jaime Bravo was on the hunt. He spent hours in the Broward Mall, the Galleria, and the Westland Mall in Miami, looking for Griselda. And Palombo was determined to get Jaime.

It was in the middle of November when they finally moved against Bravo. Palombo followed Jaime, who, followed by his bodyguards, drove to a Holiday Inn. There Bravo and his men met a couple who checked out of the hotel with two suitcases. The bodyguards were pacing around the lobby, obviously nervous. They left in two cars, followed by six DEA cars with two agents in every car. One of the cars headed north, followed by Palombo, who called the Sheriff's department and had a patrol car pull the driver over for a traffic violation very close to Bravo's official address. While the Sheriff's men gave the car the once-over, Palombo whispered to the deputy, "See if you can get them to consent to a car search." The people in the car consented, and the deputies opened the trunk. Inside were the two suitcases, but there was nothing in them but clothes. The driver had a valid driver's license; everything seemed to be in order.

"Shit!" Palombo whispered to his partner.

Meanwhile, Bravo and two of the hitmen arrived home, but one of the hitmen left the house, climbed into the Malibu, and headed out again. He passed the stopped car with the Sheriff's men climbing all over it.

"Shit and double shit!" Palombo said as the car passed them. The bubble light of the Sheriff's car was spinning red and blue rays in the night and Palombo's unmarked unit was parked directly behind the Sheriff's car.

Palombo figured that the shooter would call from his destination and warn Jaime to clear the house and hit the road.

They had to do something fast.

Palombo and Mockler jumped in their car and followed the shooter, who went to a store. The driver got out and made his purchases, then climbed back in his car. Evidently, he had not seen the Sheriff's car. The driver passed the pulled-over vehicle a second time; this time he saw what was going on. He also saw a flashing red light appear behind him from Palombo's unmarked unit.

Palombo pulled the shooter over. The driver didn't have a license. Palombo popped the trunk and looked inside. The first thing he noticed was that the trunk began where the rear window ended; a classic setup for *coletas,* narcotics traps. Palombo moved around the car. "Let me just pull the back seat. I need to have a look behind the seat," Palombo said to the Sheriff's deputies. And just as he suspected, there was a *coleta* built in behind the seat; but it was empty.

Bob walked back to his car and got on the radio. "It's time to move, guys. Let's pick up our pal Jaime." It was tricky; there was still one shooter in the house besides Bravo.

Palombo knew that the way the house was situated made it dangerous for a direct raid. It was impossible to get to the door without being seen through the front window. A clever trick to get inside was necessary, not direct force. And once they were inside the house, it was anybody's guess what would happen.

Palombo got an idea. With Special Agent Kieran Kobell at the wheel of the hitman's Malibu, Palombo drove to Jaime's house. They pulled the car into the driveway and honked the horn. Palombo and Kobell moved quickly to the trunk and opened it, staying in the shadows of the overhang. Almost immediately a head appeared at the door. "Want a hand?" someone asked.

"Yeah," Palombo mumbled, keeping his own head out of sight. The man opened the front door, took the three steps of the porch in one hop and moved down the side of the car. Palombo kept crouching with his hand on the bag in the trunk with agent Kobell farther behind in the shadows.

As the shooter rounded the corner, Kobell sprang out of the shadows. Palombo turned, gun drawn, and whipped out his badge as Kobell grabbed the hitman. "Police," Palombo whispered, flashing his badge. "Stand still and be quiet."

The killer's eyes stared at him, unblinking.

Kobell quickly patted him down for a weapon. "He's clean, let's go." Kobell and Palombo both moved behind the shooter while Palombo grabbed him by the scruff of the neck. Palombo ran him up the steps, using him as a human shield, with backup agents from the other cars following. If any shots were fired, they were going through the Colombian first. Palombo wasn't about to get his ass shot off by Jaime Bravo. Guns and badges out, they pushed the Colombian through the door and saw Bravo sitting on the couch. Kobell spun the shooter out the front door into the arms of the backup agents.

In front of Jaime on the coffee table was the leather attaché case. Inside was the Browning high-power and two clips of ammunition. Palombo held his gun with both hands, looking down the barrel, as his eyes met Bravo's.

There was no question in Palombo's mind that there could be shots fired, and if there were, he was going to fire them. "Police. You're under arrest. Put your hands up. Do it now."

Bravo sat up straight, still looking at him, staring with the same dead killer-eyes of the other two men they had grabbed. Palombo knew those eyes well. He had seen eyes like them many times before.

Palombo's brain was racing. "Go ahead, asshole, make a move, grab that fucking Browning. It'll be your last move," he said to himself. Bravo must have heard his thoughts. He stared at Palombo for a few more long seconds, then slowly raised his hands over his head. He seemed to be relieved that they were cops, and not Colombian shooters sent over by Griselda to kill him.

The agents searched the house and found three more automatic handguns: another Browning, a Smith and Wesson, and a Baretta 92S. They showed Jaime the weapons. "I want to cooperate now," Jaime told Ernie Pérez, the Spanish-speaking agent.

"The first way to cooperate is to let us search your residence," Palombo told him.

"Okay."

"We need written permission." Palombo knew how careful you had to be in obtaining permission to search. If there was any sign of coercion or force, the defense lawyers could have the search thrown out of court. The Colombians knew this, too. Palombo continued, "You look like you want to cooperate, or you wouldn't be talking to us. If you want to cooperate with us further, then consent to a search. If you don't want to cooperate, then don't consent to a search. It's up to you, just don't waste our time."

"Fine, you can search it." Jaime knew they would get a search warrant if he did not sign. What Jaime did not know was that the agents knew of his second residence. They took him there and found two automatic Mac-10 machine pistols with silencers.

After Jaime and his shooters were taken to jail, Palombo turned to the other agents and said, "We might as well make a clean sweep of this; let's go visit Mario Betancourt." They did, and got him to let them search his house, where they found two kilos of coke. Betancourt was promptly arrested, but he wouldn't testify against Jaime. "I'll do my time, but I'll stay alive," was his response. They learned later that Betancourt, who also owned a body shop, was building the narcotics traps in the cars.

The three bodyguards were deported and Jaime was later tried and convicted in front of Judge Eugene Spellman, a man who was to come back into the lives of both Griselda Blanco and Bob Palombo. Jaime got nine years in prison for the weapons violations.

It was almost the end of November now; Jaime was gone, the three hitmen were gone, and Betancourt was gone. It was a clean sweep; maybe now Griselda would return to Miami.

But there was no sign of her as time went by. Where the hell was the Godmother? Palombo was getting nervous now; he'd had her right in the palm of his hand on several occasions, so close that he could have reached out and slipped the clippers around her wrists. Yet he had held back, done nothing, hoping to bust her entire empire.

Would she move, now that Jaime was off the streets?

CHAPTER 17

Greenback Stew

Not much happened in November of 1984. The hundred-kilo reverse-deal was dying a natural death of attrition. Palombo had heard that Griselda had traveled to South America. Her first stop was Brazil, to meet with Isaac Pessoa and José Ali Parada, then she was supposed to be on her way to Colombia for *Carnavál*.

Palombo was facing problems with the prosecutors. They still wanted a cocaine transaction. A lot of documentary evidence had been accumulated in the form of tape recordings, photos, and corroborating evidence. Bob Palombo believed he had enough to sink "Mom and the Boys."

As a bonus, they had Isaac Pessoa and José Ali Parada, two of the biggest smugglers in Brazil, on conspiracy charges. Palombo could document and track a dusty white trail from the jungles of Brazil to the hands of the Godmother and her sons, including her distributors, hitmen, and methods of delivery. Palombo had Isaac Pessoa admitting on tape that he was a partner of the infamous José Ali Parada.

And Palombo had the boys admitting their guilt, bragging about the amounts of dope they were moving. The sons, because of their braggadocio, were giving themselves up to Gerry Gómez. Palombo believed that if the prosecutor presented the case properly and forcefully, and charged the jury with evidence that showed it was a clear-cut case of conspiracy, a conviction would follow. As far as Palombo was concerned, for a good prosecutor it was a bunt.

But the U.S. Attorney in Miami, Steve Schlessinger, still believed that the venue for the Godmother and her sons was Los Angeles, primarily because the money transactions took place there. Palombo, on the other hand, believed the venue could be Miami because many of the conversations emanated from Miami, even though they were phone conversations.

Palombo agreed to present the case to Jim Walsh, the head of the Central District of California Organized Crime Division for the U.S. Attorney's office. Jim Walsh had been the unsuccessful prosecutor of John DeLorean.

Palombo and Dan Moritz worked night and day for weeks on their presentation to Jim Walsh. They had the phone conversations and meetings transcribed from Spanish to English by an expert court-approved translator. They had surveillance photos; they even had an exact chronology of events from the 1974 Operation Banshee to the present. They called it the "Godmother bible." Palombo had lived this case; he could recite it chapter and verse, with exact dates, places, names of the players, and details from the various informants.

Bill Mockler, their supervisor, watched with interest as they prepared the case for presentation to Walsh.

"Need any help?" Mockler asked.

"No thanks, Bill," they answered.

"Well," Mockler stood to leave, "if you need any

help, I can fly out to California with you. Hell, I like movie stars too."

"No thanks, Bill."

"Just don't fuck it up, boys," Mockler said as he walked out of the squad room.

"Hey, Bill, don't worry; you can count on us," Moritz yelled as Palombo pulled the string on Coconut Man. His raucous laughter split the air. "We won't fuck it up, we promise."

Mockler said nothing; he just shook his head and left the room.

They were sure of themselves; they had rehearsed long and hard for their California presentation. They anticipated a slap on the back from Walsh and his all-out cooperation when they had completed their pitch.

"Well, you guys have done a nice job here. I want you to know that," Walsh said after reviewing their presentation. "But out here in California, we're looking at the big picture."

"There isn't a bigger dealer in the United States right now than Griselda Blanco," Palombo interrupted. "She's the biggest female dope dealer ever, and one of the biggest dealers of this century."

"You know the FBI has looked into this case out here," Walsh said, ignoring the comment.

Things were starting to haze over, get political; Palombo could feel it. "Look, Jim," Palombo said, "we've been working this case exclusively for almost two years, and on and off for ten years. I knew Griselda Blanco's operation back in 1974 in Queens County, New York. This is a DEA case and we're ready to move."

"I think it should be an Organized Crime Division case and the FBI should run it. They should be the lead agency."

"What the hell are you talking about?" Palombo

asked, feeling as though someone had just punched him in the stomach.

"It looks like a real good case. I'll think about it."

Palombo and Moritz looked at each other in disbelief as they were dismissed.

Palombo and Moritz wished they had their "frustration wall" in front of them now. Mockler had recently had a cork wall built where the agents hung pictures of people they disliked, and threw darts at them. They discussed hanging a picture of Jim Walsh on the wall.

Nevertheless, Palombo put together a special package of information to leave with Walsh. He had had too much experience to withhold information. He knew that later the other agency could always come back and say, "Why did you hold that back? We could have made the case if only you'd told us." Palombo believed that if the FBI got there first, fine. If the DEA got there first, that was fine, too.

But Palombo knew he had the trump card in his hand: Gerry Gómez. Without Gerry, the rest was just paper. And Palombo knew that Gerry was not going to cooperate with anyone unless he personally gave Gerry the green light.

They still did not give up on the California prosecutors. On one occasion they even brought Steve Schlessinger, the Assistant U.S. Attorney from Miami, to meet with Walsh. Steve said, "If you guys want to prosecute this case out here, I will be only too happy to assist. I believe the venue is better out here, although the case *is* prosecutable in Miami."

"Then that's your best bet. Prosecute it in Miami," was the response.

Palombo was disappointed, but he was determined to nail Griselda and her boys. The prosecution was fucking them over, and now they couldn't find Griselda. Where the hell was she? Was she still in South America? Had she cooled off on Gerry? She wasn't answering his calls. And now his own agency, the DEA, was wavering in their support.

"What am I, stupid?" he thought. "I'm sacrificing all this time away from my family and everyone I love, and no one seems to give a shit. This is fucking ridiculous. I've got to be a fool for doing this."

Palombo's family life had been put to the test. He was on the road all the time to California, Washington, and New York, and when he was home in Miami, he put in late nights on surveillances, and filling out reports. All the dull, everyday drudgery and frustrations were starting to eat away at him. His two boys missed their dad and all the fun they used to have. Why? To take some female criminal off the streets? She would only be replaced by another dealer.

But Palombo was driven to catch her. He was going to put her out of business.

Fuck them, he thought. She's going down, and it's going to be by the book, and it's going to stick.

But Palombo wasn't alone; the Miami office was behind him. Jack Lloyd was the assistant Special-Agent-in-Charge of Palombo's division, and he had lived the case along with Palombo, Moritz, and Mockler. Palombo went to him. "Hey, Jack, we've got to go back to California; we're so close on this."

"Let's get it done. What do you need?"

Palombo handed him a request sheet. "We need four or five agents to go with us. We need to take some radios with us. We'll be doing independent surveillances, and we're going to need a lot of help from our Santa Ana office. We'll use rental cars and continually rotate them."

"I'll contact Frank Briggs in the Santa Ana office. That it?" Jack Lloyd asked.

"Yes."

"Well, what's the holdup? Get going," Lloyd said. "I want to meet that lady and her boys. I want to talk to them in jail."

Later, Mockler came into the squad room to say goodbye. "So, it's off again to Tinseltown, huh."

"Yeah, we're goin' to get a chance to lie around, surf a little, check out the movie stars," Palombo said.

"Well, I can dig it. I hope you nail her this time."

"Me too; this time we got no choice," Palombo said as he hurled a dart into the frustration wall, directly into a picture of Griselda.

"Not a bad shot, Bob, not bad at all," Mockler said. "See if you can aim that well out West."

"You bet, Bill," Palombo said.

"Good," Mockler mumbled as he made it through the door of the squad room and down the hall in silence. The silence increased as the other officers waited expectantly for the familiar demented laughter. Just before he entered his office, Mockler made the mistake of looking back at Palombo, who was standing in the squad room doorway, holding the string. Mockler saw the Coconut Man's jaw drop as it started to howl with laughter. This time he closed his own door.

The California surveillance began in January, 1985.

They decided to stake out the active addresses from previous surveillances. On the first day, Moritz and Palombo spotted Griselda. And for the first time, they saw little Michael Corleone Sepúlveda. That made them feel good; maybe his mother was going to stay there a while.

They made a list of the cars and the licenses. The same players were present: Carlico Tavera and Jaime Arroyave.

For the next two days, the agents were almost frantic, following the dopers as they came and went from the house, like soldier ants feeding the queen. They saw packages change hands that they believed were full of money or dope.

On February 2nd, Palombo drove by a 7-11 store. The Colombians made many of their calls from the phone booths located outside, and as a matter of habit, Palombo always checked the booths as he drove past. Just by luck, he saw Jaime Arroyave at a phone. Palombo wheeled into the farthest corner and waited. After Jaime had finished speaking, he drove off, Palombo in tow. Bob alerted Moritz by radio; Dan said he'd try to catch up with them.

It was Saturday morning and the road was wide open. After about twenty minutes, Moritz caught up to Palombo. Arroyave made a few evasive moves, but the agents stayed with him. He pulled into a shopping center, and the agents watched him meet with another man, who they would find out later was another Gerardo Gómez, no relation to Gerry Gómez. Arroyave took a blue box out of his car and entered the passenger side of Gómez's Buick. Slowly the Buick circled the parking lot of the shopping strip, looking for a tail. Palombo radioed for backup. Then suddenly Arroyave hopped out, leaving the blue box with Gómez, who drove off. Palombo and Moritz both followed Gómez and, after some discussion via radio, decided to pull him over. Palombo saw the blue box in the back seat with one end ripped open. "You don't have anything to hide from us, do you?" he asked.

"No," Gómez answered.

"Can we look in that box in the backseat?"

"Yeah, sure, go ahead; it's not mine, anyway."

Palombo looked and found that it was full of cash: $99,850, as they found out when they counted it later.

"Hey, that's not my money. I'm just driving the car."

"Why don't you tell us what's going on?" Palombo said gently. "It's the best thing to do here."

"I was just told to meet a man in the shopping center parking lot; then I was supposed to wait for another telephone call and I would be told where to deliver the money. I got no idea whose money this is."

"Do you mind if we take you home? Then we can look at your passport and papers," Palombo said.

"Okay. No, I don't object, you can come to my house."

By now there were four cars and four agents; Kieran Kobell and another DEA man had joined them. They took Gómez to his house, where they discovered he was in the United States illegally. The agents asked him if they could search his house, and he agreed. Palombo called the Orange County Sheriff's department and asked that a dog be sent over. An officer and his dog Winston showed up. As a test for the dog, Palombo hid the $99,850; he knew it would have the residue of cocaine from the dopers' hands. Winston found it immediately. They searched the house for weapons, narcotics, and currency.

Palombo sat down and examined one of the utility bills that was lying out on the desk; it showed one of Griselda's sons' addresses. Bob realized they had stopped Gómez seconds too soon. "That son of a bitch," Palombo hissed to Moritz as he stormed over to Gómez, waving the utility bill.

"Listen, shithead. What's this?" He thrust the bill under the guy's nose.

"I don't know."

"Do you know anybody at this location?"

"No. I don't know anybody there."

"I'll tell you what. We're going to find out. You're going to come with us, and we'll see what's what."

"Okay."

The four agents headed over. Palombo had searched Gómez's car and removed a battery-powered garage door opener that he had found. As they drove toward the second address, Palombo was on the radio. "Should I try it?" he asked, referring to the opener.

"Sure," Moritz said.

"If this thing opens, I think we're in fat city." When they arrived, Palombo hit the button, listened to the hummmmmm, and watched the garage door rise.

"I've got the back door," Kieran Kobell said, parking.

Palombo went to the front door and knocked. The door was opened by an Hispanic man. "Police, federal officers," Palombo said, flashing his badge. "You got any identification?"

The man was shaking so badly that, when he opened his wallet for his identification, everything spilled out and fell on the floor.

"Can we come in?" Palombo asked of the man on his knees picking up the contents of his wallet.

"Yes, sure, come in."

There were three other men in the house; Oscar Rojas Velásquez identified himself as the sole resident. "The rest of these men are visitors," he said.

"Can we search your house?" Palombo asked.

"Yes, sure."

To be sure to avoid legal problems later, they got permission from Velásquez in writing. Winston the dog also showed up to help in the search. He hadn't made it through the door when he took off running into the living room. He leaped over the couch and started tearing at the gym bag hidden behind it. The bag was packed solid with cash.

Palombo and Moritz moved into the kitchen and started opening drawers; they were packed with cash. Money was stuffed into pots, rammed into bowls, and jammed into every drawer. The agents told the Colombians to sit at the kitchen table. As the agents found more and more cash, the Colombians started to laugh.

"Hey," Palombo said, lifting the cover of a pot, "you guys making a pot of vegetable soup here? No, I think this is what's called cash soup."

"Yeah," Moritz said, looking into the pot filled with cash, "greenback stew, looks great!"

What they had busted was apparently a "money house" for the Medellín Cartel. The Cartel was importing massive amounts of coke from Colombia into California. The Los Angeles DEA office had named the investigation of these people *"Contadora,"* Spanish for bookkeeper. Palombo had stumbled upon it simply because Griselda was a client.

There were record books also, previously seized by the Los Angeles office, that tied "Betty" and her organization directly into this group on the receipt of at least 250 kilos of cocaine. Palombo was familiar with the case; he was the coordinator for Miami.

"This is a continuation!" Palombo whispered to the other agents. "These record books correspond to others seized in July. I bet Rojas here is the fucking bookkeeper."

"But it ain't going to bring Griselda down," Moritz added.

"No, it isn't, but it's more evidence, another nail in her coffin." Palombo thought, *Maybe this will make the California U.S. Attorney change his mind about prosecuting.*

The total amount of money seized was $365,698. Palombo called in the Santa Ana DEA office and asked it to assist. The seizure belonged to the Santa Ana office, since it was the office of record and Palombo's crew were Miami agents.

The four Colombians were collected by the LAPD and put in the slammer. They could be held until Monday, when formal charges would have to be made. Palombo called the Los Angeles DEA office and explained what had happened. "Listen, we got four guys, and this guy Rojas looks like the bookkeeper. You got the old record book from Miami; this is a continuation. It'll bring you right up to the present. We're talking beaucoup bucks here."

"Yeah, it sounds good, but we're up to our asses in stuff here right now," the agent on the other end of the line said.

"It's Saturday; the LAPD can only hold them until

Monday, then they'll have to cut them loose. They really have nothing to charge them with."

"Well, like I said, Bob, we're real busy right now."

"I don't know how to say this any clearer; I'm calling from the Santa Ana office. We got all this fucking money, we got records, we got hot telephone numbers, and I can't be involved in this shit. This is not why I'm out here. I'm trying to get someone interested, for Christ's sake, but no one seems to believe me. I'll send you these goddamn books; at least this gives you the opportunity to pick them up when they get released. That'll help you start your surveillances again; I know they're all cold right now," Palombo pleaded.

"I can't promise anything. But send me the books."

"Hey, it's your case. Do what you want; all I can do is tell you what's going on," Palombo said, and hung up.

On Monday, the four Colombians walked. The books were examined later and agents were sent to their address, but it was cold. The money was held for civil forfeiture. Rojas got a receipt for the money and was told he could petition for the mitigation of the forfeiture, which he never did.

At the end of the day, Moritz turned to Palombo and said, "Hey, you know what?"

"What?"

"I think we just paid for this investigation for the entire past year with that money today."

"I think you're right. I only wish we could have nailed those four Colombians."

"We did what we could."

"Yeah, we did, didn't we. Greenback stew? Where the hell did you ever come up with that one, Dan?"

CHAPTER 18

Boxes of Cash

On February 4, 1985, they followed Uber to the exclusive La Belage Hotel near Beverly Hills. The Los Angeles DEA people told Palombo they thought that Osvaldo was also in the posh hotel, and that Griselda might be meeting with him. The IRS had an informant who had told them, "It's getting close to Griselda's birthday, and the sons are going to buy her a Rolls-Royce. She's staying at La Belage Hotel. She's been partying and having a good time smoking a lot of *bazukos.*"

The next day, a white Rolls-Royce was observed in the garage of the hotel. Later, Osvaldo left in the Rolls, returning with a very attractive Anglo female, probably a high-priced hooker.

On the following day, Palombo and Moritz followed Osvaldo as he drove to a parking lot. He went to the trunk of his Rolls and took out a large white box about the size of a coat box. He carried it over to a station wagon occupied by a man and a woman, and placed it inside. The driver of the station wagon, followed by a Cadillac, drove to a nearby public garage. The Cadillac driver climbed into the station wagon and the three took off together. The agents followed the station wagon to a Bob's Big Boy; there, the three Colombians got out and hung around the parking lot until the gray Mercury Marquis that had been used to deliver the $500,000 to Gerry Gómez at the L.A. Airport Hilton arrived. Minutes later, a pickup truck arrived with a man and woman inside.

"Hey, we got a real convention happening here," Moritz said.

"Yeah, a convention of real assholes. This looks as though it could get complicated. I'm going to call up the chopper."

In a while the driver of the car went to the back of the station wagon and took out two white boxes. The large one that Osvaldo had delivered was put into the trunk of the Marquis, and the smaller white box was placed behind the driver's seat of the pickup truck.

Minutes later, as soon as it had pulled out of the parking lot, the pickup truck was pulled over by the West Covina cops, who'd been called by Moritz.

"Why did you stop us?" the driver asked.

"I could have sworn that I saw you ingest something in your nostril while you were parked at the Bob's Big Boy. Are you under the influence?" the officer asked.

"No, no, everything is fine."

"Let's see your driver's license and registration." As the officer checked the documents, he asked casually, "By the way, what do you have in that box?"

"Oh, nothing, nothing at all."

"Would you mind if I looked?" the officer asked.

"No, go ahead and look if you want."

Officer Lindsay of the West Covina police pulled out the box and opened it up. It was stuffed with cash. "What's this?"

"Oh, that, that's the proceeds from the sale of my business in New York City."

"Really?" The officer called in their sniffing dog, who gave the box a positive hit for the presence of dope. The money, $144,060, was seized, and the driver, whose name was Zapata, was given a receipt. Eventually, Zapata sued for the return of the money, and Palombo would have to make five trips to California to appear for depositions and testimony. An expensive lawyer was hired from Marvin Mitchelson's firm to act for Zapata.

On one of these occasions, the judge said to Zapata, "What I can't understand is why you're going through all this for the return of this money, when in all likelihood you're paying that much or more in lawyers' fees to get it back."

But Palombo knew why; Osvaldo was footing the bill. He wanted to know why, within five days, he had been hit twice for half a million dollars. He wanted to know who the rat was within his organization. And if the government wanted to keep the money, they would have to produce their informant, Gerry Gómez, to justify stopping the pickup.

Ultimately, the judge didn't accept the probable cause for the stop, and he gave the money back to Zapata. Palombo might have been able to stop the return of the money, but he refused to give up Gómez.

Meanwhile, Palombo and Moritz followed the Mercury Marquis until it became obvious that it was headed for San Francisco, at which point they abandoned the surveillance.

That night over dinner they did a tally. "That makes $365,698 plus $144,060 in five days," Moritz said. "That should make Uncle Sam happy."

"It's not Uncle Sam we have to worry about. It's the damned U.S. Attorneys we have to make happy," Palombo retorted.

CHAPTER 19

Fresh-Cut Flowers

By February 8th, Palombo was starting to feel frustrated. He wanted Griselda off the streets. He needed to flush the boys out, get some action and get them arrested, all of them.

He had an idea. He called Gerry Gómez, who was in Miami. Gerry had been acting strange, negative and slightly uncooperative. Palombo was in no mood for any attitudes at this point in the investigation. "Gerry, I want you to catch a plane out here tomorrow. I want you to meet with Osvaldo. There's a plane that gets in at around three; I'll pick you up."

"Well . . ."

"Hey, there's no 'well' involved here. You know what's at stake; just get your ass on a plane and get out here."

"I can't meet with Osvaldo. They don't return my phone calls."

"Gerry, trust me; just get the fuck out here."

The next day Gómez arrived in Los Angeles and Palombo told him about his idea. "Gerry, we got a scam worked out. Osvaldo hangs out at the Rodeo

Coach exotic car dealership on Wilshire almost every day. He knows the owner or the manager, and he's bought a lot of cars there. He uses it kind of as his informal base of operations. He's living up at Belage Hotel and hanging out five or six hours a day at the dealership. You're going to register at the Beverly Wilshire Hotel across the street. You got it so far?"

"Yeah, and I'm not liking it."

"Everybody, including Osvaldo, knows you are very interested in cars, because you had a speed-shop in Medellín. You are just going to cross the street from the hotel and be looking at a car when lo and behold, you bump into him. And when he sees you, you are going to tell him you are here to launder some money for some other organization. He knows you are in the money-laundering business. You point across the street at the hotel and tell him you're staying there, and you just walked over to look at the toys."

"I don't think this is a good idea."

"I don't give a shit what you think, Gerry. You are going to get your ass out there and do as we ask, and we are going to end this thing with this family. We're going to put them all away. Now, are you cooperating with us or what?"

"All right, all right, but I'm not thrilled."

"Personally, I don't give a shit whether you are thrilled or not, Gerry," Palombo said. "Just do it!"

That afternoon, as they sat in Gómez's hotel room, Palombo spotted Osvaldo in the showroom of Rodeo Coach. "Okay, on your way!" The next thing Palombo saw through his binoculars was Gerry Gómez embracing Osvaldo.

"Man, how you been?" Osvaldo said.

"This is a great coincidence," Gómez responded, and they proceeded to get reacquainted. Gómez told his story exactly as he had been coached to tell it, and Osvaldo bought it.

Thirty minutes later, Osvaldo left the dealership alone in his Rolls. Gómez came scurrying back to the hotel and told Palombo the scam had worked. Osvaldo had moved his base of operations from San Francisco to Los Angeles, and was presently using Rodeo Coach as a meeting place. While he had been with Osvaldo, they had strolled through the showroom.

"Hey, man, want to see a few cars I bought?" Osvaldo had asked.

"Sure," Gómez had responded, and Osvaldo had pointed out the cars: a white Rolls-Royce, a blue Mercedes 500 SEL, a beige Porsche 911 Carerra, and a black Aston Martin. Osvaldo had gone on to tell Gerry that he had paid $87,000 for the Rolls, and $34,000 for the Mercedes; he did not divulge any other prices. The agents checked later; Osvaldo had purchased more than $250,000 worth of cars.

"Wanna see a picture of my house?" Osvaldo had asked next. "I'm real proud of this place. The joint belongs to Pia Zadora. You know, the actress."

Gómez had just nodded. He had never heard of Pia Zadora, but the house was beautiful.

"It's in Beverly Hills. I'm renting it now, but I plan to buy it," Osvaldo had said.

Later, Palombo located the house. The rent was $16,000 per month. The rental agent spoke in awe of Osvaldo. "My god, yes, I know who you're talking about. He has the pool sprinkled every day with fresh-cut flowers, orchids and gardenias. Must cost him a fortune." The flowers came from the florist in the Beverly Wilshire Hotel. Palombo checked with the florist, and the rental agent was right; they did cost a fortune.

Osvaldo had gone on to reminisce about old times, and had said he'd be back at Rodeo Coach with his bodyguard around four o'clock.

Palombo reassured Gómez that everything was going to be okay, and sent him back to wait at Rodeo Coach.

Osvaldo did return with his bodyguard, a massive

black ex-fighter who was formerly employed by a famous pop singer as security, and had done three years in prison on a drug rap.

Osvaldo and Gómez left in the Rolls for Belage Hotel with the bodyguard trailing in the Mercedes. On the way to the hotel, the cars pulled down a side street, where Osvaldo removed two packages from the trunk of the Rolls and placed them into the trunk of the Mercedes. After this, they went to the hotel, where Osvaldo asked Gerry to rent a room for him, since he had forgotten his credit cards. Gómez did as he was asked, and the three men proceeded to the room.

Osvaldo placed a local phone call to his mother. When Griselda got on the line, the phone was handed to Gómez.

"*Hola,* Griselda," he said. "I bumped into your son in the car dealership."

"He told me. How is it you were in the car dealership?" Griselda asked suspiciously, her antennae out.

"I'm staying across the street at the Beverly Wilshire, and I was just looking at the cars. Osvaldo says that you are going to join us tonight."

"Maybe. I'll try to make it. But I'm very busy right now." Gómez told Palombo later that he'd noticed a definite coolness in her voice, a tone that had sent chills running down his spine.

The conversation with Griselda had left Gerry shaken, but he covered it up as Osvaldo's aunt and uncle appeared and were introduced simply as *Tia* and *Tio*. The aunt was Griselda's sister; it was the same couple that Palombo had seen the night before when the agents had seized the $144,000.

The five of them left the hotel and were driven to La Scala restaurant in Beverly Hills. After they were seated, two other Colombians joined them. Osvaldo didn't introduce them to Gerry by name, but he told him they were from the family's main suppliers; one was from Fort Lauderdale, and the other was from the Los Angeles area. The two men represented different suppliers in Colombia. One of the sources was the famous Ochoa family from the Medellín Cartel. The Godmother's family owed both suppliers money, and the purpose of the meeting was to compute how much was owed for prior shipments, and to pick up the money.

"Hey, Gerry, will you help me to figure out this shit?" Osvaldo asked.

"Sure," Gerry said, taking his pen out of his jacket pocket.

Sitting at the next table was Linda Evans. They started doing the computations; Gómez found it unbelievable to be sitting in La Scala next to Linda Evans, figuring out how much coke had been smuggled in for Griselda and her sons in November.

At the same time, Palombo, Moritz, and Kieran Kobell were watching from across the street at a pizza place, eating slices of pizza and drinking diet Cokes. "It was good pizza though, Gerry," Palombo later told Gómez during the debriefing.

The calculations showed that in November of 1984, Osvaldo had received sixty-five kilos of cocaine at a price of $18,000 per kilo for a total owed of $1,170,000. The Godmother's organization had already paid part of the amount; they were left with a balance of $700,000.

"When and where are you going to pay?" the two men asked.

"Hey, no problem," Osvaldo told them. "You will receive your money tonight."

Gómez figured that the money was in the trunk of the Mercedes. Almost immediately, the bodyguard left with the two men. A short time later, he returned to the table.

At eleven o'clock, Osvaldo, Gómez, the bodyguard, and the aunt and uncle headed for the Voilà discotheque. Palombo and the rest of the DEA agents dropped the surveillance at this point and headed for their hotel. They had all been up more than twenty-four hours, and they were beat. Besides, it was starting to piss them off that Gómez was inside these lavish places having a good time, while they were sitting in cars sipping coffee, wolfing down pizzas, and waiting for something to happen.

Gómez was dazzled as they walked into the Voilà. The maître d' snapped to attention, as did his staff. They knew Osvaldo well. Osvaldo shook the maître d's hand with a palm full of hundred-dollar bills.

"Ah, Señor Johnny Corleone." (Osvaldo told Gómez later that he insisted that they call him this.) "It is so good to see you."

"These are my family and friends," Osvaldo said, with a sweeping gesture of his arm. "Do you have a good table for us tonight?"

"I'm very sorry, Señor Corleone, but tonight we are jammed; you saw the line waiting to get in. I'm very, very sorry, but I'm afraid you must share a table," the maître d' said, almost bowing in apology.

"Fuck the line at the door! And fuck sharing! I don't want to share a table with nobody. This is family, strictly family. You understand?"

The maître d' said nothing. He walked over to the best table in the house and simply said to the occupants, "Get out." The table was quickly cleared and the "family" group was seated.

Osvaldo told Gerry, "Everyone here knows I'm Don Corleone." Gómez scanned the room. It was packed with glitzy men and beautiful women. Within a few minutes, Osvaldo ordered a couple of bottles of Dom Perignon and waved at two beautiful young girls who joined the table. But it wasn't the young girls whom Gómez wanted to join the table; he wanted Griselda. But she was too paranoid to accept any story of a chance meeting at a car dealership showroom.

At around two o'clock, they gave up waiting for Griselda and Gerry, Osvaldo, and the two girls returned to Belage, where they had wild sex for hours. At six in the morning, Gómez returned to his room in the Beverly Wilshire.

Later that day, Gómez told Palombo and Moritz, "Last night, Osvaldo said he has three front corporations that he uses to launder his money. I got the names of two. He also told me he uses a San Francisco attorney who handles the actual money laundering for him."

"Did the old lady show up?" Palombo asked.

"No." Palombo noticed that Gómez's hand shook slightly at the mention of Griselda. Gómez continued, "She said she would, but I never believed she would actually show, and she didn't."

"Why?" Moritz asked.

"I don't know, but I think she saw through me. Anyway, at the end of the night Osvaldo asked me to launder a hundred grand for him right away. He wants it sent to his aunt Nuri Restrepo in Medellín. The money is supposed to be delivered to me in Miami in the next few days."

"What else?" Palombo prompted.

"He's got a California driver's license in the name of Winston Muñoz and a bunch of other phony ID that I was unable to get the details on."

"That's it?"

"Yeah; so what do I do now?"

"Go back and wait for Osvaldo to give you the $100,000 to launder," Palombo said.

The call never came, and the Godmother disappeared. The Belage Hotel surveillance went cold, and Osvaldo stopped visiting Rodeo Coach. It was February 10th now, and they hadn't seen Griselda since January 31st.

Palombo called Gómez. "What's happening? Have you heard anything?"

"Not a thing; I'm getting the cold shoulder. Osvaldo won't even answer my calls. I think we're being screwed. Griselda didn't buy that bullshit story I fed Osvaldo, not for a second," Gómez whined.

"I'm afraid you're right, and now I think she has gone under. We can't locate her anywhere. Shit, shit, shit," Palombo mumbled as he hung up the phone.

It rang a few seconds later; it was the Miami office. He had been away a long time, his cases in Miami were building up, and his superiors wanted a full status report. The team was called back to Miami to regroup and rethink their strategy.

"Where the fuck is Griselda?" Palombo thought to himself as he packed his bags to return to Miami. "Have we really blown it this time? Has she returned to Colombia?"

It was a long tense flight back to Miami, but at least he would see Grace and the kids. He hadn't seen them in almost three weeks.

PART VI

THE CORNERED SPIDER

CHAPTER 20

A Kiss
on Each Dimple

Palombo was now totally consumed with catching Griselda. He even carried her picture on his key ring. Grace wasn't thrilled. She half-joked with him, "It's so nice of my husband to drop by to see me and the kids.

"And look at this," Grace fingered her husband's key ring. "He doesn't have a picture of me; he's got a picture of *that woman* on his key ring. He's gone over the edge. He's possessed by her; the Godmother has crept into his brain."

Palombo laughed, but he knew Grace was almost right.

Palombo, Moritz, and Bill Mockler, who was about to be transferred to headquarters in Washington, D.C., sat around the Miami DEA office discussing their options. They were joined by Pete Gruden, the Special-Agent-in-Charge, and Jack Lloyd, his assistant. Dan Moritz had just been assigned to Group 6, so he knew he would not be going back to California, but he was still vitally interested in the outcome of the case.

"There's no question that Gómez is currently *persona non grata* with the Godmother organization, and he will soon lose contact with them totally," Palombo said, starting the discussion.

"It's just pure bullshit when those boys say Mom isn't in control anymore. She is. They're just macho assholes spouting off. But when she winds up in the joint, she's going to have to relinquish control and let them actually run the organization. Then wham, bam, we nail their asses," Moritz offered.

"The joint? Who says she's going to wind up in the joint? Where the hell is she? We've had her within our grasp so many times now, and each time, somehow, she slips away. Suppose she's in Colombia and never returns? We're screwed if that's the case. And I hate the thought of facing the Washington know-it-alls who are going to be all over us like white on an egg for not arresting her when we had the chance," Palombo said.

"What about the New York U.S. Attorneys?" Gruden asked. "How do they feel?"

"How would you feel about prosecuting a ten-year-old case? The New York attorneys would have to dig up all the old Banshee records, find the fucking witnesses, and there wouldn't be a lot of profitable publicity in it for them. But they did say, 'Okay, grab her ass, we'll do the best we can.' We called them yesterday," Palombo smiled.

"And Miami?" Gruden continued. "How about the Miami U.S. Attorney's office?"

"Steve Schlessinger, the Assistant on the case, says he needs some more time to finalize their case. But he said, 'Go for it!' He's ready to roll. He thinks he's got a terrific case; he just needs a little time to polish it up. If things get hairy, we have plenty of Immigration stuff we can use to hold her for at least several months."

"Anything else?" Lloyd asked.

"Yeah," Palombo said. There was no question in anyone's mind that Palombo was eating, drinking, sleeping, and not-sleeping the Godmother. He had covered every angle in his mind. "If we grab her now, then we won't blow Gerry's cover, so maybe he can help us nail the Brazilians, Isaac Pessoa and José Ali Parada. Or maybe we can activate him again with the sons; they're pretty stupid and full of themselves, not like Mom."

"So, Bob, what do you want to do?" Jack Lloyd asked, already knowing the answer.

"Jack, we gotta go back out and do it. It's got to be done."

It was February of 1985, and Miami was seething with lawless Colombians; there were shootings and murders every day. All the agents in the room understood that the office was understaffed and overworked on a twenty-four-hour basis. All eyes turned to Pete Gruden and Jack Lloyd.

"California wants nothing to do with this case?" Lloyd asked.

"No, they want 'powder on the table' or they want us to fuck off and not bother them," Palombo said, rubbing his aching arm, thinking about his meeting with Walsh. He avoided Moritz's eyes, fighting to keep his temper under control.

"Yeah, California was great, just great," Moritz added, feeling bad that he wouldn't be there for the finale, if there was a finale.

"All right, do it. It's got to be done; let's go," Jack Lloyd said. "What will we need to nail her? I don't suppose you have a list with you, Palombo?"

"Well, it just so happens that I do have a little slip of paper here. It's just a rough list . . ." Palombo pulled a carefully folded, fully typed sheet out of his pocket.

"Did you ever think you could be a little overconfident, Palombo?" Jack Lloyd asked. "It's not like we need to send our top agents running off to California; we've got plenty doing here in Miami to keep us busy."

226

"Well, we gotta give it a shot. Think positive," Palombo said, and they all laughed.

Jack Lloyd examined the list while Palombo continued to talk.

"Frank Briggs out there has been great to us; he'll be our contact."

Jack Lloyd handed the sheet back to Palombo and turned to Bill Mockler. "Well, Bill, we better give him what he wants. I've got a feeling Palombo's gonna get it anyway, and he's not going to be any good until he does what he's always said he would do: give her a kiss on each dimple before he takes her away."

On February 16th, Kieran Kobell accompanied Palombo to Los Angeles. Palombo called the Santa Ana office and was informed that on the previous night agents had seen a woman they thought was Griselda. Palombo and Kobell headed for the Santa Ana office, anxious, wondering if they really had seen the Godmother.

At the office, Palombo told Frank Briggs, "Listen, we're here for the duration, and we're going to sit on this until either we get this woman, or we can't stay here anymore." Palombo did not really know what the "duration" was. He figured he had two weeks, tops, to catch her, and then they would have to go back to Miami. And the Los Angeles DEA office gave the Godmother case a no-priority rating; if Palombo missed her this time, she would probably walk, unless she blundered right into their arms.

Palombo and Kobell went right to work. They set up a surveillance at the best address they had for the family. They remained until midnight, or three o'clock by Miami time.

Palombo and Kobell picked up the surveillance again at eight the next morning, a Sunday. They didn't speak much; there wasn't a lot to say; either she was in the townhouse or she wasn't.

Frank Briggs and two other undercover units showed up. They all picked their spots: Palombo and Kobell chose the parking lot of an apartment complex directly across the highway from the townhouse. This location gave them a clear shot of the front door.

At around nine o'clock, a chunky young Hispanic woman came out the front door. She was followed into a delicatessen, where she bought a few provisions and then returned to the townhouse.

"Shit, I thought we had something," Palombo said to Kobell, who watched the young girl through binoculars as she closed the door behind her.

Two hours dragged by, until eleven, when the front door opened again and little Michael Corleone Sepúlveda, age six, came out the front door. He stood there alone for a second, looking lost as the door closed behind him. Seconds later, the front door opened again and out stepped *La Madrina,* the Godmother.

Palombo and Kobell looked at each other, grinned, and started punching each other in the arms and shoulders. "All right! It's her. It's her! For Chrissake, it's her!" Palombo yelled.

"She's out! We've got her now!" Kobell responded.

"Oh my God, here we go!" Palombo shouted.

They calmed down in a hurry. Palombo got on the radio to Frank Briggs. "You see what we see, Frank?"

"Sure do! I already called for backup, and they're here."

"Okay, you call the shots, you're the supervisor; however you want to do it," Palombo said into his radio.

"It's your case. Take it."

"All right, two teams cover the back door," Palombo ordered. He had already worked this out in his head a hundred times that morning. "Kobell and I will pop the door after she goes back inside. Frank, you and your partner follow us inside. Let's watch and see what happens now. I'll give the signal to move, but cover that back door right now. Clear?"

"Couldn't be any clearer. We'll stand by," Briggs said, signing off.

They watched as the young Hispanic girl, who was the housemaid, joined Griselda on the porch. Griselda stood there as the housemaid and Michael walked to a park located about a block away.

"You got the warrants?" Kobell asked.

"Hey, is the Pope Polish? I've been carrying around the old New York arrest warrant for years. And thanks to Steve Schlessinger, I've got this nice fresh search warrant for the townhouse. In fact, I've got a warrant for every location," Palombo waved three pieces of paper in front of Kobell, keeping his eyes on Griselda, who left the porch and entered the house.

"Okay, let's roll! Let's do our thing," Palombo shouted as he drove over the highway and right onto the sidewalk. Frank Briggs and Bob Corso pulled in right behind him. Palombo took the steps two at a time, Kobell on his heels, with Briggs and Corso trailing.

Guns drawn, badges out, Palombo knocked on the door. It was opened by a wizened old lady whom they had never seen before. Later they found out this was Griselda's mother. "Federal agents," Palombo announced as he eased her out of the doorway and entered the house. He did a fast scan of the living room, dining room, and kitchen; nobody there.

Frank Briggs took the old woman aside and explained to her in Spanish what was going on, while Bob Corso opened the back door to let the other agents into the house.

Palombo finished his quick sweep of the downstairs —no males, no guns. He knew she was upstairs. Palombo and Kobell flew up the stairs as fast as they could go, hearts pounding. From the top of the landing, they could see three bedroom doors and in the master bedroom at the end of the hall, they could see Griselda. Startled by their sudden appearance, she looked up from the Bible she was reading, right into the eyes of Bob Palombo. She was in bed with a pillow propped up behind her.

Palombo and Kobell entered the bedroom. Palombo took a quick look around and said, *"Hola, Griselda."*

Still in shock, she looked at Palombo and answered, *"No, me llamo Betty."*

"Oh yeah?" Palombo responded.

Griselda stood in her housecoat, dazed, completely surprised by the raid. For reasons he has never understood—relief, satisfaction, respect or admiration for a great adversary—Palombo did what he had always promised to do when he caught her. Satisfied that the area was clean and secure, he holstered his gun and kissed her gently, first on the right cheek and then the left. Kieran Kobell did the same.

It was almost like the kiss of death, the kiss goodbye.

He called Special Agent Bobby Pias into the room. Pias spoke perfect Spanish. "I don't want anything to go wrong here," Palombo said. "I want you to read her her rights slowly and carefully; make sure she understands. I want everything done exactly by the book."

As her rights were read to her, Palombo watched one of the Santa Ana agents slip the clippers on her wrists.

While this was going on, a careful search of the house was made. The agents came up with various papers, about $5,000 in cash, and a Venezuelan passport in the name of Lucrecia Adalmez, with her picture in it. They made note that she had recently come from South America through Houston; the rumors of her being "down south" had been true. Palombo couldn't help but feel relieved, because now in addition to the Operation Banshee charges, they also had her on a falsified passport rap, which carries a penalty of five years in jail.

Ever-deadly, next to her bed she had placed a turban, the kind she was so fond of wearing. Inside was a .38-caliber revolver and a box full of cartridges.

Michael Corleone Sepúlveda arrived back at the house with the housemaid. They had seen the police activity from the playground, and they came back to investigate. Michael stood in the doorway, eyes wide in bewilderment, staring at the handcuffs snapped around his mother's wrists. An agent noticed, and slipped one of her sweaters over the handcuffs to hide them from the boy's view.

He, like his mother, was stunned, and stood there in the vestibule of the house in a state of shock. Finally, he ran over to his mother and buried his head firmly on her shoulder as she knelt to hold him. He remained with his face buried in her shoulder for several minutes. No one disturbed them until it was time to leave. Michael, the housemaid, and the old woman were told they would have to go to the police station also, and that they would travel in a car separate from Griselda. Palombo helped her down the back stairs to a waiting car, her sweater still covering the handcuffs.

Bobby Pias, Frank Briggs, and Bob Palombo made up her escort, and were to drive her to the Irvine Police Department station house. The minute she sat down in the backseat of the car, she started to shake and moan.

"What is it?" Pias asked in Spanish.

"I have pains, terrible pains in my chest," Griselda answered hoarsely.

"Do you think she's having a heart attack?" Briggs asked Palombo.

"An anxiety attack, maybe. We should take her over to emergency just to be sure. Where's the nearest medical center?" Palombo asked.

They sped her to the closest hospital, which was

only a few blocks away, and the duty doctor examined her. He sedated her slightly, but said she was fine, just stressed out.

Shortly after they arrived at the station house, Palombo and Frank Briggs addressed about a dozen Sheriff's deputies and local police officers, along with a few of the Santa Ana DEA agents who were waiting for them. Briggs had put out the call for them to come in.

Palombo briefed them about the two additional search warrants he had with him. When he had finished, Frank Briggs assigned the specific jobs of searching the two other locations. They were told to wait until they got the signal from Palombo and Briggs, who wanted to be there when they hit the houses.

When the briefing was complete, Palombo and Frank Briggs walked back out to the waiting area. Little Michael sat on a bench and watched what was going on in the station house with great interest. He sat quietly with his hands folded. The housemaid sat at his right, indifferent to her surroundings. The dark-skinned wizened old lady was on the loose, wandering around the station house, endlessly chain-smoking cigarettes and speaking in a rapid-fire Spanish. "Give me a cigarette!" were her only English words. Whatever she was saying was amusing because everyone who could understand Spanish was laughing. Palombo saw Griselda actually crack a smile at the old lady's antics.

Both Griselda and the old lady had their pedigrees done: personal histories, photographs, and finger-prints. While this was being done, Palombo went over to talk to Michael.

Palombo started to chat with him. At first, he thought he might be able to get some additional information on the brothers, but he was wrong. The minute he got near anything sensitive dealing with the family, Michael changed the subject.

It was as if Michael had been tutored from the day he was born. He was very precocious about "the business" for a six-year-old boy.

Frank Briggs was listening. He and Palombo walked to the coffee machine. "I can't get over it; it's amazing," Briggs said. "His antennae are set. He isn't going to give us anything."

"Well, I can't bring myself to give the kid any kind of third degree. He reminds me too much of my own sons. I don't want to pursue it," Palombo said.

"Hey, I understand. Let's drop it. It's too bad the kid has a gangster for a mother."

"As bad as she is, he's still only an innocent kid. I hate to see it; maybe there's something we can do."

"Forget it, that ain't your job. You're just supposed to take the bad guys off the street," Briggs said.

"Sometimes it bothers me to see what gets swept up in the net. This shit has got to stop somewhere. It's an endless chain. Look at his brothers: hardened criminals, murderers, destined for big-time trouble; if they make it to jail without being killed, it will be a miracle. They're fucking doomed. And what about this kid? His old man is dead, killed by his mother. Who the hell is going to speak up for him? He's a cute kid."

"Bob, take it easy here. This is deep water, where you could easily drown. Don't even harbor those thoughts. They'll just tear you up. You better cool it."

"I know, but look at him sitting over there. He looks just like my Rob or Richie. He should be home playing, having a shot at a regular life. Shit!" Palombo said, staring at Briggs.

"Hey, it ain't my fault, Bob. I didn't engineer this shit, you know. I'm just one of the players, a good guy, like you. Don't think about this stuff anymore; it isn't professional."

"Yeah, I know," Palombo said, avoiding looking at Michael.

"It's time we took Griselda over to the Orange

County Sheriff's department to book her," he added. "We've already searched the housekeeper and the boy. We should let them go back home."

"I agree," Palombo said.

They drove Griselda to the Sheriff's department and headed to one of the other family addresses, arriving at the same time as the raiding party. Frank Briggs volunteered to cover the back while Palombo entered through the front.

Briggs got a surprise. He reached over to unlock the fence from the inside, and he came face to face with Griselda Blanco's rottweiler. The dog's mouth was inches from his hand. The other agents tensed up, wondering what was coming next. The dog moved suddenly and licked Brigg's hand playfully. Briggs withdrew his hand, and then the dog hunkered down and became aggressive, growling and snapping at them. The Orange County Animal Control was called to take the dog away.

Nothing of any importance was found in either location, nor were any people present.

The following day, Palombo, along with another agent from the Santa Ana DEA office, picked up Griselda at the Sheriff's department. They were taking her to be arraigned at the Los Angeles Federal District Court. She was seated alone in the backseat of the car. Halfway to Los Angeles, she started to get the dry heaves.

"Hey, calm down, take it easy," Palombo said, trying to help her. "It's only the arraignment."

But it did no good; she vomited her breakfast into a bag they kept in the car for that purpose.

When they got to the courthouse, Palombo was surprised to see the security precautions that had been arranged. The courthouse was crawling with federal marshals, DEA agents, and court security personnel. Palombo asked them, "You expecting John Dillinger or Al Capone today?" But he didn't get any laughs.

The Godmother was handed over to the marshals, and she was escorted into the courthouse to a waiting Federal judge. The L.A. U.S. Attorneys still wanted nothing to do with Griselda Blanco. They, along with the FBI, had an ongoing investigation of the boys, and were still searching for a bust that would leave them with "powder on the table."

Before the judge, the Godmother continued to insist she was Lucrecia Adalmez, not Griselda Blanco.

Palombo had already contacted the Houston U.S. Attorney's office. It was ready to indict her on immigration charges immediately, if requested. The lawyers told Palombo, "We think she's going to get slam-dunked by the charges pending, but if there is any problem at all, if things look as though they might fall apart, we'll get an indictment and an arrest warrant real quick. How's that sound?"

"Sounds good."

"If the worst possible scenario happens, and she gets acquitted on the old Banshee case and the Florida U.S. Attorney doesn't nail her on the *Los Niños* case [the original Miami case], well, we'll have her for a nickel down here."

"Okay, that's the way we'll play it," Palombo agreed.

Griselda Blanco was given no bond, and was ordered to New York to stand trial.

Palombo returned home to Miami and to his wife and family. Grace was overjoyed at the news of Griselda's capture, but she was not overjoyed at her husband's shocking suggestion.

Palombo told his wife, "You know, honey, honestly and truly, if I thought there was a way that I could take this kid and adopt him, I would. I really would, you know?"

"Now I know you're crazy. I only suspected before, but now I know. You're gonzo."

"Somebody has to do something for this kid. I mean, look at him." Palombo had brought home a picture of Michael at play in a schoolyard. He handed the photo to Grace. "He's cute, isn't he?"

"I agree that he's a cute kid, he's a doll. But you've got to remember where his roots lie. I don't think his mother would think it's too cute, your adopting her son. I mean, how much sense does it make? You chase this woman for ten years—one of the worst criminals of the century—until you put her in jail, and now you want to adopt her son?"

"He's part of an endless chain of cruelty and violence. Somebody's got to break the chain."

"What about your own sons, and the safety of your own family? No, Bob, this is all just too stupid to even be talking about. This woman is supposed to be a cold-blooded murderer, who has supposedly ordered the death of more than a hundred people, and you want to take her youngest son? Forget it."

"I'm not saying that we could ever pursue it, because obviously we're not going to be able to. No one is going to give this kid up, and he's going to be well taken care of. She's never going to get out of prison anyway, if I have anything to do with it. But I agree you're right. It would never work. I just thought . . . well, you know, it's sad."

"I know what you thought, and you know what?"

"What?"

"That's why I love you, for what you thought and the way you think," she said, kissing him. "So, what do you do now that your obsession is behind bars? What will make you go to work early and stay late?"

"I'm not finished with the family yet."

"No?"

"No. I'm going to put her boys away next."

"That's great. You want to adopt her youngest son

and put her other three boys in prison. Men; what minds!"

"Hey, it's my job."

"There's more to your life than just your job. I haven't seen you in weeks," she said, taking his hand and leading him into the bedroom.

CHAPTER 21

Kickin' Ass

The New York U.S. Attorney's office is located close to the World Trade Center in downtown Manhattan. Assistant U.S. Attorney Arthur Mercado stood in his office looking directly across the street at 26 Federal Plaza, the massive building that holds many of the New York Federal Court records. There was a knock on his door and his boss walked in.

"Got a hot case for you here, Art: Griselda Blanco —ever hear of her?"

"Vaguely. Wasn't she part of that old Operation Banshee indictment in the early seventies? Wasn't that the first major conspiracy case involving Colombians?"

"That's the one. They nicknamed her *La Madrina,* The Godmother."

"Yeah, and later Pepe Cabrera, her partner, was charged for murder."

"That's it, Art. They just nailed her in California on the old New York warrant. You got the case."

"That case is at least ten years old!" Mercado exclaimed.

"Give you a chance to stretch your research skills. The DEA is assigning an agent named Mary Cooper to work with you as your chief investigator. She's new, been out of the academy six months."

"What about witnesses? Where the hell are they after ten years? And the wiretaps; I'm sure they're all in Spanish," Mercado said, turning to look back at the bleak gray records building across the street.

"Well, you're half Puerto Rican; it'll give you a chance to practice your Spanish. By the way, Art, you're looking in the right direction; all the old records are over there at 26 Federal. I'm told there's around a hundred boxes that deal with the old Banshee case."

"What other support do I get?"

"The usual. It's your secretary and you."

"My secretary works for two other people besides me!" Mercado exclaimed.

"Yeah, well, it's going to be a challenge. There's an agent that chased her for ten years. He's the guy that finally nailed her. His name is Bob Palombo; he'll help. He wants to see her put away."

"How long do I have? When's the trial?" Mercado asked, turning around to face the U.S. Attorney.

"Sometime in June. Have to give her a speedy trial."

"June! It's March now!"

"Yeah, and that's not all; there's going to be a hell of a fight at the bond hearing. She's being held without bail right now."

"Who's representing her?"

"Jack Litman; he shouldn't give you any problem," the U.S. Attorney laughed. Jack Litman was one of the best and most famous criminal attorneys in New York City. A few years later, Litman would defend Robert Chambers at the infamous Central Park yuppie murder trial. His experience was extensive, and his success record was one of the best.

"No, no problem *at all;* I'll just kick his ass. I've had

six previous court cases, and now you give me a nice fresh ten-year-old case that no one gives a shit about. The headlines happened in 1974 when the arrests were made; that's when everyone cared. I'm going to get killed on this case; I can feel it."

"Hey, Art, think positive. You're out of law school two years, and you get a chance to go up against Jack Litman and kick ass. Think how many young guys would like to be in your place. Here's her file with the indictments and other paperwork." The U.S. Attorney dropped the file on Mercado's desk. "See ya in court, Art. Good luck." The U.S. Attorney walked out of Mercado's office.

Arthur Mercado was twenty-six years old, a graduate of Columbia Law School and Pace University. He had joined the U.S. Attorney's office March 5, 1984, almost exactly one year before the Griselda Blanco case was plopped onto his desk.

Years before, when Arthur had seen a TV movie called *Prince of the City,* he had said to himself: "One thing I never want to be is a United States Attorney. I never want to do criminal work." So he went to work in a firm doing securities work, class action suits for small stockholders who had been defrauded. But he discovered that he wanted to get more involved with people, so eventually he applied to the U.S. Attorney's office on a whim, and was accepted.

Arthur opened the file on the desk and scribbled down the case number of the old Operation Banshee trial, where only twelve of the original sixty defendants had been prosecuted. Griselda had been arrested on this same ten-year-old warrant; now it was her turn to stand trial. The Miami case was not yet ready for trial and the prosecutors welcomed the extra time to prepare. He gazed once again out his window, across the concrete canyon, and wondered about the records. Where the hell were they? What kind of shape were they in? And what about Griselda Blanco, rumored to be one of the most ruthless and dangerous of all the Colombia dopers?

The next day Arthur was introduced to Mary Cooper.

Mary's involvement had begun in February, the day Griselda Blanco was arrested in Los Angeles. Palombo had called Heather Campbell, Mary Cooper's supervisor, and told her of the arrest.

Mary was working surveillance on the street when she got beeped and was told to come to the office immediately.

"Griselda Blanco's been arrested," Campbell told Mary.

"After all this time, it's hard to believe somebody nailed her. I'm surprised. I wasn't sure we would ever get her," Mary responded. The hunt for Griselda Blanco was well-known inside the DEA, especially in the New York office, where they held all the fugitive warrants for the Operation Banshee case.

"You're going to be the case agent for the trial," Campbell said.

"The case is more than ten years old!"

"Yes, and we have to win it. Other charges are being prepared in Miami right now, but they're not sure what's going to happen. The key is to win in New York," Campbell said.

"Are you sure you want me on this case? Maybe someone with more experience . . ."

"Mary, you can do it. I have every confidence in you."

"But we'll have to find the witnesses and all the old evidence . . ."

"Mary, no one said it was going to be easy. Just follow your training and seek help from senior agents when you need to. Anything I can do for you at a higher level, just call. Okay?"

"Okay," Mary said, leaving the room. Bob Palombo's hunt for Griselda Blanco was a legend in the office. A legend that no one really believed would ever have an ending.

Griselda was famous for slipping away like the melting mist in the morning. Mary wondered why she had not run to Colombia. Why was she still in the United States? Too many enemies; that must be it. She was a ruthless death-dealing doper who never showed any mercy. And now she was going to be tried on a ten-year-old indictment; and Mary Cooper, fresh out of the DEA academy, was the trial case agent. Mary felt tense and excited as she read the case file. This was a big one.

Mary Cooper was a slim blonde with a slight trace of freckles, and blue eyes that sparkled when she talked about her job. She loved law enforcement, both the action and the purpose. Working on the Griselda Blanco case was like a dream come true, because it represented a great challenge, far from a cut-and-dried, well-documented case. But that only steeled Mary's resolve, because Griselda Blanco represented everything on the far side of the law. It was why Mary was a cop.

She had graduated from the DEA academy in July of 1984. She had only been on active duty seven months.

The first battle came almost immediately. A bail hearing was set before Judge Motley.

The judge listened carefully to Arthur Mercado, who was on his feet for about half an hour, citing case after case of Colombians who had jumped bail. Jack Litman was up next, and he gave an eloquent plea to the effect that all people should be allowed bail; it was one of the basic constitutional and human rights. No one had ever convicted Griselda Blanco of a crime. There was every reason to believe she would not flee.

The judge saw it differently. Judge Motley was the first black woman ever to be appointed to the federal bench, and she was serious about her job. Based on the history of Colombians jumping bail, it was her decision to leave Griselda with no bail.

Griselda was furious. She instructed her lawyer to appeal the verdict, something rarely done in the judicial system. Litman took his appeal to the Second Circuit. Litman seemed to be saying, "I'm going to fight you tooth and nail, every inch of the way; you better not make one tiny mistake, or I'll demolish your case and your career along with it."

The bail appeal was heard quickly. Within three days of Judge Motley's ruling, both attorneys handed in their briefs. The appeal court studied the case and came back swiftly with the decision that Judge Motley had properly considered the facts and the law; Griselda Blanco would not be granted bond.

On the way out of the hearing, Jack Litman whispered to Arthur Mercado. "Well, this is only round one. Get ready to try this case right away." Litman knew that since this was an old case, the evidence and witnesses had probably gone stale. So, like the excellent attorney he was, he placed *speedy trial* on the top of his strategy agenda. He didn't want to give his opponents a chance to get organized.

Suddenly, Griselda fired Litman as her attorney. Mercado and Cooper suspected that it was because he had lost the bond hearing appeal, but they were never sure. She replaced him with Frank Mandel and Nathan Diamond.

When Arthur Mercado got the news that she had fired Jack Litman, he breathed a huge sigh of relief. Although he had looked forward to testing himself against Jack Litman in court, he knew his chances to win were better now that Litman was gone.

243

CHAPTER 22

Raiders of the
Lost Archives

The Operation Banshee evidence was stuffed into one hundred boxes marked BLANCO. The boxes were located on the fifth floor of 26 Federal Plaza, a huge building that rises from the bedrock of Manhattan like a monument raised to the might of bureaucracy. When Arthur Mercado and Mary Cooper walked onto the fifth floor, it reminded them of the last scene of *Indiana Jones and the Raiders of the Lost Ark,* where the ark is placed in an enormous airplane-hangar-size room with thousands of other crates, all marked TOP SECRET. The fifth floor held hundreds and hundreds of boxes, all marked CONFIDENTIAL. The walls were lined with locked file cabinets that held thousands of now-meaningless secrets, and evidence that had once determined the course of many lives.

"Where the hell do we start?" Mary Cooper asked.

"Brown boxes. We're looking for brown boxes marked BLANCO."

"They're *all* brown, Art."

"Yeah, I know. The BLANCO boxes are supposed to be together, but they're not. They're all over the damn place. If a box shows no markings, then you'll have to look on the other side, the bottom, the top, all over, until you find a marking. We'll get the custodian to stack them for us, and when we're done we'll take them across the street to my office."

"Your office is tiny, Art."

"I know. Let's worry about that after we have the boxes together."

For the next week, Mercado and Cooper wandered around the fifth floor shouting as though they had discovered gold whenever they found a BLANCO box:

"Hey! I've got number 67! It's on the bottom of this pile. Send over the clerk."

"I've got number 28 over here! Only ninety-eight boxes to go!"

When Bob Palombo and Dan Moritz heard of Mercado's plight, they could envision losing the case because certain key evidence had not been found. They knew what a mess records rooms could be, especially to the inexperienced. They volunteered to help, and came to join in the search.

During the week of the box hunt, Mercado was able to scrounge a small windowless room slightly bigger than a broom closet on the third floor, very close to his office. This was dubbed "the war room," and day after day the boxes were carried in from across the street, until the room was bursting with them. When the recap was done, all but one of the one hundred boxes that were supposed to be in storage had been accounted for. "Watch, the missing box will be the most important one," Mercado said to Mary Cooper, joking.

He didn't know how right he was.

Parts of the Operation Banshee case had been tried twice before. The first part was in 1975, after the raid that resulted in eighty-eight arrests, when twelve people were tried and convicted. The second part was the Pepe Cabrera trial. Arthur knew that Pepe was Griselda's original partner with Alberto Bravo. Arthur Mercado called the prosecutors of those trials; they were polite and cordial, but not very helpful. They just confirmed what he had surmised from the beginning: he was on his own on this case.

Next, he received twelve thousand pages of transcripts from the first trial, and he read them looking for an angle, something to use to corroborate his only good witness against Griselda, Carmen Cabán. From what he had been told, Arthur Mercado was sure she would not cooperate with them.

Carmen had been busted in late 1973; she did two years on Riker's Island, where she was left high and dry by Griselda and Pepe Cabrera. Finally, she turned witness against the original Operation Banshee defendants and testified in the 1975 trial.

The U.S. Department of Justice called on her again in 1981 to testify against Pepe Cabrera. But Cabrera was given bail and he skipped. This meant that the prosecutors no longer had a need for Carmen, so she was abandoned, and all the promises made to her were either forgotten or reneged on. She had been promised a residence visa and protection in the Witness Security Program. This promise was recanted, and she was told to get lost.

So in 1985, Mercado was informed that Carmen was hostile and unwilling to testify. Carmen was a crucial witness if Mercado was to win his case. He needed help, so he called Bob Palombo.

Palombo was not thrilled with Arthur Mercado as the choice for prosecutor. Out of 140 prosecutors in the New York office to choose from, the U.S. Attorney had selected a green kid with almost no trial experience. It rankled Bob; it reminded him of Jim Walsh in California, and the shoddy treatment Bob felt he had received there.

mPalombo had bragged to Steve Schlessinger, the Miami U.S. Attorney on the case, "You think this bullshit would happen in New York? If the New York U.S. Attorneys had this case, they'd be jumping up and down to indict this woman; they would put their best people on this case and kick ass. They've got the best attorneys in the world there." Now he realized he might have to eat his words.

Palombo had even gone so far as to call Mercado when he was assigned the case to say, "Listen, I'm going to tell you quite frankly that this is what I think you should do . . ." Palombo then read a long list, laying out what he thought Mercado should do, whom to contact, and how to proceed. When he was through, he said, "Well, that's it. That's my advice; what you do with it is up to you. As far as I'm concerned, I'm here to help you. I'm ready to testify whenever you need me."

"Well, I'll think about it," was all Mercado said, and he hung up.

Mercado called back a few weeks later, inquiring about Carmen Cabán. Bob told him, "She's going to be hostile because she's been fucked over in the past. You have to contact Luis Ramos and Bobby Nieves. Carmen trusts them because they've always been square with her; maybe they can help. They speak Spanish perfectly."

"Nieves is in Costa Rica," Mercado said.

"Yeah? Well, see if you can get him brought back. And while you're at it, get hold of Sammy Weidl and Mike Cunniff; they were all part of the Operation Banshee investigation. In fact, Mike Cunniff is going to be able to tell you about what's in those ninety-nine boxes you've got, where the hell to look, what's good and what isn't. Mike, Bobby Nieves, Luis Ramos, Vinnie Polizatto and myself put the whole damn indictment together in the first place. If you want us to come over and sit down with you, we will—might save some time."

And that's what they did.

Bobby Nieves came up from Costa Rica. Luis

Ramos, Mike Cunniff, Vinnie Polizatto and Palombo came in from various DEA offices. They sat together and reconstructed the 1974 Operation Banshee investigation. They blew the cobwebs off the boxes of information, and helped make sense out of what Mercado was reading.

While they were doing this, they discovered what the missing box number 100 contained. It was the most important box, because it contained all the physical evidence: the specially designed shoes, girdles, brassieres, suitcases, and birdcages used to deliver dope into the United States from Colombia.

"Of all the boxes not to be there, it had to be the damn evidence box!" Mary Cooper said.

"Well, we'd better find it or we're in deep trouble," Mercado said.

They all searched again, but to no avail. The box was missing.

"Do you suspect foul play?" Mary Cooper asked Palombo and Mercado.

"No, just a bureaucratic fuck-up. It's probably in this 'well-organized' records room somewhere," Palombo said.

But where? Where the hell was it? Mercado thought to himself. Without the evidence and a decent witness, it was going to be almost impossible to move a jury to a guilty verdict, and Mercado knew it.

"What do we do about it?" Mary Cooper asked.

"We keep acting as though there's no problem and prepare the case," Mercado said.

"And pray that the stuff shows up," Palombo added.

"Right," Mercado confirmed.

"Good luck," Palombo said. "If you need me, you can contact me in Miami. I'll help you guys any way I can."

Arthur Mercado's next step was to try to contact Carmen Cabán. He followed Palombo's advice and first got a Hispanic officer whom she trusted, Luis Ramos, to talk to her.

After speaking with Ramos, Carmen agreed to talk to Mercado, but she promised nothing else. Carmen had a serious problem: her son was in jail in Medellín, Colombia, for car theft. The problem was compounded because Griselda's brother was in the same prison.

Mercado was surprised at how extremely soft-spoken Carmen was. Looking at her, no one would think that she had ever been involved in crime, even murder. He met her in a hotel room in New York, a "safe hotel" run by the DEA. Carmen spoke through an interpreter. She was so shy and polite that she had asked through the interpreter, "May I go to the washroom?"

Mercado was very forthright with her. "Carmen, I can make no guarantees except that I will try to help you if you cooperate with us. I am not a prosecutor who will make anybody promises at any time, just to get what he wants. I'll just promise that I will do the best I can for you. I know pledges have been made to you before, pledges that were not kept. What is it you want?"

"I want to be allowed to live and work in the United States, that is all. And I want my family in Colombia protected."

Mercado interviewed her at length, and Carmen told her story. It seemed impossible to Mercado that this woman could have had such a violent, incredible life. It was as if she were two separate people. She was very helpful.

"Who else was with you when you met with Griselda, a witness who might verify your statement?"

"My sister was with me on one trip to Colombia, and met with Griselda," Carmen said softly.

"Will she testify?"

"Perhaps; I can ask her."

The sister agreed; she would testify. This was great news for Mercado because it corroborated Carmen's testimony.

But it was dangerous for Carmen; it was inevitable that news would leak out that she was going to testify and her son's life would be placed in danger. The Witness Security Program offered sanctuary in the United States for Carmen's family members. Only her brother accepted the offer.

Mercado looked everywhere for another informant who knew Griselda. He scoured the entire DEA until ultimately he came up with the name María Gutierrez, the travel agent and long-time "friend" of Griselda's who had informed on her to the DEA in Medellín. She could only testify on a small part of the case, but it was an important aspect.

María could testify that Griselda knew she was a fugitive, and that she was closely involved with Alberto Bravo. The defense was going to try to establish that she never knew she was indicted, and therefore could never give herself up.

María was found inside the Witness Protection Program and transported to a "safe house" in New York City to await the trial.

Arthur Mercado and Mary Cooper had an impossible job ahead of them, sorting out the evidence and cataloguing the facts and players. Mercado asked for a paralegal assistant to help, and was refused. There was a severe shortage of paralegals, but he was given a law student to assist.

The boxes were full of information, including thousands of pages of wiretap transcripts. Mercado read them all. The conversations included Alberto Bravo, Pepe Cabrera, a male named Mono, and Mario Rodríguez. All the important players were recorded on the phone except Griselda. The only reference that was ever made to her was the name "Gris." This occurred on six different occasions.

Many of the conversations were in code. These conversations were useful as backup material, but Mercado knew that this kind of material would never convict her. They would need a key witness to convict her. They had Carmen Cabán, but how would she be on the stand?

There had been many career promotions as a result of the 1974 Operation Banshee bust, but one NYPD officer who had worked very hard on the wiretaps hadn't received any recognition or a promotion—apparently because his contribution had been behind the scenes. He had seen almost everyone around him move ahead, but he was still walking the beat. His name was Frankie Teraldi, and when Mercado contacted him, he volunteered to help. He reviewed all the conversations, and later testified as to the legal procedures followed to get the tapes—how they were recorded, whose voices were on the tapes, and the exact dates and chronology of events. This was essential to establish the conspiracy and to allow the tapes to be admitted as evidence. After Teraldi explained the tapes in detail, the judge finally agreed to allow about twenty tapes into the trial record, six of which connected Griselda directly to the conspiracy.

Mike Cunniff, a top DEA agent, also stepped into the breach and helped Cooper and Mercado. He was stationed in Maine, and many weekends he drove down and helped Cooper and Mercado go through the evidence boxes on his own time. Mike Cunniff knew the codes, and he was able to explain much that looked like gibberish to the uninformed. He also explained exactly how the voluminous mountains of information were catalogued by both the DEA and the NYPD. Cooper and Mercado referred to Mike as "the human index," and they leaned heavily on him to locate key evidence.

There was a piece of evidence that looked insignificant at first, but that intrigued Arthur Mercado. This small detail was to play an important role in convicting Griselda Blanco. It was a birthday card from Griselda to a man named Romero, who was arrested for bringing in from Colombia a dog cage that was full of cocaine. Mercado had come up with a strategy: he was going to connect Griselda with as many of the players indicted in Operation Banshee as he could.

Mary Cooper talked to Mercado, and suggested that they reindex every single thing in the case. They first had to find the log, the exhibit book. They did, and with the help of Mike Cunniff, they reindexed every important exhibit in the file.

They were working nights and weekends with no exceptions except for Saturdays, when Arthur Mercado would slip away for two hours to go to the closest synagogue for services.

The days sped by. Finally, a week before the trial, Mercado was ready to try the case except for one giant problem: they still had not found the box with the physical evidence.

It was at this time that Griselda's lawyers, led by Frank Mandel, tried to make a deal. They came to Mercado and said, "How about we plead her guilty for jumping bail?"

"She never jumped bail; she was never arrested," Arthur said.

"You know what I mean. Plead her out to five years. It's better than losing the case. The most you can get here is fifteen years, and it's unlikely the judge will give her the maximum sentence even if you win."

Mercado mulled it over carefully. He had no physical evidence, his case depended on one witness who might flake out on him during the trial, and the damn case was ten years old. And what about his career? He had been handed his first big case; suppose he tried it and lost it? His career would go right into the crapper. And Miami might still indict her, so she could face charges down there. There was a lot to think about.

"I'll let you know," he said to her defense lawyers. He immediately called the Texas U.S. Attorney's office, and the lawyers agreed to proceed on the Immigration violation if he wanted them to, but if he won the case in New York, they would drop the charges.

Next, he called Jim Walsh's office in California and asked if the attorneys there would be willing to prosecute Griselda. They told him, "No, we've already told the DEA agents we have no interest in her. We need powder on the table, and they didn't get it. We think you're going to have one hell of a time convicting her." Mercado thanked them and hung up.

Mercado and Cooper visited Rhea Crekor, Mercado's immediate supervisor at the U.S. Attorney's office, to ask for advice.

"I'm inclined to plead her out to the five years," Arthur said. "We still haven't found the physical evidence, and the trial will turn on this Colombian witness Carmen Cabán."

"You know who this Griselda Blanco is? You know the things she has done?" Rhea asked.

"Yeah, we've heard the scuttlebutt about her," Mercado replied. "She's nasty."

"Believe it! The agents I've talked to have convinced me that this is one of the worst excuses for womanhood ever created. She makes Al Capone look like a sissy."

"But the damn case is ten years old," Mercado insisted.

"Arthur, you're a lot better prosecutor than you think you are. You're going to knock 'em dead in court."

"So?"

"Whether you win or lose, just try the case. She's too significant to let off with a five-year slap on the wrist. We have to go for it. Now why don't both of you go look for that missing box of evidence?" she said, smiling.

Three days before the trial, Mercado was hit by an urge to search an area that they had missed. He went to the evidence room and talked to the custodian. "I want to search that far corner for the missing Blanco box."

"Do what you want, Chief, but we've already looked, and it's impossible that it would be over there. We don't keep the *B*'s over there."

"How about if I look anyway?"

"Look, it's a complete waste of time, but do what makes you happy. But you're going to have to do it on your own. I ain't wasting my time. I'm busy."

"Okay," Mercado said and headed over to the mountain of boxes. The custodian went back to reading the *New York Post*.

Not one of the box markings began with a *B*. Slowly and methodically, he started to move the mountain, one box at a time.

As he piled the musty boxes on top of each other, the air slowly thickened with dust motes that sparkled in the morning sunlight. After half an hour, Mercado had penetrated to the center of the mountain. He sensed what it was, even before he turned the box over and saw BLANCO marked in bold black letters on the side. With trembling hands, he ripped it open. For Arthur Mercado it was like finding treasure. Inside the box were the high platform shoes that were so popular in the early seventies, a brassiere designed to hold coke, a false-bottomed bird cage, and a special compartmentalized girdle.

He sat down on the nearest box and took a deep breath and sneezed. Then he laughed out loud. He couldn't wait to tell Mary. "Hey," he yelled to the custodian, "how about helping me with this box? It's a big one."

"What box is that?" the custodian asked, dropping his paper, walking over.

"The BLANCO box that's not here," Mercado said, trying to hide his smile.

CHAPTER 23

Pulling the Tolls

The trial began on June 26, 1985, before Judge John M. Cannella, the same judge who had tried the Operation Banshee case in 1975. Judge Cannella had suffered a heart attack a few months after that trial; many people believed it was a result of the stress of the Banshee trial. He was very familiar with the facts of the case.

Arthur Mercado had worked for days on his opening address to the jury. He began: "It was in a country called Colombia. They were in a city called Medellín. Pepe was there, Albertico was there, Doña Gris was there, and they were talking about how to get the merchandise from Doña Gris in Colombia to Pepe in New York where Pepe would sell it.

"Pepe said, 'Let's bring it in a dog cage,'" and Doña Gris said, 'Let's bring it in in bras and girdles.'

"Pepe's name is José Cabrera. They call him *El Tio*, The Uncle.

"Albertico's name is Alberto Bravo; sometimes they also call him *Trapito*.

256

"And Doña Gris's name is Griselda Blanco. They also call her *La Madrina,* The Godmother.

"The merchandise that they were talking about, ladies and gentlemen, was cocaine. They were figuring out a way to get that cocaine from Doña Gris and Alberto Bravo in Colombia to Pepe Cabrera in New York, where he could resell it, and that's what this case is about." Arthur moved as he spoke, making eye contact with the jury, concentrating on each of them. "This case is a conspiracy case. The people that I have mentioned didn't carry the cocaine themselves. The evidence will show that they paid other people to bring the cocaine from Colombia to New York, inside shoes, in bras, in girdles, inside this cage . . ." Arthur held up the dog cage for the jury to see. The cage made it all real; he could feel the jury respond. ". . . and in other ways you will hear about."

Mercado also took his opening address as an opportunity to introduce Carmen to the jury. "You will meet Carmen Cabán, who was once a member of this conspiracy. She will tell you about crimes she committed, that she lived with Pepe Cabrera for a while, and that she carried drugs for him. We will also learn that she was arrested in 1973."

Mercado went on for half an hour, talking with the intensity and skill of a seasoned barrister, his thin wiry body and off-the-rack suit contrasting with the expensive clothes of the team of defense lawyers.

And so the trial began. Bob Palombo was back in Miami, working cases, but he followed the case with great interest, talking to Mary Cooper on an almost daily basis. He still wanted the sons, but he wasn't getting very far. The boys were in California, and he was in Florida with a desk full of cases. He called Mary. "How's it going?"

"Okay; depends on how Carmen holds up under cross-examination. What's up with you?"

"I still have a score to settle with Griselda's boys.

257

Has anything strange been happening in court, anything at all?"

"No, Bob, I haven't noticed anything strange."

"Well, the boys have got to want to know every detail of what's going on at that trial; just keep your eyes open."

"Right, I'll let you know," Mary said, hanging up. After that conversation, Mary Cooper took a much stronger interest in who came into the courtroom.

Mercado had already decided to be aggressive and go for a quick strike. He called his key witness first. Carmen Cabán took the stand. Dark-haired, attractive, dressed in a print dress, she looked vulnerable and feminine. She spoke in her very soft, almost soothing voice; trembling hands were the only betrayal of her nervousness. Griselda stared directly at Carmen with a cold, chilling hatred that Carmen could feel slither over her body like a wet cloud. Carmen had been warned that Griselda's lawyers might coach Griselda to try to intimidate her. Carmen feared for her family still in Colombia, but she stared straight ahead with an occasional glance in the direction of Griselda.

Mercado knew immediately that she could captivate the jury. He prayed she didn't get caught in a lie. It would be death for a witness like her, whose testimony hung on the edge of credibility. A push either way could either destroy her testimony, or give her the highest credence. It hung by a thin thread.

Mercado established that she had known Alberto Bravo, Pepe Cabrera and Griselda for years; had lived with Cabrera, visited Colombia, and run both drugs and money as a mule. And how everything connected, like small rivers running to the ocean, to the Godmother.

"Pepe opened the false bottoms of the shoes and took out bags of cocaine," Carmen said to Mercado and the jury.

"Did he make a phone call?"

"He called Colombia, to *La Madrina.*"

"Who is *La Madrina?*"

"Griselda Blanco."

"How do you know he called her?"

"Because I placed the call myself," Carmen said calmly in her soft voice.

Mercado wanted to establish her as an expert, and at the same time to explain to the jury that these were sophisticated, high-level smugglers, involved in a major conspiracy, who used code in their conversations, even on a telephone line that they thought was clean.

Carmen explained, "If somebody called from Colombia and said, 'The fellow has left from the farm,' it meant that he had come here to this country. If they said somebody was 'ill' or 'sick,' that meant the person was in jail."

"What else?" Mercado asked.

"If they spoke about *nieve,* snow, that meant cocaine. *Maria* meant cocaine, and *camisa,* the word for shirt, meant marijuana."

Mercado had delivered the 1975 Operation Banshee case testimony to Griselda's lawyers just days before the case began. Carmen had been a witness in that case, and Nathan Diamond, one of the defense lawyers, was trying to go through her testimony in the prior case and listen to her on the stand.

Mercado asked Carmen about the time she had spent with Griselda in Colombia. Carmen explained. "I went back to Griselda's house with Griselda and Diana. We met with my sister and Araceli, who were in the living room."

"What happened next?" Mercado asked.

"Diana went to her room and returned with a different dress on. 'How does she look?' they asked. I said she looked fine. They asked me whether I knew what she had on. I said no. Diana lifted her skirt; she was wearing a girdle and a brassiere filled with cocaine."

Carmen went on to testify that she had seen suitcases torn apart and drugs removed, and many pairs of shoes with the false heels removed in Pepe's apartment in New York, where the drugs were weighed and bagged. These had all been sent from the Godmother in Colombia.

While Carmen was testifying, Mary Cooper observed Griselda. The defense lawyers had dressed her in a matronly way, but it didn't soften her appearance. Her eyes betrayed her; they were cold dark orbs of death. She didn't blink very much, and she stared straight ahead at Carmen with no betrayal of emotion.

Mary noticed another woman enter the courtroom and take a seat; she looked distinctive, and she paid absolute attention to every word of the testimony. The woman appeared Mexican or Oriental, an exotic look that caught Mary's eye. Somehow, Mary believed she was connected to Griselda, although this was just intuition.

Mary Cooper and Mike Cunniff sat together for much of the trial. On the first day, he noticed three rough Hispanic males sitting in the back of the courtroom. They kept getting up and leaving the courtroom, then quickly returning. It seemed to Cunniff that they were making faces at Carmen as she testified. They glowered at her in a very threatening way. Mike eased out of his chair, walked around to the back of the courtroom and tapped the leader on the shoulder, motioning with his finger for them all to leave and follow him. Mary watched the door close behind them as they left. Mike Cunniff returned to his seat ten minutes later.

"What happened with those guys?"

"Nothin', I just asked them for some identification and what they did for a living. Court security is important, you know, and we as officers of the court have to keep that in mind. Nasty guys."

"I notice they didn't return," Mary said.

"They suddenly remembered they had another appointment," Mike said, turning his attention back to the court proceedings.

The prosecutor didn't miss the scene, and he called it to the judge's attention at a conference at the bench, complaining that it could prejudice the jury.

The judge replied, "There have been some incidents in this building connected with trials. The security has been increased. I'm not going to second-guess security and be carried out of here on a stretcher or watch somebody else leave that way. Let's get on with the trial."

Carmen remained on the stand for the entire first day as Mercado questioned her. That night Mary Cooper called Bob Palombo in Miami, and on instinct told him about the strange-looking woman she had seen in court.

"That sounds like Gloria Naranjo. She's a close friend of Griselda's. I made her years ago in Queens, but I could never bust her. Have her followed home tomorrow and get her address."

"Okay."

"How's the trial going?"

"So far so good, but it was our turn today. Tomorrow the defense cross-examines our star witness."

"Good luck. Let me know what happens," Palombo said.

The next day, the defense attorney hammered away at Carmen, trying to discredit her. She had been instructed to tell the truth. She had immunity, and the key was to stick with the unblemished truth. If she did what she was told, the defense would only dig a deep hole for themselves, because they would prove she was part of the conspiracy.

The defense tried every trick in the book to establish that she was lying. Nathan Diamond asked, "At the bottom of the United States passport application, do you remember there being a statement that you swear that the items above are true and correct?"

"Yes," Carmen answered.

"And you signed, knowing you were lying?"

"Yes, I did," Carmen admitted, almost whispering.

But these were petty things, and lawyers' tricks that often backfired if it appeared that the witness was being browbeaten or abused. The defense also made a mistake in the cross-examination, a mistake that Mercado was sure the jury picked up. Nathan Diamond asked, "During the search of that apartment, they found approximately four pounds of cocaine, a .22-caliber Colt revolver, a .357 Magnum, a Western revolver, a Luger, four boxes of ammunition, $15,000 in cash, and drug paraphernalia, which included hypodermic needles and scales, is that not a fact?"

"No, sir." The courtroom went absolutely silent, and Arthur Mercado's stomach snapped into a knot. "Not hypodermic needles."

"What about the other items, did they find those?" the defense lawyer persisted.

"Yes, sir."

Mercado almost let out a rebel yell. It was the best answer he had ever heard a witness give. If it was a trap, a lie designed to catch her, she had slipped free. And at the same time, she had established her credibility; it was as though she were saying, I admit to everything I've ever done, but this one little thing I didn't do. It was a devastating answer.

Before Carmen left the stand, the exchanges got heated. Mercado wanted to introduce the fact that Carmen was in fear of the Godmother. And the defense wanted to introduce the fact that Carmen was present during a murder that Pepe Cabrera had committed, years before. The judge did not want either of these subjects discussed.

Mercado started the action. "Do you recall why you didn't mention Griselda Blanco to the DEA agents when you were first arrested in 1974?"

"I was afraid she might harm my family."

"What changed?"

"Some of my family was moved to safety."

"Objection," the defense shouted.

"Sustained," the judge said.

The defense lawyers quickly called a conference at the bench and said, "This clearly prejudices the jury."

"Are you making a motion for a mistrial?" the judge asked.

"Yes, sir."

"Your motion is denied," the judge answered.

Then it was the defense lawyers who attacked, in a final attempt to ruin Carmen's credibility. Nathan Diamond blurted, "You assisted Pepe Cabrera in a shooting and killing, did you not?"

Carmen had in fact witnessed Pepe shoot and kill a man in New York. He had handed the smoking gun to Carmen to hide for him. But this was not admissable evidence in Griselda Blanco's case. It had no bearing on the charges against Griselda.

Judge Cannella reprimanded the defense. "I told you not to go into that. You got a strict order from the court not to go into that area. We're not going into other cases; we are trying the case before us."

The judge turned to the jury and said, "The jury will disregard that last question. This is the only case we are trying." The judge's anger was evident to everyone in the court.

Mary Cooper noticed Gloria Naranjo once again in the courtroom. Mary had prepared a DEA team that was waiting, ready to follow Naranjo. At the first break that day, Mary pointed Gloria out to the agents. "That's her. I want you to follow her home and get her exact address." The agents nodded. Mary knew these agents were good. Gloria would never burn them.

The trial continued for the rest of the day with Carmen on the stand.

After the court was adjourned, Mary went directly to the Manhattan Correctional Center and checked the visitors' ledger to see who had been visiting Griselda Blanco. She had had only one visitor, and the visitor had come on a regular basis, Gloria Naranjo. Mary wrote down the address that she'd given when she visited. Mary went back to her office and waited. An hour later the phone rang.

"You followed her?" Mary asked.

"Yeah, we got the address." Mary held her breath as they read the address to her. Bingo, it was the same that Gloria had given in the MCC visitors' ledger.

She called Palombo. "We got it, Bob; Gloria's address. It's 48th Avenue and 43rd Street."

"A garden apartment complex," Palombo volunteered. "A five-floor walkup. Her apartment is on the fourth floor. I followed her around for days in the seventies. I can even remember where she parked her car.

"I can remember it as though it was yesterday. That's definitely the same place where I visited her ten years ago. I can't believe she hasn't moved."

"You going to want what I think you're going to want?" Mary asked.

"Yeah, I want you to pull the tolls. We're especially interested in the California numbers. She's gotta be talking to the boys," Palombo said.

"I'll call New York Telephone tomorrow and get all the long distance calls for the last three months."

"Great; keep me posted."

"Don't worry, I will. This is starting to get exciting," Mary said.

"It's always exciting when it comes to Griselda. And Mary . . ."

"Yeah?"

"Great work!"

"We'll see," she replied.

That night when Carmen returned home, she had an urgent call from Colombia. She returned the call and listened as her hysterical sister told her that her son had been stabbed three times in jail, but he was still alive. Carmen collapsed in a heap, sobbing, wondering when the violence would end. Why had she agreed to testify, against the advice of her brothers and sisters who still lived in Colombia? But Carmen knew she had never really had any choice at all. She wanted to stay in the United States, and there was always the overt threat that she could be deported at any time because she had no papers. She was trapped.

The next day, the defense tried a new tactic. They tried to prove that Griselda did not know she was a fugitive from American justice. The burden of proof lay on the prosecution. But Mercado was ready.

He called a surprise witness into the courtroom: María Gutierrez, Griselda's "long-term friend" and confidante. As María entered the courtroom, Griselda's stony countenance twisted in disbelief. The one person in whom she had confided her every little secret was now walking down the corridor of justice to testify against her.

Griselda Blanco had told María Gutierrez on many occasions that she was running from the U.S. law. In fact, Griselda had asked her to look after her jewels, including the Perón diamond, when she disappeared into hiding.

As María passed Griselda on her way to the stand, she did not look at her. But she heard Griselda whisper, "Not María! It cannot be you to speak against me, María."

María took the stand and told her story, but it was only a small part of the story she knew, because she had to restrict her testimony to pertinent issues that dealt with the Operation Banshee case and the fact that Griselda knew she was a fugitive.

This was the only time during the trial that Griselda displayed any emotion. She sat ashen-faced, in shock, as María told her story to the jury. Arthur established her credentials: an Olympic-class swimmer, a concert pianist, daughter of one of the first families of Colombia, and Griselda's travel agent. It was a very short testimony, with no cross-examination. The defense did not want María wandering into other areas that could be devastating to their client.

María was followed on the stand by Charlie Cecil, who explained that he had met with Griselda's lawyer, Jorge Valencia, in Colombia to offer her a plea bargain, immunity for testifying. Charlie Cecil explained to the jury, "I was called back by Jorge Valencia, Griselda's lawyer. Jorge said that he had spoken with his client, and she was turning down the deal I offered."

"So was there any question that she knew that she was a fugitive?" Arthur asked.

"No," Charlie answered. "She knew."

When María and Charlie were finished, Mercado had left no doubt in anyone's mind that Griselda knew the U.S. authorities had indicted her and were looking for her.

Arthur Mercado had one more trick up his sleeve. Early on the first day of the trial, he had introduced a birthday card into evidence. At that time, Mercado was careful to inform the jury that the birthday card had been taken off a man named Romero when he was arrested in a New York airport with a dog cage that had a false bottom filled with cocaine. The card was signed by Griselda. He was also carrying a card with Griselda's and Pepe Cabrera's phone numbers.

On the third day of the trial, Mercado reactivated the birthday card by asking the defense to stipulate, or agree without argument, that it was truly Griselda's signature. The defense lawyers refused to give up that easily. The judge ruled on the issue and ordered Griselda to provide a sample of her signature. It was perfectly legal for the judge to request this, since she was not confessing to anything; she was just writing her signature.

Reluctantly, she signed her name on a sheet of paper for the court. It was at this moment that she made a monumental mistake. She attempted to disguise her handwriting, and she fell headlong into Mercado's trap. He took one look at the signature, smiled, handed it to the judge and walked over to his desk, where he picked up a piece of paper.

In her normal signature she had a very distinctive *G,* but on the sample she submitted to the court, she had changed it dramatically. Arthur Mercado had a true sample of her signature on the bottom of a legal document he had obtained for just this purpose. He handed the proper signature to the judge, who looked at it and just shook his head. Arthur let the jury come to the same conclusion as he pointed out which was the true signature. It did not take a handwriting expert to tell that she had tried to delude the court. Mercado let the documents do the talking. It was like shouting to the jury, "Ladies and gentlemen of the jury, she's trying to fool you with this petty trick. She's disrespectful of this court *and* she thinks you're stupid."

There was another incident where the defense lawyers were asked to stipulate to a piece of evidence: an address book that had been found in the apartment of a major female cocaine dealer in New York, and Griselda's name appeared in it. The arresting officer, a sergeant in the NYPD, had found the book, and had been subpoenaed to appear with it. Arthur called the officer to ask if he would be there to testify.

"Hey, listen," the sergeant said. "I got my two-week vacation coming. I planned this a year ago."

"I'm sorry, but you've been subpoenaed to appear."

"I'm sorry too," the sergeant said. "I don't give a shit. I'm going on my vacation. I don't care if I am subpoenaed. *Adiós.*"

Arthur decided to bluff it out. He waited until after the handwriting fiasco to talk to the defense lawyers during a break. "You guys aren't going to really dispute the fact that an officer of the NYPD seized those records, are you?"

"Nah." The defense lawyers turned to each other

and shrugged. "Why don't we stipulate to it? Okay with you?"

"Sure," Arthur said. "It's okay with me."

Arthur sat down and made a big scrawling note to hammer the missing cop when the trial was over.

Mary Cooper finally received her report from New York Telephone on Gloria Naranjo's toll calls, and they found a number in California that was called on a regular basis.

Mary gave Palombo the address and asked him what she should do next.

"Have a 'pen register' put on Gloria's line to trace the numbers she calls," Palombo replied. "I'm due to go out to California in a while; I'll check the address then. It's just a hunch, but thanks."

Security around the courthouse was very high. Mary and Arthur would arrive at around eight in the morning, and often would not leave until ten that night. Mary parked outside the Federal Courthouse, where it was bleak and desolate late at night. One night, she and agent Mike Cunniff were leaving the building around ten; as Mary approached her car, she noticed a wire hanging down.

Mike Cunniff said, "Stand back, Mary, I don't like this. Get away from the car."

"Mike, what are you going to do?"

"I'm just going to have a look underneath. Believe me, I'm not going to touch anything."

Mike got down on the ground and crawled under the car very slowly.

Boom!

There was a terrific explosion about a hundred feet away from them. Mary jumped about two feet off the ground, and Mike smashed his head on the muffler. He was out from underneath the car instantly.

"What the hell was that?"

"Who cares? As long as it wasn't this damn car," Mary blurted, still shaken from the explosion. "God, my nerves are bad enough as it is. I don't need this!"

"Me either," Mike Cunniff said, rubbing his badly bruised head.

Mercado took special care when he discussed the physical evidence during the trial. The bird and dog cages were displayed to the jury. A U.S. Customs agent had made a detailed diagram of a brassiere. It fascinated the jury. There were also the platform shoes with hollow soles and heels, and the girdles with built-in panels to hold the coke. Together with the birthday card, the address book and photos of the co-conspirators, it was an impressive array of evidence. While he was making his presentation to the jury, Mercado wondered what it would have been like to prosecute without the physical evidence. He gave thanks once again that he had found it.

It was now the defense's turn to call witnesses. They had told Mercado they were going to call ten witnesses for Griselda's defense. Mercado went through his lists and couldn't find anybody that he believed they would call. They called Sam Weidl to the stand. Arthur looked over at Mary Cooper and shrugged his shoulders in disbelief. Sam Weidl was a DEA agent who was not about to help the defense. The defense had decided to persist in trying to discredit Carmen; they put Weidl on the stand and hammered the fact that when Carmen was arrested she never brought up the name Griselda Blanco. The inference was that the prosecution had prompted her to say what she did, and she was making up her testimony to please the U.S. Attorney.

Their time with Sam Weidl on the stand was more like cross-examination. But Weidl did have to admit Carmen had not brought up the name Griselda Blanco. Then it was Arthur Mercado's turn to cross-examine Weidl.

Arthur began, "Agent Weidl, when you interviewed

her, did you give her any information on Griselda Blanco?"

"No."

"Did you show her any pictures?"

"No."

"Did you in any way influence her in her testimony?"

"No."

This testimony showed that Carmen was working off memory, her own recollections; that there was no way she could have fabricated such a complex web of characters, phone calls, drug seizures and events without her story being blown apart by the defense attorneys.

And Mercado was learning fast. He saved his last blow—a reminder to the jury—until the end, knowing that the defense would object. "Agent Weidl, do you think that Carmen Cabán might have withheld the fact that she knew Griselda Blanco out of fear that her family in Colombia might be punished?"

"It's a good possibility."

"Objection; hearsay," the defense roared.

"Objection sustained. The jury will disregard the witness's last statement."

Mercado told Mary Cooper later, "Calling Weidl may have helped their case or it may have hurt it. But what we got out of him was a lot better than what they got." After recess, Mercado and Cooper went back into court to listen to the next defense witnesses. There weren't any.

The defense attorneys rose; one of them said, "Your honor, we've thought about it, and we have decided we really don't need to call any more witnesses. We believe our defense is sound as it stands."

It was just a ploy. They didn't have any more witnesses. They were trying to throw Mercado off on his closing arguments, to catch him unprepared. They knew when the trial would end; he didn't.

* * *

But it was not to be. Mercado had written his closing arguments a week before, and he had been rehearsing them every night at home.

He was ready. Arthur Mercado rose and walked before the jury to give one of the most important speeches of his life. He stood in front of the jury and began. "How did it work? They recruited young men and young women; people who were poor, like Carmen Cabán; people who liked the excitement, people who liked the money of the cocaine trade. They recruited these people as protection; Pepe Cabrera did, Alberto Bravo did, and Griselda Blanco, the woman who now sits before you, did. These people were to take the risks for them so that they didn't have to carry the drugs past Customs, so that they didn't have to carry the drugs in their shoes, or wear the girdles and bras packed with cocaine.

"That's why Griselda Blanco never had to get on a plane carrying drugs. The generals don't go into the front line. They send the soldiers, the little people like Carmen Cabán and her sister, because these generals don't like exposure. They don't take risks. That's why Griselda Blanco is still operating.

"The defendant Griselda Blanco hides behind Carmen Cabán and people like her. She uses Carmen and people like her as protection from the law."

Arthur Mercado talked for a solid thirty minutes. Carefully, he tied all the evidence to Griselda. The jury sat, absorbed in his words. It was as if he had a needle and thread; he wove a verbal web, creating a tapestry that slowly and completely encased the Godmother.

Palombo sat in the audience. He had flown up for the summation. Mercado had changed. He was no longer a green, inexperienced prosecutor, cannon fodder for a skilled defense attorney. In ninety days, he had matured into a tough adversary. Palombo wondered why. Then he realized that, like himself, Mercado had become obsessed with taking the Godmother off the streets. Now Mercado had Griselda Blanco in his grasp, and there was no way he was going to let her slip through his fingers. Palombo patted the phone records he had in his pocket, just to reassure himself they were there.

He had a hunch the California number would lead him to the boys, and he intended to follow it up. Palombo glanced over at Griselda as she sat stoically awaiting her fate. She had shown no emotion throughout the trial, except when María Gutierrez had appeared to testify against her.

Frank Mandel spoke for the defense. He defined "conspiracy" in a very powerful way. Mercado believed it was a powerful image that worked against the defense. "Think of conspiracy in terms of a pail that is on the floor collecting water from a leaky ceiling. Little by little the drops of water drip into the pail; think of the evidence as it comes from the witness chair as drops of water that are supposedly filling up this bucket."

The defense pushed ahead and tried to destroy the web that Arthur Mercado had woven so carefully. Mandel blasted away for an hour, then sat down. Mercado had his final chance for rebuttal, and the jury departed to assess their verdict. It was Tuesday, July 9, 1985. The trial had taken only fourteen days.

Palombo, Mercado, and Mary Cooper didn't have long to wait for the verdict. The jury marched back in after only three hours and pronounced Griselda Blanco guilty as charged. Palombo slumped back in his seat and let out a huge sigh of relief. Mercado, the rookie, had kicked ass.

Mercado smiled as Palombo shook his hand and patted him on the back. Mercado, with less than a year's experience, with the help of a dedicated female DEA agent with only six months' experience, had just convicted the woman the DEA classified as the biggest, most deadly female drug dealer in the history of the world.

The Godmother was sentenced to the maximum the law would allow, fifteen years, in the federal penitentiary. The judge said to Griselda Blanco, "The only reason I'm giving you fifteen years is because, unfortunately, that is what the statute forces me to do. If I had my way, I'd put you away for seventy-five or a hundred years. You are a despicable person."

As they left the courthouse, Mercado turned to Palombo and said, "Well, Bob, what's left for you?"

"Taking her three sons off the street, and prosecuting her in Florida on conspiracy."

"Good luck; I know it's important to you. It was extremely important to me that I get a guilty verdict in this case."

"I know what you mean," Palombo said as he hailed a taxi. He was off to the airport, headed back to Miami. He sat back in the cab and wondered about little Michael Corleone Sepúlveda. He knew the reality of the situation, and that his desire to adopt the boy was based more on impulse than good judgment, but he still wondered what would become of Michael now that his mother was headed for the slammer.

Yet these thoughts did not dull his desire to put Michael's brothers in jail. He felt for the bulge in his inside coat pocket. The phone records were still there. Somehow, he knew that Dixon and Uber and Osvaldo were still in California. But were they at this number? After all, it was still just a hunch. He gazed out the window as they sped along the East River Drive. He smiled, thinking of the pen register on Gloria Naranjo's number as it traced every incoming and outgoing call. He rolled down the window to get some fresh New York air.

CHAPTER 24

Something Will Fall
on Your Head

During the trial period, from May to July, 1985, Palombo had spent most of his time tracking down Isaac Pessoa and José Ali Parada, the Brazilian connection that now supplied Griselda's sons with the bulk of their cocaine. His pursuit had led him and Gómez to Brazil and Panama several times.

In July, Palombo and Gómez flew to Panama to meet with Pessoa, but he did not show. Shortly after that, the Brazilian police unexpectedly raided the ranch of José Ali Parada, and arrested both Pessoa and Parada. Palombo and the DEA followed up by issuing indictments for both men in the United States. Palombo had six people he wanted brought to justice in the United States: the two Brazilians, Griselda, and the three boys. He didn't have the Brazilians in an American jail, but at least he had them in a Brazilian jail with a U.S. indictment pending against them.

But this was only filling his days with activity and motion. It was capturing Griselda's sons that filled his mind. He wouldn't rest until they were in jail.

On October 2nd, Palombo appeared before federal

magistrate Herbert Shapiro in Miami, and watched him sign criminal complaints and issue arrest warrants for Griselda Blanco, Dixon Trujillo, Uber Trujillo, and Osvaldo Trujillo for conspiracy to import cocaine. The magistrate set bail on the boys at the same time at $10,000,000 each. The warrants and complaints were sealed except for Griselda's, which was served.

Unknown to Palombo, on September 25th, Osvaldo had been arrested by the United States Secret Service in Los Angeles, along with several other Colombians. Osvaldo was using the name Clayton Guzmán.

Osvaldo's arrest happened by accident. An apartment owner in Los Angeles was concerned because rent on an apartment was being paid to him in cash, and he was suspicious that it might be funny-money. So he called in the Secret Service to examine a hundred-dollar bill. "This money looks like shit," the apartment owner explained to the two Secret Service men who stood in the hall. "And the guys that gave it to me look like shit. Here, you guys take the fucking money and examine it. I don't want any trouble passing counterfeit money," the man said, extending the bill to the agent.

"What apartment?" one of the agents asked.

"Right down the hall. I bet those three assholes at the door are headed there." The apartment owner pointed at Osvaldo and two of his bodyguards who were standing in the lobby, waiting to get buzzed in.

The two Secret Service agents backed away into the shadows and watched the three enter the building. They lay back out of sight, and when the moment was right, they slipped in behind the men and followed them to the door. The door was opened to let Osvaldo's group in and the agents made their decision. They walked in with Osvaldo, guns and shields out, yelling, "Federal agents!"

The agents searched the apartment and came up

with twenty-three kilos of coke, $33,000 in counterfeit hundred-dollar Federal Reserve notes, $20,000 in genuine notes, and a loaded .22-caliber pistol. They also found a stash of $3,709 in good U.S. currency, false identity papers, and a Mac-10 machine gun with a silencer and several gun barrels. When the arrests were made, Osvaldo said that his name was Clayton Guzmán, and that he was a Venezuelan citizen. Osvaldo, in his interview with the agents, said that he knew there was coke in the apartment, but that he was not part of the transaction and he was not the owner of the coke.

Osvaldo, under the alias Clayton Guzmán, was sent to the Federal Correctional Institute at Terminal Island just outside Los Angeles to await processing.

Max Mermelstein had been arrested in 1985, and was also at Terminal Island. Max had secretly decided to "do the right thing" and cooperate with the government, but he had not cut his final deal.

Osvaldo had vowed long before to kill Max on sight. Max was sure Osvaldo had personally been on the scene when Marta Ochoa was killed.

Julio Silva, a friend of Max, told him that Osvaldo had just arrived on the Island. Max decided to clear the air. Max, Julio and four other Colombians waited for Osvaldo outside the mess hall. When Osvaldo rounded the corner, Max grabbed him by the throat and held him up against the wall. Osvaldo looked over Max's shoulder and saw the five Colombians standing behind him. "Listen, you little shit. I'm gonna tell you the rules and regulations here in the joint. You don't bother me and I don't bother you. You make one move against me and you're one dead little motherfucker. You got it?"

"Yeah, yeah, yeah," Osvaldo stuttered, his eyes wide in fear, his toes barely touching the floor.

"You're just a punk in here, and you'll be one dead punk if you fuck with me. I'm just being nice, giving you this warning; don't misunderstand and think it's weakness. I could already have killed your ass."

"Hey, I don't mean you any harm."

"Sure you do, so cut the bullshit, just stay out of my face. You understand?"

"Yes."

"I hope so," Mermelstein said, releasing his choke grip on Osvaldo's throat, lowering him to the floor. "I hope you're not stupid like your mother."

The next move Max made was to call Dick Gregorie, the Miami Assistant U.S. Attorney who was head of the criminal division. "Hey, you've got a guy in here by the name of Clayton Guzmán. Well, he ain't Clayton Guzmán, he's fucking Osvaldo Trujillo, and he's in here on some charges that everyone says ain't gonna stick, so you better grab him."

"What's in this for you, Max?" Gregorie asked.

"Points, and you'll be solving a little problem for me. Osvaldo and me, we don't get along so good."

Gregorie called Palombo, and Palombo sent Jeff Behrman out to the jail to rearrest Osvaldo on the Miami complaints. He was able to do this just moments before the weapons, coke, and counterfeiting charges were thrown out of the California Federal Court for illegal search and seizure procedures.

One son down, two to go.

A week later, Bob Palombo was promoted and transferred to Cleveland as the Resident-Agent-in-Charge. Jeff Behrman, a rookie, was put in charge of the *Los Niños* case. Jeff Behrman had joined the group in May, 1984, directly out of the academy, brand-new to the world of dope and dopers. Moritz and Palombo took him under their tutelage, and he got the "instant immersion" program. He traveled with Palombo on the investigation down to Rio de Janeiro, Brazil, and to Panama when Palombo was using Gómez to try to nail Pessoa and Parada.

"Jeff, every new agent should be as lucky as you. You come into this office and right away you get to chase the bad guys all over Central and South America, and you get to work with two experts like me and Moritz. Hell, I know twenty-year agents who have never been outside of New York."

"Yeah, lucky me. I get to hook up with you guys in Group 2 and risk my life every day while observing these weird dopers in their own protected turfs like Brazil and Panama, where we can't do shit if we get in trouble. I'm real lucky, Bob."

Behrman actually loved the job as much as Palombo and Moritz, and he knew the Blanco case well. Palombo believed Behrman was bound to become a terrific agent; all he needed was experience. Palombo kept in close contact with him by phone from the Cleveland office.

In November, Max Mermelstein agreed to his final deal to fully cooperate. He had been busted in Fort Lauderdale and was facing life with no chance of parole, so he made a deal, a deal that would make him the single most important witness against the Medellín Cartel. Max had spent almost two years with Griselda as her main supplier. Max was now going to talk to anyone who wanted to listen. He had a great deal to say about Griselda Blanco, her family, and the cocaine wars. And Palombo thought it would be a good thing if they went out to California and listened.

Palombo spoke to Behrman. "Jeff, I think it would be a good idea if you and Pat O'Connor went out as a team and talked to Max Mermelstein in California. I have to testify on that cash we seized out of the trunk last fall. Believe it or not, Osvaldo is still pursuing the case. He's actually continuing to pay the legal bill in order to try to find out who the snitch is—although it won't do him much good in jail. Anyway, it gives me a good reason to go out West. I'll meet with you guys at the airport and do a little snooping."

"Snooping? What do you mean, snooping? Sounds like fun," Behrman replied.

"I can't tell you right now. I just smell it; there's something at the house on Crescent Heights that Gloria Naranjo called during the trial. There's no doubt in my mind that we're going to come up with something there. I just have a feeling."

"Hey, isn't that all police work is, feeling?" Behrman laughed.

"No. There's luck, too," Palombo replied, laughing. "Remember your training: the mind can be a dangerous thing."

In a few days, Bob Palombo, Pat O'Connor, and Jeff Behrman arrived at the Los Angeles airport and rented a car.

"Should we check into our hotel?" O'Connor asked.

"Hell no, we're going hunting," Palombo said.

"Where?" Behrman asked. "As if I didn't know."

"Crescent Heights," Palombo said with a broad grin. "Showtime!"

After three hours of wrong turns, they reached Crescent Heights to find a young man and woman standing idly by a BMW, right in front of the address.

"Oh, shit. What the hell is this?" Palombo whispered.

"I'm going to go down the block. Let's park the car and take a walk," Behrman said.

Palombo, Behrman, and O'Connor walked up the opposite side of the street. Just as they passed the BMW, a head popped up in the backseat. It was Uber. He had a telephone in his hand; he was making a call from the backseat.

"Holy shit, there he is," Palombo whispered out of the side of his mouth. "Let's not get him nervous; we don't want him running into the house on us. It's just us, no backup; the L.A. office doesn't even know what the hell we're doing. I don't want to have any problems; let's do this nice and easy."

The threesome walked up a little farther, crossed

the street, and came back down the block toward the BMW. When they were fifteen yards from the car, Palombo realized he only had on his ankle holster. He wouldn't be able to get to his gun without flagging the bust. "Got a gun?" he asked both men.

"Of course we've got guns," Behrman said. "What the hell do you think?"

"Fuck you. Pat?" Palombo asked.

"Yeah, I got my piece."

"You better use it, because I can't get to mine. When I say, "Now," you guys do it. We gotta be sure it's Uber."

The three agents were within three feet of the car. Palombo stepped slightly ahead to look in the backseat. Uber looked up into Palombo's eyes. A look of doom crossed his young face like a dark cloud. He knew it was over before Palombo said, "Now!"

Jeff Behrman whipped out his .9-mm automatic and dropped into a three-point stance, drawing down on Uber. "Federal agents; freeze."

Pat O'Connor covered the two people leaning on the BMW.

"Okay, asshole, out of the car," Palombo said. "Now stand up against the car. Keep your hands behind your head. Nice and easy, now." Uber leaned against the car and "assumed the position" as Palombo frisked him. "How you doin', Uber? Not too talkative right now, huh? I can understand that."

"What's going on?" the young woman asked.

"Just calm down, no problem, we're federal agents." Palombo flashed them his shield. "We have an arrest warrant for you, Uber."

"Who are you?" Uber asked.

"My name is Palombo."

"Oh, you're Palombo."

"That's right."

"You're the one that locked up my mother."

"You're right again." Palombo finished searching

Uber. "Stay leaning against the car." Palombo hand-cuffed him while Jeff Behrman read him his Miranda rights in English; Uber spoke very good English.

Palombo turned Uber around. "Can I contact an attorney?" Uber asked.

"Yeah, no problem." Palombo replied.

"Can she go inside?" Uber nodded at the girl.

"Yeah, sure. Okay, go on inside. What's your name?" Palombo asked the young man standing next to her.

"Oscar Jaramillo Naranjo." Palombo stared at him for a second; he had the same last name as Gloria. Was he Gloria's son? Palombo said nothing. "This your house?"

"Yes. If you want, you can wait inside," Oscar Naranjo volunteered.

"Thanks. We need to use your phone to call the office. Uber, by the way, where's your brother Dixon?"

"Oh, he's out of the country."

Gerry Gómez had picked up a rumor that Dixon was in Argentina. "Well, two out of the three boys ain't bad," Palombo thought to himself.

Just then, the girl stuck her head out the door of the house and yelled, "I couldn't get hold of the attorney. But I talked to Dixon, and Dixon said he is coming over right now."

Palombo and Behrman looked at each other and raised their eyebrows. It must be Christmas in November, they both thought. Dixon, too; what a present!

"Okay, let's go; let's get out of here," Uber said.

"Where do you think you're going?" Palombo asked, knowing what Uber was thinking. "What's your hurry? We will have to wait for the other agents to come. Besides, I don't know my way around Los Angeles."

"That's for sure," Behrman added.

"Hey, if we hadn't gotten lost, we might have missed Uber, here, and that would have been a damn shame. Wouldn't it?"

Uber rolled his eyes and looked away.

"We'll take your friend up on his offer and go inside the house and wait."

Once they got inside the house, Uber spieled off a barrage of angry Spanish at the girl.

"Hey, no talking in Spanish. Cool it!" Palombo yelled over at Uber.

They walked through the house. Playing in the back room with another little boy was Michael Corleone Sepúlveda, Griselda's youngest son. *"Hola, Miguel,"* Palombo said, smiling.

"Hola," Michael responded. He stood there for a second, staring at Palombo, then went back into his room to play. Palombo was not sure if Michael remembered him.

Palombo called the L.A. office of the DEA and told them what was happening. "We're expecting visitors, so if you're going to come over, don't park anywhere near the damn house, *capisce?"*

They waited. Palombo and Behrman took turns looking out the front door peephole.

"So you're the one who arrested my mother?" Uber asked.

"Yeah," Palombo answered.

"And now you're arresting me."

"Looks that way," Palombo grunted, looking out the peephole.

"Something will fall on your head," Uber mumbled.

"What?" Palombo asked, turning from the peephole, motioning for Jeff Behrman to take over. "What the hell did you say?"

"Oh, nothin'."

"Hey, Bob, he's out there. Dixon. He just pulled up. Have a look."

Palombo looked out the peephole. "He looks weird through this, like a bloated fish with black hair."

"What's he doin'?" Behrman asked.

"He just passed by the front door and looked this way," Palombo said, taking the .38 snub-nose chief special out of his ankle holster and jamming it in his waistband.

"Pat, you stay here with this happy threesome. Come on, Jeff, let's beat feet."

By this time, Dixon had walked almost to the end of the block. Palombo looked in the opposite direction and saw a parked Kawasaki motorcycle near the far end of the block.

They walked quickly behind Dixon until they were within a few feet of him. Dixon looked over his shoulder at two gun barrels and two fast-approaching agents. "You Dixon?" Palombo asked.

Dixon stopped and started to answer as the two agents caught up to him, braced him, and patted him down before he could get another word out.

"Federal agents; you're under arrest," Palombo said.

"Oh, shit," was all Dixon could think of to say.

Minutes later, officers of the L.A. DEA office arrived and transported the Trujillos down to be fingerprinted, photographed, and booked. They seized the BMW and the phone in the backseat.

Upon arrival at the DEA lockup, Uber had a lot to say. He began with Palombo, Behrman, and O'Connor. "Someday something will fall on your head as it has on mine today. Things will come down around you. I will remember your faces."

The agents remained still. Uber next addressed the DEA officers. "I will be out on bond by tomorrow. The judges, they are friends of mine."

When the DEA agents dropped him off with the U.S. Marshals at the Federal Courthouse, Uber turned to the agents and told them that one day he would see them on the street. He then made a gun with his hand, and pointed it at the agents.

Palombo decided to pay Uber and Dixon a visit in the lockup. He walked into the main holding cell. "Sit down, fellas. I've got something I want to say to you both." He waited for them to sit. "Don't make promises you can't keep. First of all, you're in and I'm out. And there are a hell of lot more guys looking for you two than are looking for me. I really wouldn't be so concerned about getting even with me. No, I'd be worrying about staying alive in jail, because you are not exactly the most popular guys in the world."

Palombo turned his full attention to Uber. "You know there was a time when you went into a gas station down on the Dixie Highway near Fort Lauderdale, and somebody spotted you. If you had not gassed up quick, and gotten out of there, your buddy Jaime Bravo would have caught you there. You would be history." Palombo referred to the interview with Jaime Bravo following his arrest.

Palombo continued. "Jaime's in jail, too. I'd worry about Jaime, not about me."

"No, no," Uber replied. "You misunderstood us; we don't mean you any harm."

"Well, I just wanted to let you know that Jaime's still looking for you, that's all. And sometimes assholes like you guys wind up in the same prison with other assholes that hate them." Palombo walked out, leaving them stunned. Now they had something else to think about.

They were both shipped to Miami and held in pretrial detention with no bond. Palombo had the hat trick now with the boys, three out of three, and the Godmother herself. She had been moved down to Miami to stand trial with her sons.

He had them dead, a beautiful case of conspiracy. He felt confident that they would all go away for the maximum sentence, even though there was not a speck of "powder on the table."

If the case was so airtight, then why was he nervous? He thought back to his early days in the U.S. Customs office, and to his mentor Al Seeley. Then he knew why he was nervous; the unwritten law that whatever could go wrong *would* go wrong. He rubbed his bicep and wondered why it was bugging him. He busied himself with paperwork.

THE KONKABLE

With that, Munoz's wife hears her own comments to the latent case, to her early days at the U.S. Customs Service, to his arrest of A. Soraya there in there who he was taken. In recent Hij and ing is power ordered for that home at home. He orders his cousin's home there, which was his time. For he, let him...

CHAPTER 25

Deal with the Devil

Pat O'Connor had a droll sense of humor, and he loved to bust Palombo's chops in a nice way. He called Palombo in Cleveland from the Miami DEA office. "Hey, Bob, Gerry Gómez, your star witness, has got a little bit of a problem."

"What's the little bit of a problem?"

"Oh, about three thousand pounds' worth," O'Connor said.

"What are you talking about?"

"You know that little fruit-juice importing company that he was setting up while we were getting him into the Witness Protection Program?"

"Yeah, sure I know. Get to the point."

"The same Gerry Gómez who wanted to go down and say goodbye to his family members in Colombia because he'd never be able to see them again? And you guys were nice and let him go down to Colombia as an act of good faith and humanitarianism?"

"Pat, please get to the fucking point."

"Well, it seems like he went and got himself into the

286

smuggling business instead and brought back three thousand pounds of cocaine."

"What! What are you saying?" Palombo screamed, rubbing his aching arm.

"Yeah, Sweatbands!" Sweatbands was Gómez's nickname, because when he got nervous he sweated so profusely. "He's headed for the Miami submarine right now, escorted by the marshals, and he wants you there."

"Shit, what next! I'll grab a travel voucher and be down there this afternoon."

Palombo called his wife. "Grace, I've got big problems in Miami. Would you pack me a bag for overnight? I'll be home in twenty minutes."

By five o'clock that afternoon, Palombo was in the Miami airport, where he was picked up and taken immediately to the Miami "submarine," the secure facility for federal witnesses and prisoners kept by the Marshals' Service. In Miami, the submarine was in the basement of the federal courthouse.

Gómez had been charged with conspiracy to import cocaine. To prove a criminal conspiracy, the prosecutors needed to show knowledge and intent. Palombo questioned him and Gómez stuck to his guns. "Bob, I don't know shit about this. That dope was just packed away with the fruit-juice concentrate. I have no idea how it got there. I was tricked. I had no idea . . ."

Palombo was angry. "Gerry, I think you're a lying sack of shit. You don't expect me to believe that, do you? I don't want to know. You're a piece of garbage; you are insulting my intelligence. You used me. I have no use for you unless you want to be a man and tell me the goddamn truth. If you think I'm going to believe that bullshit you're handing out, then this meeting is over and I'm going back to Cleveland."

"Okay, okay! Yeah, I met with these people in Colombia and they discussed legitimate business with me. They did at one time say, 'Why don't we try a little poison?'"

"What the hell do you mean by that, Gerry? What's poison?"

"Well, there's only one meaning for poison."

"And what did you say?" Palombo asked.

"I said, 'Hell no, I don't want to do anything like that. If I'm going to do this business, it's got to be clean.'"

"In other words, Gerry, you said no to these people."

"Yeah, that's right."

"Okay, I can't take this anymore. Let me tell you something: You're full of shit. You're lying. That's it. Goodbye." Palombo started to leave.

"Hold it, Bob, hold it, for Chrissake," Gómez pleaded. "You want the truth? I'll tell you the truth." Gómez did not realize that what he was about to say would put him in jail for fifty years. He was trying to exculpate himself from guilt, and instead he dug his own grave. Gómez believed that if he didn't have anything to do with the smuggling directly, then there was no conspiracy. "Yeah, I knew that they were eventually going to bring drugs in."

"They gave you front money?" Palombo asked.

"A hundred and fifty thousand dollars. And they told me, 'You don't owe us any money back, because what's happening is, we're sending you up this fruit juice. It's a dry run, to see if the shit gets through Customs without getting hit, and to see if you can get it cleared and out onto the street. So we don't care, we don't want any money back from the fruit juice.'"

"And you went along with this, Gerry. Why didn't you just turn them in to us? Hell, you would have been a big fucking hero. You could have picked up a little cash and a new identity. I don't understand you."

"Look, I didn't do anything wrong here. I was going to let them do what they wanted to do. I didn't care what they did with the cocaine, because I was going to be gone in the Witness Security Program. See, I would stall them off until I was gone."

THE GODMOTHER

"Gerry, I don't believe you. You're some piece of work. You take the $150,000 from these assholes, and then you want to be gone when they come to collect what they paid for? And you want to use the DEA to help you do it! I can't fucking believe what I'm hearing."

"Look, Bob, I'm only telling you what happened. I'm not involved."

"Gerry, you are a brilliant person in some respects, and as stupid as they come in others. You're your own worst enemy. You don't learn by your mistakes. I gotta go," Palombo said, and left the submarine.

What the hell would this do to the *Los Niños* case? Gómez was the chief witness. He decided that he'd better go talk to Steve Schlessinger.

Schlessinger's boss was Dick Gregorie, chief of the Criminal Division for South Florida, and one of the best federal prosecutors in the country. But it was Steve's case; Gregorie let him call the shots.

Steve had received the same bad news about Gómez. He had originally lobbied a judge in Oklahoma where Gómez had been busted for coke, into releasing Gómez into their custody for the Godmother investigation. Steve had lobbied the same judge into a travel permit so that Gómez could go to Colombia to say goodbye to his relatives before he entered Witsec, the witness protection plan. "Shit, shit, shit!" he repeated to his empty office and slammed the phone into the receiver.

Still, they had a terrific case. They now had Max Mermelstein, who had been Griselda's supplier and money launderer, as a witness. They had María Gutierrez, her confidante, who was ready to testify. And they had Fernando López of the Brazilian National Police, who had agreed to travel to Miami and testify to the physical evidence, which included bank accounts and code books found in Brazil. These documents linked the Godmother directly to the

Brazilian cocaine connection, Isaac Passoa and José Ali Parada. It made her an international criminal involved in a worldwide conspiracy.

Palombo and Steve Schlessinger talked about the possibility of the defense coming in with a deal, a plea bargain for Griselda and the boys. Palombo was strongly against any plea agreement. "Steve, no deals. Understand? I don't give a fuck about Gerry Gómez being caught on this conspiracy rap; we still have a great case. If we start cutting deals, I'm going to be real pissed. No deals, please, unless they are willing to plead straight up to the indictment with absolutely no recommendation for sentencing. That's fine; you can't stop 'em from doing that. But as long as that's understood, no caps, nothing. We go for the whole enchilada, nothing less. Okay?"

"Bob, I'm with you. I won't plead them out."

But there was another plan afoot that Palombo and Schlessinger knew nothing about.

The trial had been set to be heard on July 21, 1986, in front of Judge Eugene Spellman. Roy Black, a top Florida defense attorney, had been retained by Griselda.

The first inkling that there was something seriously wrong occurred on July 15th, just before the trial date. Judge Spellman called a special meeting in his chambers. Present were Steve Schlessinger, who was trying Griselda, and the three U.S. Attorneys who were prosecuting the boys. Dixon, Uber, Osvaldo, and their attorneys, Alan Baum, Richard Beiley, and Miguel Orta, were also present.

One of the defense lawyers spoke first. "Judge, our clients are willing to plead guilty, but we would like an indication from Your Honor as to what sentence the court would impose."

"Well, from what I know about this case, and from what I know about these defendants, I'm going to give them ten years."

Schlessinger stepped forward. "Your Honor, this is a *major* conspiracy. Although these are young men, they are still leading players in the cocaine business, and we feel that if you were to hear the evidence at trial, you would sentence them to considerably more than ten years."

Spellman snapped back at Schlessinger, annoyed. "You're not even part of this conversation. You are prosecuting the mother, so you are not really part of this." Spellman calmed down and continued. "I wish to resolve this case with these young men. If they plead guilty to one count, I am telling you that the maximum sentence they will get is ten years."

The prosecutors were in shock. It was the first time they had heard of this offer. One of the U.S. Attorneys spoke for them all: "Your Honor, as Mr. Schlessinger says, we have a very strong case and these are serious offenders. You know that the maximum here is twenty years, and we think we can get them convicted."

Judge Spellman bulldozed ahead. "Well, okay, you have made your objection. Despite that, I am advising everyone that the sentence is going to be ten years."

Schlessinger and the other prosecutors were dazed. They walked out of the judge's chambers confused and shaken. It was clear that there was no choice. The judge was implying that if they tried the case and lost, the Trujillo boys would walk, and if they won, the most they could hope for was a ten-year sentence. So, obviously, accepting the ten-year sentence would be the smart thing to do.

"Shit," the prosecutors said, almost in chorus, beaten before they had started. They stood motionless, numb, in the Miami federal halls of justice. "How the hell can Spellman do such a thing?" echoed down the empty hallway.

"I don't know, but I think he just did it," they answered themselves.

The prosecutors marched back to see Leon B. Kellner, the U.S. Attorney, and Dick Gregorie, their

RICHARD SMITTEN

immediate boss. The senior attorneys listened carefully. "Bullshit, they can plead straight up or they can go to trial."

The prosecutors went back to Spellman and said, "Your Honor, they can plead straight up to the indictment or go to trial." Spellman only stared at them with no comment.

Two days later, on the 17th of July, the three sons pled guilty.

Palombo got the news the same day and exploded. He called Schlessinger and vented his rage.

Schlessinger waited for Palombo to cool off before he spoke. "Bob, I'm telling you right now, I don't give a shit whether we go to trial with the boys or not, it's ten fucking years. That's what Spellman says. He made it clear he's going to give them ten years if they are convicted. And that's that."

"All right, I guess we're fucked on the boys. What about the old lady?" Palombo asked.

"There are no deals with the old lady."

"You sure?"

"Yeah, Roy Black approached me and I told him no deals. Griselda has to plead straight up to the charges and face the full twenty-year sentence."

"You're sure!"

"Positive."

"Is there any chance we could nail her on a CCE?" Palombo asked.

"Well, we have the five elements we need, but the main witness, Gómez, is shaky as hell. We can't chance it. Gómez is too unstable, especially now that he's up on these new charges; if he starts jerking us around on the stand, we're fucked. And there is no telling what Black will do to him. He may demolish him as it is," Schlessinger said.

"Shit, what a jerk. He could have been a hero."

"So could Nixon, but he got caught, too. At least we're gonna put the Godmother away for a long time."

292

"I hope so. She's one powerful, tricky woman," Palombo added. "I don't think this is going to be over till it's over."

Palombo's words were prophetic.

There was already a private deal between Judge Eugene Spellman and Griselda's attorney, Roy Black.

Roy Black, months later, on the stand himself, under oath and an agreement of immunity, would have to disclose what that secret plan was.

According to Griselda's attorney, a bargain had been struck between him and Judge Spellman, a deal that did not include the U.S. Attorney. Later, the U.S. Attorneys would say privately that making a secret deal with Griselda Blanco was like making a deal with the devil.

On July 17th, Judge Spellman asked Roy Black if Griselda Blanco's case could be resolved with the government so that it wouldn't have to go to trial. It was going to be a long trial and he had a full court calendar.

On July 20th, Roy Black met with Griselda and explained that the government might drop the charges from two counts to one count, but she would have to plead guilty with no deal. That meant facing a twenty-year consecutive sentence. Griselda said no to the offer. She did not want to plead to a count that could get her twenty years on top of the fifteen years she had received in New York. She preferred to go to trial and take her chances.

Roy Black passed this information on to Judge Spellman. No deal; the trial would have to proceed.

On July 23rd, jury selection began and continued on to July 24th. On the morning of July 24th, Roy Black testified, he received a message in his office to call Judge Spellman in his chambers. Black called immediately. In his later testimony Black related the conversation.

"Roy," Judge Spellman said, "if Griselda Blanco

will plead guilty, the maximum sentence I will give her is ten years. That, however, will have to be a consecutive sentence. Now, the U.S. Attorney is going to object to this, so don't say anything to Steve Schlessinger about this conversation we're having. Convey this offer to your client and see if she will plead guilty to resolve the case. Roy, the ten years is not that much more time than she is due to serve already."

Roy Black returned to the courtroom and immediately spoke to Steve Schlessinger. "Are you still willing to take the top count on Griselda Blanco?"

"Yeah. We would take the top count, no deals, straight up. She would face twenty years."

"Okay, I want to confer with her, but I'm disposed to recommend to her that she take it. The only reason I'm doing this, Steve, is because I have conferred with experts in parole and I can tell you that the difference between her pleading to this count or not isn't going to substantially change her parole situation."

"Hey, look, I don't care. If that's your feeling, fine." Schlessinger figured that Black was just trying to fold his hand gracefully before he pled guilty, to save face.

The next morning, July 25th, Roy Black spoke at length with his client. Present were his partner Frank Furci, George Thompson, a parole expert, and Sylvia Hauser, the translator.

Black told Griselda what was going on. "Judge Spellman called me and said if you plead guilty, you will get the same sentence as your sons are getting, ten years. However, it will be consecutive to the New York sentence. I believe if you go to trial the sentence will be much more severe."

Roy Black spoke slowly so that the translator could keep up and Griselda could think about what he was saying. He resumed. "This is not part of any plea bargain arrangement with the government. The U.S. Attorney has not agreed to this. This is strictly be-

tween us and the Judge, and Judge Spellman said not
to mention it to anyone."

According to Black, George Thompson explained
how the parole system worked, and that ten years on
top of her existing fifteen would have no effect on her
parole eligibility. Under Judge Spellman's proposal of
a ten-year sentence, she would still be eligible for
parole after 120 months—ten years. So when it came
to Griselda's parole possibilities, the tacking on of ten
years was meaningless.

Griselda Blanco accepted the secret deal.

Black gave her a final reminder. "Now, remember,
you are never to say that the judge has offered this deal
of only ten years. Judge Spellman is a man of his
word. He will do as he has promised. Do you understand?"

"*Sí*," Griselda said when the translator had finished. "*Yo comprendo.*"

Steve Schlessinger had not heard from Roy Black
again. The jury had been selected, and he was ready to
try the case. He was reviewing his paperwork when
Roy Black suddenly rose and stood before the court.

It was 2:30 P.M., July 25th, and the courtroom was
packed with law enforcement people who had chased
Griselda: Bob Palombo, Al Singleton, Dan Moritz,
and Jeff Behrman, to name just a few.

There was immediate silence as Roy Black spoke. "I
have had a number of discussions with my client, and
we have decided that we are going to enter a plea of
guilty to count one of the indictment."

Palombo was shocked, as were the rest of the law
enforcement people. Schlessinger was annoyed that
Black had not had the courtesy to at least call him first
and tell him she was pleading out to the charge. It was
customary in this kind of plea to at least notify the
prosecutor. But he was happy she was pleading to the
full charge of count one. He still had the Gerry Gómez
bust to deal with.

After her plea, Griselda Blanco took the stand for her rights to be explained to her. Judge Spellman interviewed her. A translator was used to make sure there were no misunderstandings. "How old are you?"

"Forty-six years old."

"Are you married?"

"No, I am a widow."

"Yeah, a black widow!" someone in the gallery whispered.

Judge Spellman continued. "What has been your primary occupation during your adult life?"

"Housewife."

"Do you desire to plead guilty to count one of the indictment in this case?"

"Yes, Your Honor."

"Do you understand that in pleading guilty to count one of the indictment, you subject yourself to a possible term of twenty years, a fine of $250,000, and that sentence may be in addition to any sentence that you have presently imposed upon you?"

Griselda Blanco remembered Roy Black's words: "Remember, you are never to say the judge has offered this deal."

"Yes," she said.

"Is your decision to plead guilty a free and voluntary one?"

"Yes," Griselda said.

"Anybody threaten, coerce, or intimidate you in any way to plead guilty?" Spellman persisted.

"No."

Judge Spellman proceeded to tell Griselda that the U.S. government was obliged to prove its case, and to fully inform her of her rights and loss of rights under the plea she was making. He concluded, "Therefore, you must understand that the Court has the prerogative of imposing the sentence within the guidelines indicated by law. Do you understand that you are giving up all of your rights that I have just indicated to you insofar as you have entered a plea of guilty? Do you understand that, Mrs. Blanco?"

"Yes."

Griselda Blanco took her seat.

Spellman then addressed Roy Black. "Let me ask this question. The Court is treating the plea as a plea by the defendant based on her admissions to this court that she is, in fact, guilty of the offense charged. Do you have any questions in your mind about that, Mr. Black?"

"No, not at all, Your Honor."

Judge Spellman was anxious to wrap it up. "Are there any other terms, conditions, or agreements?"

"No, Your Honor," Steve Schlessinger said.

"Mrs. Blanco, is this your understanding of the plea agreement?" Spellman asked.

"Yes," Griselda lied.

"And Mr. Black, is that your understanding?"

"Yes, Your Honor, that is correct."

Spellman ended the session. "The Court now finds that the defendant is alert, competent, intelligent, and that she fully understands the nature of the charges against her and the full consequences of pleading guilty. Most important, she understands the rights that she has given up by virtue of her plea."

Palombo couldn't have been happier as the judge wrapped up his comments. It was a slam dunk—three pointer on the Godmother. She was gone for twenty big ones plus the fifteen in New York, for a total of thirty-five years.

Spellman continued, "The Court is also satisfied that your decision to plead guilty is a free and voluntary one, not as a result of any force, threats or promises, and that you are pleading guilty because you are, in fact, guilty. The Court does hereby find you guilty as charged. Sentencing will take place at 9:00 A.M. on September 5th."

Bob Palombo was ecstatic. They couldn't have done any better. She pled guilty with absolutely no deal, full-up to the indictment. He met Steve Schlessinger in the hall after the trial and shook his hand.

"Congratulations, Steve, on her pleading out."

"Well, I was as surprised as you. It's the first I'd heard of it. Black didn't even call me to tell me he was going to plead her out."

"Well, I would have been happier with a CCE, for life with no parole, but this is great. Do you think she will get the full twenty?"

"After the judge reads my presentencing memorandum, I believe he will have no choice. This is one hell of a vicious bitch."

The time dragged by for Palombo from July 25th to September 5th. He was busy as the Resident-Agent-in-Charge for Cleveland, but it was nothing like the drama and excitement of South Florida and chasing the Godmother. He was anxious to put his ten-year chase behind him and clear his mind for what lay ahead in his career.

On the flight to Miami for the sentencing, he thought of all the agents who had been involved over the years in trying to catch the Godmother. All the lonely nights, missing his wife and family. But somehow it was worth it.

Palombo sat in a crowded open court surrounded by other officers who had pursued the Godmother and her sons, and who were instrumental in getting Griselda Blanco into court, in front of Judge Spellman, waiting to be sentenced.

Roy Black had his chance in front of the Court before the sentence was passed and he used it aggressively, attacking Steve Schlessinger, primarily for withholding evidence. This shocked Schlessinger, since there had not been a trial in which to present any evidence.

Steve Schlessinger summed up the government's position. "I would ask the court to consider the people who are not present in court today, but whose lives have been ruined by the kind of poison that these individuals have distributed throughout the United States." Steve Schlessinger looked over at mother and sons for a few long moments, then turned back to the judge. "Those people are not here. They can't be here. Where is justice for the people whose lives have been destroyed by cocaine? Who is going to listen to their cries?

"Before I sit down, Your Honor, I would just like to publicly pay homage to the efforts that were made by the investigating agents in this case. They have come to court this morning: Special Agents Bob Palombo, Dan Moritz, and Jeff Behrman. These agents, Your Honor, made a complete and total commitment to this investigation, and it is through their efforts that this case was brought to a successful conclusion. They have done everything that agents could do in a case. Your Honor, if there is to be any good to come from this, they now turn it over to you for an appropriate sentence.

"They can do no more. Thank you, Your Honor."

Judge Spellman was also particularly eloquent that morning as he addressed the court. "From the standpoint of this case, if there ever is a case other than the Ma Barker case that has been in a courtroom, and that truly demonstrates what a mother's influence ought not to be, this is one.

"It is incredible for this Court to believe that what we in effect have is three seasoned veterans who collectively, adding up their ages, don't come to seventy. I have to say to the mother who sits in this courtroom and who constantly continues to influence what is said and done by these young men, that this is the most incredible thing I have ever seen.

"I truly must suggest to you that if the good Lord

really had you in mind, that he might have given some real consideration to a substitute for motherhood."

Judge Spellman proceeded to sentence each of the sons to twelve years. Then he moved on to the Godmother. "There is nothing unpredictable about the damage that you have wrought. It seems almost uncanny to me to believe that a woman could take three young men that left her womb and do what you have done to these three young men. It is just incredible!

"It is the order of this Court that you be hereby sentenced to a term of twenty years and to pay a fine of $250,000. This sentence and fine will be consecutive with the sentence you have heretofore been ordered to serve by the Southern District of New York."

The judge rose to leave and the courtroom stood as a body as he exited.

Griselda Blanco stared at Roy Black with anger and confusion in her eyes. She had been double-crossed!

Black didn't wait long to discuss it with her. Griselda Blanco was not a person to make angry.

The court was adjourned; the law enforcement people had all they could do to restrain a rebel yell in the courtroom. Steve Schlessinger, Bob Palombo, and Carol Wilkinson, an Assistant U.S. Attorney, were filing their way out of the court when Roy Black ran up to Steve Schlessinger.

Roy Black said, "Spellman wants to see us in chambers."

"Who?"

"Everyone, including the boys' lawyers."

Once in chambers, one of the lawyers for Griselda's sons spoke first. "Judge, we had an agreement for ten years for the sons, and now you gave them twelve years."

Judge Spellman explained how he thought he was doing them a favor. With the twelve-year sentences, the sons would be eligible for parole at any time.

The attorney responded, "Don't do us any favors; give us the ten-year sentences."

Judge Spellman said, "Okay, I'll do it."

"Judge, what about our understanding?" Black asked.

"Well, you know, I don't recall . . ."

"What about the forecast you made, that you'd be giving my client ten years?" Black asked.

Schlessinger broke in and said, "There is no such promise, there was never any promise made by the government. There really wasn't even a promise with relation to the sons; they pled straight up to the full sentence. Twenty years, that's what they could have gotten. Your client, Mr. Black, was never a part of any kind of *forecast;* she was never part of any deal. There *is* no understanding!" Schlessinger spoke angrily.

The judge said he wanted to think about it some more. Schlessinger and Black walked out of the judge's chambers together. Schlessinger turned to Black as they reached the door and said, "What the hell's going on here, Roy? What are you guys talking about?"

Roy Black stopped at the door and looked Steve Schlessinger directly in the eye, and said with a sly smile, "You'll find out, Steve. You'll find out."

Schlessinger rejoined Palombo, Wilkinson, and the other DEA agents, and they lunched together. Schlessinger had no appetite. He was distant and preoccupied. His luncheon partners noticed he was not as ebullient as they thought he should be.

"Anything wrong?" Palombo asked.

"Nah, just the letdown after the buildup." Schlessinger forced a smile, not wanting to discuss what he had just heard in the judge's chambers.

Palombo didn't believe him, and decided to stick close to him.

While they were lunching, Roy Black was in his office, frantically phoning the judge. He finally reached Judge Spellman and said, "Judge, you have obviously forgotten the conversation we had with regard to Griselda Blanco. She was to receive the same sentence as the sons, ten years; do you recall the conversation?"

"I'm not sure," Black claims Spellman responded, "but I'll accept your statement that we had such a conversation."

Steve Schlessinger and Bob Palombo returned to Steve's office after lunch, where Steve was handed an urgent message, a message he was dreading. "Call Judge Spellman immediately."

Fifteen minutes later, Steve was standing in the judge's chambers while Bob Palombo waited outside.

According to Schlessinger, Judge Spellman explained, "Steve, there's been a mistake here. I'm sorry about this, but it seems that during the course of these proceedings, I had a conversation with Roy Black, in which I told Roy that I didn't see any reason why his client shouldn't receive the same ten-year sentence as the sons, and I'm afraid that Roy's been put in a terrible position because of what's happened. Would you please agree to my making a clerical change on the judgment reflecting that Griselda Blanco is to receive a sentence of ten years rather than twenty years?"

Steve Schlessinger stood stock still in shock that turned to outrage and anger. He couldn't speak; he had practiced in the federal court system for more than ten years, and he had never encountered anything like this. He was appalled that an attorney of the stature and reputation of Roy Black would sink to this level. And the final insult had happened that very morning when Black had accused the government of holding back information. Black's entire vitriolic speech now whizzed through Schlessinger's mind as a sham. "The government had withheld evidence?" My god, what about these two men, what did they hold back? What kind of conspiracy was this? Why would Black tear a strip out of the government when they had entered into this secret deal? And the judge's words, "Roy's been put in a terrible position" echoed through his head. It was outrageous.

Steve Schlessinger took a deep, cleansing breath to harness his emotions before he spoke. "I'm afraid, Judge, that we aren't going to agree to any clerical amendment. The sentence that was pronounced in open court should stand. The U.S. government was not party to any agreement that Griselda Blanco would receive anything less than the full sentence of twenty years. This woman is one of the worst criminals of the century. You read my presentence investigation memo. I'm sorry, Judge; we just can't agree to what you are suggesting."

With that, Schlessinger staggered out into the hall and came face to face with Palombo. "They're giving her the same goddamn deal as they gave the boys, ten years," Schlessinger blurted.

"What! What the hell are you talking about? Who's 'they'?" Palombo snapped.

"According to Black, he and Spellman made some kind of a secret deal. Hell, Bob, I don't know what's going on."

"This can't be; it just can't be."

"Don't get excited; we'll work it out. I wasn't there; they can't do this. This is ex parte; there is something wrong here, very wrong."

"Jesus Christ!"

"Bob, I didn't know anything about this. This is impossible . . ."

"This is bullshit, Steve. Let's go to trial. This is just absolute bullshit; we're not going to give this woman ten years. Forget about it! It took me ten fucking years to catch her!"

"We'll work it out."

"How're you going to work it out? And where do Roy Black and Judge Spellman get off making this deal, deciding the course of this trial on their own? This stinks!"

"Bob, I know it stinks; don't make it any worse than

it already is. I have to go now, and speak to the U.S. Attorney."

Steve returned alone to his office and told Joe McSorley, the First Assistant U.S. Attorney. Joe was outraged, livid—the whole thing reeked. Together, they marched into the office of the U.S. Attorney, Leon B. Kellner.

Kellner listened quietly and suggested that they wait for a day or so and think calmly about their position, which was spelled out at the end of their meeting: "Does the U.S. government attempt to vacate all the pleas and go on to trial? Or, do they vacate only her plea and go to trial against only the Godmother? Or, do they give Griselda Blanco the benefit of this secret bargain?"

Later Palombo had a drink with Dan Moritz and Jeff Behrman and told them what had happened in Judge Spellman's chambers. They sat in disbelief. Palombo let off steam. "Hell, Jeff, you and I testified in front of Judge Spellman in the Jaime Bravo case less than a year ago. I stood right before him and testified against Bravo and all this shit about Griselda came out then. Everything, the murders that were the reasons for the guns, and the vengeance. He had to remember what kind of a person we are dealing with here. Ten fucking years he gives her; I just don't believe it."

"Why the hell did he give her twenty years and then retract it?" Moritz asked.

"How the hell do I know? Mercado wins a ten-year-old case in New York with hardly any evidence, a miracle victory. We chase her for ten years and put together this airtight case in Miami, that's to be given away in a ten-minute phone call between a judge and a defense attorney, and the U.S. Attorney isn't even consulted on the deal. How the hell do I know what's going on?"

Nobody except Griselda Blanco, Roy Black, and Judge Eugene Spellman knew what had gone on.

The U.S. Attorney, Leon Kellner, decided to bring in the big guns. He appointed Larry Scharf, his own "Special Counsel," to preside over the special hearing called by the Department of Justice to resolve the controversy regarding Griseld's sentencing. Larry Scharf was known as "Dr. No" to the other Assistant U.S. Attorneys and the staff of the South Florida Justice Department. He was famous for knowing the law by heart, almost always being right, and almost always saying no to special requests and questions presented to the U.S. Attorneys. In this case, he said yes, he would preside at the hearing and try to get to the bottom of the Griselda Blanco trial. He was chosen because he did not have a regular trial schedule. He was Special Counsel; he only went to court on particular occasions. He did not have to stand before a potentially hostile judge day after day as Steve Schlessinger and Carol Wilkinson might.

Larry Scharf was a small person, slight and wiry. He stared with intelligent eyes and said little. But when he spoke, it was with the quiet confidence of being sure that he was right in what he said about the law.

The U.S. Attorneys had reported the matter to the Public Integrity Section of the Department of Justice, although they didn't expect any real action to be taken. No one liked prosecuting a federal judge.

Next, they looked up certain points of law of the Federal Criminal Code, which deals with fraud and false statements. There were severe penalties for influence, perjury, false statements, and false declarations before a court.

After reviewing the law, the U.S. Attorneys decided that in order to get to the bottom of this matter they would have to offer Roy Black immunity from prosecution. Black accepted the deal, and said he would speak truthfully at the hearing about exactly what had happened.

The Department of Justice agreed to call in another federal judge, Kenneth Ryskamp, to conduct the hearing. Scharf began the proceedings in front of Judge Ryskamp to determine what had transpired at the mysterious trial that never was.

Griselda Blanco was first to take the stand. Scharf asked Griselda Blanco, "Is it fair to say that you relied upon Mr. Black's statement about what Judge Spellman had offered in coming to your decision to plead guilty?"

"Yes. I would not have done so otherwise."

"Before you entered the plea, did you have a conversation with Mr. Black about what would occur when you went before Judge Spellman?"

"Mr. Black said I should not say anything to the Judge regarding the ten years that the Judge had offered me, and that I was going to be asked if I would waive my rights. Mr. Black told me about all the things the Judge would be asking me."

"Anything else?" Scharf asked.

"Mr. Black said that I could not say that I had been made the offer of ten years by the Judge, or that anyone had promised me anything, or that anyone had forced me, just to say that I had made the decision myself."

"Did Mr. Black tell you that when your plea was taken you would be placed under oath?" Scharf asked in his steady, deliberate way.

"Yes."

"Didn't you ask Mr. Black, 'Why am I being asked to lie under oath?'"

"No, I didn't ask him anything."

"And he didn't explain it to you?"

"No," Griselda replied.

The next issue Scharf covered was the sentencing of her sons. "Were you told that the U.S. Attorneys would not agree to a ten-year limitation on the sentence your sons would receive, but that Judge Spellman made that agreement anyway?"

"Yes," Griselda answered. "The attorneys told my sons that Judge Spellman had offered ten years."

Scharf zeroed in on the issues of perjury and conspiracy. "On the day of your trial, did you hear Judge Spellman say to you, 'The court is also satisfied that your decision to plead guilty is a free and voluntary one, and not as a result of any force, threats or promises, apart from the plea agreement; that you are pleading guilty because you are in fact guilty of the offense charged in count one of the indictment.' Mrs. Blanco, do you recall Judge Spellman saying that?"

"Yes," Griselda whispered.

Roy Black was next on the stand to be questioned by Lawrence Scharf. "Would you agree that certain untrue statements were made during the plea colloquy?"

"Yes."

"And what were they?" Scharf asked.

"I believe that Griselda Blanco's response to the fact that she didn't know there were any other promises is untrue," Roy Black said.

"And what about your response, Mr. Black?"

"My response as well."

Scharf could smell the blood. "Did Judge Spellman specifically tell you not to convey his offer of ten years to Assistant United States Attorney Schlessinger?"

"Yes. He said that he knew Mr. Schlessinger would object, and asked me not to say anything."

"Incidentally, did you ever tell the government prosecutor?"

"No."

"Mr. Black, did you tell Griselda Blanco that the U.S. Attorney was not to know?"

"Yes. I told her that Judge Spellman said not to mention that he had called and offered the ten-year sentence."

* * *

Bob Palombo knew that they weren't going to get anywhere. He was a veteran of the system, and from the second Steve Schlessinger had explained Black's story that a secret deal had been cut, he knew the issue of a twenty-year sentence was dead.

He sat in the Miami office, rubbing his arm, thinking of all the peaks and valleys he had experienced in the hunt for the Godmother. The other agents noticed him rubbing his arm and teased him, "Hey, Bobby, must be some real good news you're not telling us, the way you're rubbing that arm; wanna share your good fortune with us?"

Palombo got up and went into the nearest office, slamming the door so hard that the only picture in the Miami squad room fell off the wall.

Nothing had come easily. For every peak they ascended, there was a vertical valley they fell into. If they weren't battling with the FBI in San Francisco, it was the U.S. Attorney in Los Angeles or the Miami U.S. Attorneys or the San Francisco U.S. Attorney. And how many times over the last ten years had he carried his work home with him and said, "Grace, you're not going to believe this! You're just not going to believe this! I can't believe it! I've taken it in the shorts on this case too many times, this is the last straw." But he always went back to the chase.

As Palombo had predicted, the Ryskamp hearing went nowhere. At the end of the hearing, the U.S. Attorney was given the choice of accepting the original verdict or a new trial. It was October now, and the dynamics had changed. Their star witness, Gerry Gómez, had been convicted on the smuggling charges against him, and the Spellman fiasco had taken the heart out of the U.S. Attorneys. They acquiesced and accepted what they referred to internally as the "corrupt deal" that they believed had been made between the judge, the defense attorney, and Griselda Blanco.

There was never any further inquiry into what Judge Spellman and Roy Black had done, and Judge

Spellman would never agree to discuss his side of the story, whether or not it was obstruction of justice, perjury, an indictable offense, or an ethical violation. The matter simply faded into foggy "legalese" and was filed deep inside the bowels of the Miami Federal Courthouse.

After the hearing, Steve Schlessinger stood looking out over the Miami skyline from his office window, wondering what the hell had really happened. What a way to end a ten-year investigation. He did not believe any of it. But it was Miami, and anything could happen in South Florida.

Had Roy Black been more involved than he said?

Had Judge Spellman been manipulating Roy Black, or vice versa?

Had it really been Griselda behind the scenes pulling all the strings, using her immense fortune somehow to change her fate?

Steve Schlessinger shrugged, flicked his office lights out, and watched the Miami skyline glow softly in the tropical sunset as the red and orange hues covered the buildings like a warm blanket before night fell.

He wondered in silence. He believed he would never know the truth.

High overhead, flying into the red molten ball was Bob Palombo. He was flying back to Cleveland; back to Grace and his two boys. He thought of Al Seeley, his mentor, and those early days in New York, when he'd been out on the streets chasing the bad guys. Things hadn't gone too well. He wondered what Al would have said, and he thought about all the battle-scarred, jaded cops he knew, and he felt for all of them.

He ordered a scotch and looked out the porthole window as the plane banked low over Miami and headed up the gold coast.

The waves looked red in the sunset as they broke on the beach, almost like blood. He remembered what Seeley had told him: "It's persistence that pays. Never give up on a case, because chances are those same people will cross your path again, and you'll have another chance at them. It's God's way; everybody has to pay for what they do. Sooner or later they pay, Bobby."

Palombo sipped his scotch. He knew that it might be over for him, but it wasn't over for Griselda. There were dead souls she would have to account for.

He felt good. His arm didn't bother him at all.